EXPOSE-DESTROY- HEAL-
REPLACE!

EXPOSE-DESTROY-HEAL- REPLACE!

גָּלַע חֲבַל רָפָא חָדַשׁ

KENNY BROWN

Kingdom 2 Enterprises, LLC

Contents

Exposed Destroy Heal and Replace by Kenny Brown
Published by Kingdom 2 Enterprises, LLC
1309 Coffeen Street, Suite 1200
Sheridan WY 82801

Visit the authors website at https:// authorkennybrown.com/
Cataloging-in-Publication Data is on file with the Library of Congress.
International Standard Book Number: 979-8-9905530-3-3
Paper back ISBN: 979-8-9905530-4-0
E-book ISBN: 979-8-9905530-5-7
Printed in the United States.

I want to dedicate this book first and foremost to my Heavenly Father-The One True God, His Son Jesus the Christ, Yeshua Hamashiach, and His Holy Spirit without whom I am nothing!

I also want to dedicate this book to my family— Topaze my wife; and my four children, Jessie, Brooke, Tatum, and Grant and their families along with my granddaughter Chloe.

Chapter 1

Expose Destroy Heal Replace

Have you ever been so sure about, so convinced, so confident about an aspect of your life, your place in this world, the reason you are here that you could stake your claim and say, "This is who I am, and this is what I am here for!" But then everything you were so sure about falls apart all around you, and now you don't know what you are sure about, what to trust in, and if everything you have done or believed in is even valid anymore. When everything you have been working towards—a successful marriage, a successful career, successful church attendance, and service for the Lord—was all going as planned and according to what the world says the path to a beautiful life should be. It all blows up in your face and falls apart all around you in a successive series of events, and all you can do is question everything!

- You question who you are, what your life has become, and why it is at odds with how you had anticipated it.

- Have you ever felt that no matter what you do, how you plan, and who you strive to become, everything seems to go differently than you had hoped?
- Have you ever wondered why are you this way? Has God made a mistake? Maybe He is too busy to notice the circle of insanity you live in. Does he have more important things to take care of and more important people to look after?
- Have you become so beaten down, so broken down, so oppressed, so depressed that there is nothing left to do but throw your hands up and cry out?

"WHAT DO I DO NOW?"

It's difficult to understand why all this may be happening. We may believe that as long as we are going to church or synagogue, following the Lord, doing the right things, trusting, and being good Christians, We will never have to worry about failure, divorce, job loss, betrayal, or even the feeling of not fitting in with the church. We may believe that as Christians, we were shielded from all of this, that we have a sort of insurance policy that keeps us from the effects of these types of life circumstances. The whole reason for being a Christian is to ensure that when we die, we have our ticket to heaven and that as long as we stay in His will, all of the terrible things that the rest of the world experiences won't happen to us. We may have even told people that if they accept Jesus Christ as their Lord and Savior, they too will go to heaven, and until then, while they are waiting here on earth, they can be blessed, prosperous, not have problems, and live problem-free. How many sermons have we heard? How many bible studies and testimonies have we heard that have professed this very thing?

Through our shake-ups, epiphanies, and wake-up calls, we need to take a step back and look at our life, particularly our

Due to this fallen state and His unrelenting love for us, the Lord is perpetually recalibrating, realigning, and setting back to order what He originally intended for His Kingdom, for His purpose, how He is to be worshipped, served, represented, and His intentions for mankind from the beginning of creation, in the way a caring parent course-corrects one of their children who has veered off the path. Whenever He sees disorder, dysfunction, and misalignment in the representation of Him, He **Exposes, Destroys, Heals, and Replaces** these flawed perceptions to right standing in His sight. He does this for us individually but also for church service, ministries, and organizations that are established in His Name and for His purposes, but have become and are operating from a self-centered, needs-based perspective that comes from a skewed mindset that we are serving and ministering to others– all in the name of the Lord. When, in reality, we are serving the Lord to satisfy OUR need to feel wanted and valued, to feel that WE are making a difference, and to make US feel good when WE have helped, blessed, and served others. We intend to be witnesses, represent the Lord, and draw them to Him, but in reality, we may be doing it for our affirmation... GULP!

Let's take a closer look at the principle of the **Expose, Destroy, Heal and Replace** concept:

EXPOSE!

Our Father, the Lord God, desires to lift the veil of blindness, deception, and falsehood that the evil state of this fallen world is using to cover our eyes and our minds. He intends to **EXPOSE** our self-centered approach to serving, worshipping, and representing Him.

Has it all become filthy rags? Is it all skewed? Is it misplaced? Has it become what it was never intended to be? Our walk, ministry, and witness may all be based on a self-centered, self-serving, and self-focused agenda that is misplaced and misaligned. It may be missing the mark because it may be about US when HE is to be the focus of it all. He is to be the One to receive the glory for it all. What it has become is that it is more for OUR feeling valued, noticed, and appreciated so that others can see that WE are good Christians when it should be for us to reflect Him, for others to see Him in us, and to get a revelation of Him through us!

The Lord also wants to expose that since the Fall of Adam, this fallen world and the devil are constantly trying to deceive, distract, and deter us from our created identity, mission, purpose, and destiny. The goal of this evil state is for us to remain off course, ineffective, and not be impactful for the Kingdom. The Lord wants to expose the tactics that the world and Satan use to accomplish this deceptive strategy, which is primarily through infusing **defining moments** into our lives that cause us to fear, be ashamed, isolate us, blind us, and keep us in a constant state of self -pity and away from our intended roles in the Kingdom.

Examples of defining moments are events in our past that have happened to us, disturbing, shameful- humiliating experiences, and moments in time that are so traumatic that they have defined us and are still affecting us years later. Events such as our parents divorcing, being sexually molested as a young child, abandonment, betrayal, or belittling, embarrassing moments that have so affected us that when we think about them or we have a similar current circumstance, we are triggered back to those defining moments- and it's as if we are experiencing those events in real-time all over again. These defining moments keep us emotionally stuck and trapped and won't allow us to move on, sometimes for decades, and ultimately have become so much a part of us that it has become our identity. These moments can be events that happened to you during your upbringing that you may have even repressed and forgotten, but then something will trigger you, causing you to respond in alarm, skepticism, and apprehension without you even realizing why. These defining moments define everything we now do and how we respond. We have become victims; we are 40-year-old adults still stuck as a hurting 10-year-old child. These defining moments keep us in a state of neediness, shame, and pity and cause all of our interactions to be based on our need to be soothed of our traumas and defining moments.

When these triggers happen, we become fearful, guilty, and ashamed of ourselves, and we often will pull away from everyone who loves us: our family, friends, church, and God. We may feel that we are flawed and unworthy. We can no longer move forward, and we usually get self-conscious. Then we either become introverted- separating ourselves from everyone and everything- or we become combative, fight, and lash out at everyone and everything! These defining moments can render us impotent in our connections, walk, interactions, relationships with others, and connection with the Lord. This isolation causes us to become even more self-conscious. We withdraw or lash out even further, which then can alienate us so much that we begin to identify ourselves as this hurting, shameful, unworthy person who has no mission, purpose, or destiny outside of survival, hiding our secret, and protecting our emotions and feelings from the world around us and even from the Lord.

DESTROY!

The Lord wants to destroy the things that separate.

- All of the **defining moments**, the barriers, the fears, the shame, the lies, the hurts, distractions, and deception that separate us from Him.

- The things have defined and that hide and hinder us from our intended created identity and value.
- Things have defined and hidden us from our purpose and mission here on this earth.
- The things that separate us from our inheritance, legacy, and lineage that we were created for initially.
- Our masks, camouflage, coverings that hide who we have become, to cover the shame, guilt, and feelings of unworthiness.
- All of the self-centered agendas that skew our focus, beliefs, and perspectives to where we can never clearly see ourselves, see others, see who He is, or see why we are here.
- He also wants to destroy all those things that have become misperceptions and misunderstandings of who He is and His true intentions for His Kingdom. He wants to destroy the works of oppression, depression, and obsession that the world and the devil have used to enslave us. We were never intended to be enslaved to the things of this world but to be children and heirs to the King who rules and reigns alongside Him with dominion while we are here on earth and in heaven to come!

HEAL!

Through all of the trauma and conditioning of the life we live- such as with our desire for overachieving and ambition- to win the race that never satisfies and distracts us from keeping our eyes off God and to focus instead on ourselves. The things we have experienced in the past, the defining moments, the shame and pain we have suffered our entire lives, the hatefulness and evil that we have had to endure, it's no wonder we have strayed from and lost who we are, who He is, and why we are here!

But the good news is, the Lord wants to **heal** us!!!

In 2 Chronicles 7:14 it states:

> *"If My people, who are called by My name, will humble themselves, pray, seek My face, and turn from their wicked ways, then I will hear from heaven, forgive their sins, and heal their land."*

He wants to heal our faulty/skewed belief systems, our spiritual blindness, and our prodigal self-centered state. He is a caring, loving, judicious Father who wants to make all things come together for our good. Everything we have been through and that has happened to us, whether good or bad, does not have the final say. He has the final say, and as it states in this scripture if we will humble ourselves and pray and seek His face, and turn from our wicked, flawed, and self-centered ways, He is faithful to heal our land (our hearts, our emotions, our relationships, our connection with Him) ... Hallelujah!

He is the God of yesterday, today, and forever! As the God of yesterday, He can go with us back to our past defining events and show us how He was with us in that moment all along. He can show us how and why this happened to us, He can help us process the event, and He can help us heal from it. We are healed by recognizing that that event was not intended for us in the first place, that it was thrust upon us, and that defining moment was never supposed to have the power to change who we are. He will show us that He is more than capable and willing to heal us- that is why He sent His Son, that by His stripes, we are healed. We can be healed of everything past, present, and future. Jesus' sacrifice, stripes, and blood are more than sufficient to cover all time, dimensions, and eras- past, present, and future!

The key, then, is for us to surrender the defining moments. Often, the defining moment has become so entrenched and part of who we are that we won't surrender the event to the

One who can heal and restore us. We may believe He can, but we don't feel we are worthy or that it will be real or will last. We may think, "All these years, and it's still there, it still triggers, it still stops me in my tracks, and nothing has healed it before; what makes me think it can be healed now?"

Back to the scripture of 2 Chronicles,

> *"If My people, who are called by My name, will humble themselves, pray, seek My face, and turn from their wicked ways, then I will hear from heaven, forgive their sins, and heal their land."*

This statement contains a qualifier, IF. We must get past the IF. That is the first step to healing.

This qualifier lies with us; it lies with us having to decide. Our God is not a dictator, and He didn't create us to be robots. He made us in His image and His likeness; in that likeness, He created us with free will. True worship can only come from free will. So, we have to use our free will. We have to decide. We have to choose to surrender the IF. We have to make a stand for this to happen. We have to make a stand that we are going to BELIEVE! We have to make a stand that we will have to TRUST!

- We have to believe and trust that our God is faithful. He will meet us at the intersection of BELIEF and TRUST and be faithful to do what He said He would do. He WILL heal our land- our hearts, hurts, hang ups, trauma, and **defining moments.**
- We have to believe and trust that He loves us, that He loves us so much, and that He demonstrated His love by giving us His one and only Son for us!

In 1 John 4:19, it states that,

> *"We love because he* **first** *loved us..."*

And then In John 3:16, it states,

> *"For God so loved the world, that he gave his only begotten Son, that whosoever believeth in him should not perish, but have everlasting life."*

Most of us have heard, are familiar with, and can repeat this verse verbatim, but do we truly understand its impact and depth of meaning, or has it become a platitude? When God makes a statement, it is fact; it is truth; He cannot lie, and once stated, it is the absolute truth! Once spoken, it cannot be taken back, so what God says, we have to believe and trust that it is!

So, in these verses, the statements are based on Him loving us FIRST, and so much so that He gave His only begotten Son. The statement that He loved us first leads to His love being unconditional. It is not based on whether or not we love Him. He already loved us from the beginning, before we were even in our mother's womb (Jeremiah 1:5). It's not based on whether we are perfect; it is not based on our sin, our pain, our shame, or if we are too far gone.

IN OUR CURRENT STATE, whatever state we are in, it is in **that** state to which He loves us so much that He gave His only begotten Son for us; how could any Father give His only begotten Son without an unexplainable, supernatural love that goes beyond understanding?

In the rest of the verse in John 3:16, we also see the qualifier, "that whosoever believeth in Him..."

Here we are again, back at the intersection of BELIEVE and TRUST. We must settle in our hearts that we CAN believe and trust that He loves us so much that He sent His only begotten

Son. We must know that He wants to heal and restore us. We have to settle in our hearts. We are worthy of being healed; we are worthy because we are LOVED unconditionally! Our **worth** is based on His **love**! We have to settle in our hearts to get past the IF. We must settle in our hearts to surrender our hurts, traumas, defining moments, and self-centeredness so that He WILL heal our land!

REPLACE!

The Father intends to restore all things to what He intended them to be in the beginning! He intends to restore and replace what was lost:

- Our understanding of Who He is. To know Him, to have a relationship with Him, and to know that He loves us beyond all understanding!
- To restore who we are. Our original created identity. In His image, to re-present Him as His children and heirs to the King, and no longer slaves to sin and the world.
- To restore our mission, purpose, and destiny. To become a family again.
- He desires to walk with us in the cool of the garden, side-by-side, to be in each other's presence, to rule and reign in His Kingdom together- while here on earth.
- To restore us to right standing with Him in His sight. We no longer have to hide from Him, be ashamed, and be separate from Him.
- To restore us into alignment with Him. So that we can hear from Him so that we can know His purpose, so that we can be filled with His love, anointing, knowledge, revelation, and power so that our cup is overflowing, and we are no longer needy, pitiful, hurting, and self-centered victims. To restore us so much that we are abounding

with His love and that when others see us, they don't see US; they see **HIM** in us!

Hallelujah!

We are going to embark on a journey to see how the Lord uses this template of **Expose, Destroy, Heal, and Replace** throughout the Bible to realign His children from their fallen state and their self-centered focus, which has corrupted and turned their eyes from Him, and how it restored them back to their intended created identity and mission purpose and destinies. We take this journey to understand who He is, who we are, and our purpose.

We will see how.

- Like the Prodigal son, we will learn to recognize the defining moments, the trauma, the fears, the shame, the lies, the hurts, distractions, and deceptions that have affected us our whole life.
- Like the story of the Leper, we will learn to recognize the things that have kept us from and hide who we truly are!
- Like King David, we will learn to recognize the things that have defined and hidden us from our purpose and mission here on this earth.
- Like Adam and Eve in the Garden of Eden, we will learn to recognize the masks, camouflage, and coverings we have created to hide who we have become and our shame, guilt, and feelings of unworthiness.
- Like the story of Gideon, we will learn to recognize all of the self-centered agendas that skew our focus, beliefs, and perspectives where we can never see our true self, higher calling, or why we are here.

Chapter 2

What Is Man?

"Lord our Lord, how majestic is Your name in all the earth!

You have set your glory in the heavens.

Through the praise of children and infants, You have established a stronghold against your enemies, to silence the foe and the avenger.

When I consider Your heavens, the work of Your fingers, the moon, and the stars which You have set in place, what is man that you are mindful of him, and the son of man that you would consider him?

You have made him a little lower than the angels and crowned them with glory and honor. You have made them rulers over the works of Your hands, You put everything under their feet, all flocks and herds, and the animals of the wild, the birds of the sky, and the fish of the seas.

Lord our Lord, how majestic is Your name over all the earth!"

Psalms 8: 1-9 (NIV)

David, when writing this Psalm, is most likely out in the desert running from King Saul, who is trying to kill him. For

Saul fears and knows that the Lord has anointed David as the new King and that the time for the reign of Saul will soon end, Saul is trying to stop the process by killing David.

David is in a very contemplative state, and when we look at his journey to this point, we can understand why.

- He was anointed to be the next King over Israel when he was very young, estimated to be between 10-15 years of age, by Samuel the prophet, almost as an after-thought, as all of his seven older brothers were first considered before him. But finally after they had been disqualified-rejected by the Lord, Samuel had his father Jesse call him from the field where he tended the sheep to come in and was anointed the next King in front of, to the astonishment of, and perhaps in the frustration of his family, because the Lord had chosen David specifically stating that David was a man after His own heart.
- When David was anointed, he, along with anyone else, would have expected that he would have been taken to be groomed as the new King of Israel but was sent back to continue his hum-drum life of tending his father's sheep. At the same time, his brothers served in King Saul's army as soldiers for several years. David had been tending sheep and was roughly 17-19 years old, when he was tasked by his father to take lunch to his brothers on the battlefield and to check on them, where he met, confronted and defeated Goliath and was exalted into the King's court as a hero.
- After serving in the King's court and eventually as a commander in King Saul's army, where David exceeded Saul's abilities as commander of his army, upon return from one of the battles, the women upon the army's return sang:

> *6 the women came out from all the towns of Israel to meet King Saul with singing and dancing, with joyful songs and with timbrels and lyres. 7 As they danced, they sang: "Saul has slain his thousands, and David his tens of thousands."*
>
> *8 Saul was very angry; this refrain displeased him greatly. "They have credited David with tens of thousands," he thought, "but me with only thousands. What more can he get but the kingdom?" Saul was very angry; this refrain displeased him greatly. "They have credited David with tens of thousands," he thought, "but me with only thousands. What more can he get but the kingdom?"*
>
> *1 Samuel 18:7-8 (NIV)*

- From that point on, Saul hated and tried to kill David, so David had to flee for the next seven years in the desert and even hide among Israel's enemy, the Philistines.

Somewhere in this backdrop, David wrote Psalms 8. He is in a quandary as to where he fits in this world and if his calling, anointing, and purpose is even valid now. Thus far, it was not going the way he would have envisioned his path to *KINGSHIP* should have gone, and he has been fleeing for his very life! At every opportunity, King Saul pursued and attempted to kill David in the palace. King Saul's army has been chasing David all across the region. David has hidden in caves, nearly starved to death, and on a couple of occasions, while Saul was pursuing him and caught up with him, David had snuck up into Saul's camp and had the opportunity to kill Saul but refrained, for David would not harm God's anointed. Even though Saul would not have given David the same deference, when presented with the same opportunity, David respected God's chosen, God's anointed, so much so that he refused to kill Saul. David would wait for the Lord's timing and justice if and when it happened. The search for David had been so intense that David had to resort to hiding and living with his and Israel's enemy, the Philistines.

On the other hand, he can hear from the Lord and feel the Lord's hand directing him. David had a great victory over a lion and a bear while tending his father's sheep; he had victory over the giant Goliath, the Philistine's champion, on the battlefield after 40 days of Goliath taunting the Israelites and their God. He has had tremendous victories on the battlefield, so much so that the women were singing his praises to the jealousy of King Saul, and the Lord has sustained him while he was fleeing King Saul and while he was amongst his enemies and in the desert.

I imagine him gazing up at the desert's starry night sky and being overwhelmed with the Magnificence of God Himself, Jehovah, Adonai, YHWH, and His vast and fantastic creation. I am sure He was thinking, "Of all the things YHWH has created, the stars, the moon, the sun, the desert, the mountains, the ocean, lakes, and rivers, the trees and forest, all the amazing animals that walk over the land, all of the creatures that swim in the sea, all of the types of beautiful, amazing birds that fly through the air... What is man that you are mindful of him, and the son of man that you would consider him?"

I can imagine David thinking, "Of all the magnificent things that You created that You could focus Your attention on, why, man? What catches Your attention that You would notice him?"

I am sure David even took it further and asked, "Why me?"

David probably thought, "I receive no other consideration from any other source, not my family, not my nation, not the Philistines, not my friends... so why do You, the Great YHWH, consider me? Here I am herding sheep, or hiding in a cave, or consorting with the enemy because the King of my nation seeks to kill me! By any other consideration, I am a failure, I am an outcast, I am a traitor, I am the least in my family, the least in my tribe, I have been anointed King of Israel by the mighty prophet Samuel, and yet here I sit in the desert a fugitive wondering why You even consider me. I challenge that I don't feel worthy of such attention and mindfulness!"

To pursue this revelation, we do what David did and go back to the beginning, to the book of Genesis.

> *In the beginning, God created the heavens and the earth. Now the earth was without form and void, darkness was over the surface of the deep and Spirit of God was hovering over the waters.*
>
> *Genesis 1:1-2 (NIV)*

So, in the beginning, there was nothing but darkness, chaos, and disorder. And the Spirit of God was hovering over the waters. This indicates that there is an anticipation that something is about to go down. The Spirit is hovering, waiting to be activated!

Then, in verse 3, we see the activation.

"And God said,"

Can we take a moment and meditate on those three words?

The magnificence, the simplicity, the awesomeness, the amazing economy, and the ease of the Lord God that all He has to do to make anything happen... is to speak! That will activate and get the Holy Spirit to move- when God Speaks!

You would think that something as daunting, critical, and significant as creating the heavens and earth would take a much more concerted, coordinated strategy and force to create the world into existence, but for God, all it takes is His Word!

We are continuing with verse 3.

And God said, "Let there be light," and there was light. God saw that the light was good, and He separated the light from the darkness.

God called the light, "day, "and the darkness He called, "night." And there was evening, and there was morning-the first day.

Genesis 1: 1-25 details that God created the rest of the earth through His spoken Word. He separated the waters and established the waters from the sky, and then the Lord separated the water from dry land, and then He gathered waters to be called seas. God created vegetation, seed-bearing plants, and fruit; created the lights in the sky, established sacred times, days, and years; and established the sun, moon, and stars. God created the sea creatures and the birds of the air, then created the creatures of the land, livestock, and wild animals, and also said that they will produce after their own kind, ensuring the creation will be sustained. During each phase of this creation process, God paused and said that it was good each time.

God had created the earth in five days through His spoken Word!

So the earth was created, there is now order from disorder, function from dysfunction, and a magnificent, beautiful, wonderous planet has been created with time; there is day and night, the seas have their place, the land is established with lush and fruitful vegetation, the sea is full of life of all the created creatures, the land, and sky are teeming with birds and land creatures.

It is, in all senses of the Word, a paradise! What more could you want?

So here we are on the sixth day of creation.

We have this magnificent paradise created, and He has set aside seven days in His schedule, and there are two more days to fill in. It's almost as if God has created this beautiful paradise, and now, He needs something to accessorize it or a creature to maintain it. So what should God create to put the capstone on this glorious state? This creature needs to be worthy of this beautiful paradise, with a scope, care, and ability to cherish it to be worthy of God's unique handiwork.

So now, if we look at the creation sequence, we see God created the earth in 5 days. On the 6th day, He decides to create His next creature.

In Genesis 1: 26

> *Then God said, "Let us make mankind in our image, in our likeness, so that they may rule over the fish of the sea and the birds in the sky, over the livestock and all the wild animals all the creatures that move along the ground?*

So we see here that God is creating a creature that will be in His image and His likeness. That is a significant statement! There is none like God! God is God all by Himself! There was nothing before God; there will be nothing after God! There is nothing that compares to Him! He is so awesome, all-powerful, majestic, transcendent, grand, and wonderous that words can't do Him justice. His power and might are so complete that He just speaks, and the world is created. So, this new creature is to be created in this image and likeness. This indicates that this new creature will be distinct and special compared to the rest of creation.

If we look at Genesis 2:7

> *Then the Lord God formed a man from the dust of the ground and breathed into his nostrils the breath of life, and the man became a living being.*

So God not only decided that this new creature would be distinct and special, but the way He created him was completely different and distinct from the way He created all other creations. All other creation was created through God's spoken Word, "Let there be," and it was so. But with this new creature, God did not just speak into existence.

The Lord God reached down His hand and scooped up the dust of the ground. (Just as an aside, isn't it good to know that the almighty God is not afraid to get His hands dirty for us? Hallelujah!). Then the Lord God formed man with His loving hands, and then, once formed, breathed into his nostrils the breath of life! The Lord God breathed His Spirit, Essence, likeness, and Glory into us! And man became a living being.

Wow!

This doesn't sound to me like this creature was created to be an accessory, an afterthought, or a servant for the creation. This creature was made from tender care and intimacy that we haven't seen the rest of creation receive. The rest of creation didn't experience the Lord God stooping down and reaching out His hand to scoop it up. The rest of creation didn't experience the Lord God molding and forming it with loving care, with His own hands. The rest of creation didn't experience God looking in its face with adoration and then breathing His Spirit, His Essence, His likeness, and His Glory into it.

Another distinction we see with this creature is that when God spoke the rest of creation into existence, He said that it was good, but as each element was created, God didn't express the purpose and reason that it was created at the time He created it. But with man, immediately after he was created, the Lord God expressed what man's mission and purpose was to be, along with the purpose of the rest of creation.

In Genesis 1: 28-31

God blessed them and said to them, "Be fruitful and increase in number; fill the earth and subdue it. Rule over the fish in the sea and the birds in the sky and over every living creature that moves on the ground." Then God said, "I give you every seed-bearing plant on the face of the whole earth and every tree that has fruit with seed in it. They will be yours for food. And to all the beasts of the earth and all the birds in the sky and all the creatures that move along the ground—everything that has the breath of life in it—I give every green plant for food." And it was so.

God saw all that he had made, and it was very good. And there was evening, and there was morning—the sixth day.

So now we can see that man wasn't made for creation, but that creation was made for man! We see the full manifestation of the purpose for man and creation within these four verses. We see that creation received its stated purpose when man was created. Man is to be fruitful, to fill the earth and subdue it. He is to rule over the fish, the birds, all the living creatures, and every seed-bearing plant. This was all given to man to have dominion over. The rest of creation's purpose is to be in service to and for man. The whole reason that God created the earth was for man. He created man when He had the rest of creation established so that when He did create man, all of creation was ready for him.

Then we see in Genesis 2:8,15, 18, and 20.

8-*The Lord planted a garden eastward in Eden, and there He put the man whom He had formed.*

15- Then the Lord God took the man and put him in the garden of Eden to tend and keep it.

18- and the Lord God said, "It is not good that man should be alone, I will make him a helper comparable to him."

20- the Lord God formed every beast of the field and every bird of the air and brought them to Adam to see what he would call them. And whatever Adam called each living creature, that was its name. So Adam gave names to all the cattle, to the birds of the air, and to every beast of the field. But for Adam there was not found a helper comparable to him.

In these verses, we see the care and attention the Lord God gives Adam. He creates a special space within His creation -the garden of Eden that is set aside to place Adam to tend and keep it. Then the Lord cares and is so concerned for the welfare of Adam that He determines that it is not good for him to be alone, so the Lord God creates and presents all the living creatures to Adam to name them and to analyze if any are fit to be a companion for Him. But through this process, none is found. The Lord God determined that it is not good for man to be alone because Adam was made in God's likeness, and God Himself is not alone. The Lord God is a triune being, made up of Father, Son, and the Holy Spirit, but one God with three characteristics. So when He made Adam, He stated, "Let US make man in OUR image. So, if God is not alone, it is also not good for man to be alone. None of the creatures were suitable because they were not created in his (Adam's) likeness, not created in his kind.

So Father God has decided to make Adam a helper, a companion. The definition of Father is- to come forth from. Adam came forth from the Father God and was so much in His likeness that the rest of creation acknowledged their likeness.

Again, in Psalm 8: 5-8, David reveals that.

"For You have made him a little lower than the angels and crowned him with glory and honor. You have made him to have dominion over the works of Your hands; You have put all things under his feet, All sheep and oxen-even the beast of the field, the birds of the air, and the fish of the sea that pass through the paths of the seas."

As I read this verse, something didn't quite sit with me concerning "*for You have made him a little lower than the angels.*" I'm not challenging the revelation that David is giving, but maybe the translation. No other part of the creation story in Genesis even mentions angels, so why bring up angels now in David's Psalm? So, to investigate this, I looked back at the Hebrew meaning of the Word angel in this text. What I found is that the Hebrew states,

"and You are making lack him little from Elohim, and glory and honor."

This makes more sense to me. The Hebrew Word used here is- Elohim. This is actually one of the names of the Lord. So, in essence, this is stating that,

"*You made man a little lower than Elohim.*"

You made man just a little lower than Yourself! That's why You consider him!

The Lord God wanted to create a family! We have a created value that far exceeds any other created thing: His likeness, His image! So now we see why the Lord God couldn't find a companion comparable to Adam. Therefore, the Lord God had to create Adam's helper completely differently than He created any other part of His creation, including Adam. In Genesis 2:21-25

> *And the Lord God caused a deep sleep to fall on Adam, and he slept; and He took one of his ribs and closed up the flesh in its place. Then the rib which the Lord God had taken from man, He made into a woman, and He brought her to the man. And Adam said, "this is now bone of my bones and flesh of my flesh; She shall be called Woman, because she was taken out of Man." Therefore, a man shall leave his father and mother and be joined to his wife, and they shall become one flesh. And they were both naked and were not ashamed.*

I want to bring to your attention a few things here. The Lord God put Adam into a deep sleep and removed one of His ribs to create his companion; why did God do that?

- Similar to how the Lord God created Adam in His likeness and His image when creating Adam's companion, the Lord God wanted the companion to be in the likeness of Adam, in Adam's kind, which in turn was the likeness of God. When the Lord God created all the animals, fish, and birds, he created them to multiply from their kind. For Adam, he would need to be able to multiply from his kind.
- The statement, "*And they were both naked and were not ashamed.*" Why does the scripture point this out? What is the significance of the fact that they were naked and not ashamed?
- Man and now woman were created from perfect holiness and into perfect holiness. When He finished creating man and all of His creation, the Lord God said in Genesis 1:31 that it was "very *good*." At this point, all of creation hadn't suffered the fall of man and sin entering in through the disobedience of eating of the tree of the

knowledge of good and evil, so there was no shame, guilt, lust, or perverted thoughts or acts, so the man was naked and not ashamed due to there was no existence of guilt and shame and their bodies and existence were perfect, holy, and "Very good!"

- Also, since Man was made in the likeness and image of the Lord God, man resembles, displays, and reflects the Lord God's attributes. One of the dominating attributes of the Lord God is that His glory physically manifests through shining, radiating, and illuminating, so much so that His glory is what you see when you see Him! His glory covers over Him- this is referred to in Hebrew as Kadosh and in Greek as Shekinah glory. Since Adam and now Eve are made in His image and likeness, and as we learned in Psalms 8:5 that we were made just a little lower than "Elohim," Adam and Eve also displayed a level of this Kadosh, this Shekinah glory over them which covered over them. With this glory over them, this illuminated glory and holiness lend to no shame. It is part of the essence and connection to the Lord God.

As we study Genesis, we notice God walks alongside man in the cool of the day to commune with man. God desires to fellowship with man on the earth that He created. Scripture does not reference that God walks alongside any other of his created things. He walks alongside man because man is the only creature created in His image and likeness. Man was the only creature that when the Lord God looked upon, He would see Himself being reflected back; the Lord God would see Himself in man being reflected back to Him. That reflected image can also be explained as that when the Lord God looked on Adam and Eve, His glory would shine onto them, and then because they are in His image and likeness, that same glory would reflect back to the Lord God!

So, like David in his Psalm, we are starting to understand why God would consider man over the rest of His creation. He is mindful of him over all the other beautiful, amazing, wonderous things He created. It is because when the Lord God surveys and looks over all His magnificent creation. However extraordinary and beautiful it is, man is the only created thing that, when the Lord God looks upon and gazes upon, can reflect back His glory, essence, and Himself to Himself.

The Lord God is judicious with His glory and will not let it go to waste or return void, so when He created man in His image and His likeness, it was to create him so that the Lord God's glory would retain its value and worth and would return to Him! We have a created value that far exceeds any other created thing; that value is in His image and His likeness in us!

When the Lord God created Adam and Eve, He created them as perfect, pristine creations that perfectly reflect His glory to Himself. They were purely created reflecting surfaces that when His glory would shine upon them, their reflecting capability, their reflective surfaces were so perfect that they reflected His glory to Him without spot or blemish.

As we look at the science as to how reflective surfaces work, in particular to light, which is more closely to how the Bible describes the shekinah glory of God, and what affects a surface reflect-ability, we learn that the purity of the reflecting surface determines the authenticity and undiluted reflections of the reflected image. A high-quality mirror, for instance, can reflect up to 90 percent of the light that falls on it; the mirror absorbs the rest. Due to very few impurities, the reflection of 90 percent is considered very clear. That would be consistent with how God's shekinah glory would emanate to Adam and Eve. As we discussed earlier, Adam and Eve were created a little lower than Elohim, and it would be reasonable to assume that similar to a high-quality mirror, they would reflect back at least 90% of His glory to Him and absorb 10% as a blessing for them to experience and enjoy!

A reflector that is imperfect has blemishes or stains, pits, or is tarnished, which will not reflect back the true quality or fullness of the light being emitted but will actually absorb a higher percentage of the intended light. The more blemished a surface is, the less light it can reflect and more that is absorbed, which is different from how it was initially designed to function; it has become something other than what it was intended to be.

Another factor that determines the level and authenticity of the reflecting ability of the reflecting surface is the angle at which it is facing compared to the source of the light. When a reflecting surface is facing directly towards the source of the light being emitted, it has the best opportunity to receive and to reflect the most percentage of light back to the emitting source. The more the reflecting surface turns away- its focus is no longer true towards the emitting source, the less it can receive and the less it can reflect back, which dilutes the reflection back to the source and will deflect or refract the reflection towards the area it is focused on and not where it was intended which is the source. If the reflecting surface is turned away from the source, it can't receive, absorb, or reflect the light. Since it is no longer in alignment with the source it was created for, it receives, absorbs, and reflects what it is focused on the environment, circumstances, and experiences surrounding it, which makes it impotent to its original design and disconnected from the source of what makes it effective.

Yet another factor that determines the level and authenticity of the reflect-ability of the reflecting surface is whether the reflecting surface is covered over or veiled from its source. In modern times, when reflecting surfaces are used for the sun, for example, cloud cover will reduce the shine emitting from the source, limiting or stopping any potential for the reflecting surface to receive back. If you put a cloth or veil over a mirror, it can no longer reflect the intended image.

When looking at the reflect-ability of Adam and Eve in the garden before the fall and considering these factors, we see that they were perfect, pure, pristine reflecting surfaces for the Lord God's Kadosh or shekinah glory. They had no blemishes, stains, tarnishes, or pits on their surface that would dilute the reflecting back of His glory to Him. We can also see that their focus was always and intently on Him. Therefore, His glory was not deflected. He was intently focused on them, and they were intently focused on Him, which describes perfect alignment and synchronization in their focus on each other; their eyes were singular. We can also see that nothing could veil their ability to reflect His glory back to Him. Adam and Eve had an unhindered clarity in Who the Lord God was, who they were, and what their purpose, mission, and destiny were, which was to have dominion over all the living things in creation and to walk alongside and rule with Him in the cool of the garden, all for His glory!

In the light of this, when we consider ourselves.

How is our reflector doing?

- How clear is our surface?

  Are we reflecting back 90% to our Father and only absorbing 10%? Is our surface shiny, pristine, and clean, or is it mostly tarnished, stained, blemished, and pitted? If we're honest... is there any part of our surface that is able to reflect at all, or do we only absorb? Have we become so self-absorbed and needy that we hoard the glory for ourselves?

- How is our focus towards Him?

Are we intently searching, gazing, and acknowledging Him, or are we so self-focused, others-focused, and circumstance-focused that we have turned away from and stopped receiving Him? Is our focus distracted to the point that we have become victims, depressed, angry, hurt, vengeful, accusatory, protective, introverted, isolated, that the only thing we can reflect is our attitudes, circumstances, emotions, and experiences that surround us?

- Has our view of Him been covered or veiled?

Have we allowed our view towards Him to be clouded, veiled, distant so that, when we do look for Him, we can't see or find Him due to all of the things that we have allowed to cloud our minds and vision that we don't even know where to look?

Why is this the case? What has happened the creation of Adam and Eve as perfect reflectors of His glory, and we are so misaligned that we can't even find His glory?

We can see why we have become and act this way and why our reflectors (hence our created identity, mission, purpose, and destiny) have lost their effectiveness and shine.

6 When the woman saw that the fruit of the tree was good for food and pleasing to the eye, and also desirable for gaining wisdom, she took some and ate it. She also gave some to her husband, who was with her, and he ate it. 7 Then the eyes of both of them were opened, and they realized they were naked; so they sewed fig leaves together and made coverings for themselves.

8 Then the man and his wife heard the sound of the Lord God as he was walking in the garden in the cool of

the day, and they hid from the Lord God among the trees of the garden. 9 But the Lord God called to the man, "Where are you?"
Genesis 3:6-9

This is primarily the effect of the fall of Adam and Eve in the garden- the separation. They lost their ability to reflect Him back. Once sin entered the garden, immediately their eyes were opened, they realized they were naked, they were ashamed and began to sew fig leaves together to cover themselves. Does this sound familiar? Can you relate to this? Once Adam and Eve's eyes were opened, their focus completely changed. They were no longer focused, searching, gazing for the Father. They were focused on themselves, realizing they were naked, and because they realized their nakedness, they were ashamed of their nakedness. When we have had an embarrassing moment or situation exposed, how many of us are ashamed, and our ONLY focus is to cover it up and make it go away?

Because Adam and Eve's eyes were opened, they realized they were naked- and were ashamed, and upon hearing the voice of the Lord walking in the garden, they hid themselves! Wow!

What a turn of events! How quickly things deteriorate! Adam and Eve have covered themselves in fig leaves and are hiding from their Father in the trees. They have camouflaged themselves to look like their environment.

They have now.

- They have tarnished their reflective surfaces with sin, fear, and shame.
- They diverted their focus from the source and now are focused on their nakedness.
- They covered their reflective surfaces with the things of their environment and fig leaves and are now hiding

behind trees from the source of their purpose- To reflect the Lord God!

It's no wonder the Lord God asked the question...

"Adam, Where are you?"

The Father, the Creator, the Lord God, is asking the pinnacle of His creation, the ones He gave all dominion, to rule with Him, who were created just a little lower than Himself, who He lovingly formed with His own hands in His image and His likeness, breathing His essence into to reflect Him-to reflect His glory back to Himself.

Adam, "Where are you?"

It's not as if He didn't know where they were or why, but more along the lines of.

"Where are you?"

- Where is your focus?
- What state are you in?
- What have you lost?
- What have you become?
- Why are you hiding?
- Why do you fear?
- Where is My reflection?
- Where is my glory?

When the Lord God was walking in the garden in the cool of the day, he was surveying His creation, expecting to see His dear children reflecting back His glory. He could not find His glory, His image, being reflected back. Where was it? Why was it lost?

And now the question for us is, "Where are YOU?"

- Where is your focus?
- What state are you in?

- What have you lost?
- What have you become?
- Why are you hiding?
- Why do you fear?
- Where is your Father's, your Creator's reflection?
- Where is your Father's glory?

We have become the fruit, the lineage, the legacy of this tragedy of the fall many generations later.

What will it take for us to give our Father His glory back?

Is there no hope?

Is it lost forever?

Chapter 3

The Fall

"NOOOOO!!!!!!"

My wife woke up screaming in a cold sweat, heart pounding, tears running down her face... I sat up startled, realizing that she was having the dream again, and I also began to cry and pull her to me; we both sat in the dark, holding each other and crying ourselves back to sleep. Even after all of this time, several years now, we still were not over the loss of our child, even our adult child.

When we got up the following day, my wife was already sitting outside our dwelling, looking out over the countryside in the pre-dawn light. Evidently, she hadn't slept much and looked haggard and deep in thought.

Putting a hand on her shoulder, I offered, "I miss him too."

"Which one?" she asked.

I hesitated before I answered, "Both," I conceded.

It has taken a while, but enough time has passed to admit to missing both of our adult children.

It's hard, but how can you not think of one without thinking of the other? A tragedy that pierced the family in such a way that, as a parent, you can't get the event out of your head, and you wonder if you can ever move on.

I sit outside our dwelling on a bench beside her and stare out over the fields of crops while the sun is coming up; even now, I can tell it will be hot. I would have to go out and tend the crops today, but I just wanted to sit for now. My thoughts began to linger, and I recollect our two sons as young kids so full of energy, running all over the fields chasing each other, playing hide and seek, wrestling and roughhousing, giggling, and on occasion, someone would get hurt and cry and come running to me with a scratch or cut. That was something I could never get used to, the sight, smell, and mystery of blood and bleeding; I thought I could hear the blood crying. At first, I didn't know how to respond or take care of the injury, so I would send them over to my wife to nurture them back to health. She somehow would know what to do and what to say to soothe them, and they would be off and romping through the fields again.

Over the years, the boys grew up to be hearty men and became actively involved in the family business of raising crops and tending the flocks. The older son oversaw the crops while the younger managed the flocks. They were both capable in their respective roles. As time went on, though, there became a distinct difference in their personalities and demeanors. The older son, though capable, would easily get distracted and tired of the ongoing routine and diligence necessary to raise crops. The constant monitoring to ensure that the thorns and weeds didn't overtake the fields, fending off the locusts and insects that would come to feast on the crops, the turning of the soil and digging trenches to retain the water so that the crops wouldn't dry up and wither away all seemed to be never-ending and became arduous to him. When harvest time would come, there was the rigor of gathering all of the crops, the threshing and processing, the storage, and ensuring that it wouldn't spoil. It had all become more of a burden than a livelihood to him.

The older son would then often complain of the tediousness and effort required. The scratches and cuts, the filthiness of working the soil, the heat and sweat that led to the overall weariness and exhaustion that he felt at the end of each day would annoy and frustrate him more and more as time went on. Then, there was the offering I insisted would be brought to the Lord God, the Creator of all things. I instructed my sons to get the first and best of each harvest to show gratitude and reverence to the Lord God for blessing, providing, and sustaining us. This also frustrated my older son, though he never mentioned it out loud. Why would he have to show gratitude to the Lord God for blessing, providing, and sustaining us when the older son perceived that he was doing all the work? He tried to understand the explanation that I offered that the Lord God miraculously made the seed burst forth in the soil, causing the sun to nourish the plants, the dew to provide water, and the increase for the crops to blossom and bear fruit. I would go on to explain that it is through our tending that we can partner with the Lord God to participate in the blessing, provision, and sustenance that He has provided and also to keep us from becoming proud, relying on our strength, which could lead to turning our focus from Him, and to acknowledge that He is Lord overall. We are created to reflect His goodness. My older son would dutifully perform his tasks, but it was becoming more and more apparent that he was becoming increasingly frustrated with the performing of those duties.

On the other hand, my younger son seemed to relish his role of managing the flocks. He would rise before everyone else just as the sun rose. He could be heard singing songs to the Lord God in his still, calm voice that would soothe the flocks and keep them quiet. When moving the flocks, you could see him singing, dancing, and skipping through the fields, leading them to better grazing grounds, and the flocks would happily follow him. The flocks had become so familiar with his voice that they no longer followed any of our voices; they only followed him and his voice.

When bringing his offering to the Lord God, my younger son would take care and prepare to choose the choicest, most healthy, and fatted selections from the firstborn from the flock to present to the Lord God as his offering. The younger son did so cheerfully and believed that the Lord God provided all of the increase of the flock and that the Lord God would also give the future increase of his flock. He believed by faith that the Lord God sustained the health and multiplication of his flock because of the Lord God's blessings. The Lord God always seemed incredibly pleased with the younger son's offerings, which made me, his father, very proud and grateful for the younger son's heart to honor the Lord God in such a way. The countenance of the younger son was glowing; you could see the effects of the Lord God reflecting through his son, and it made his heart swell.

I could tell that the older son was growing increasingly more and more jealous of his younger brother in virtually every way. The older son had an undertone of cynicism when talking with or about his younger brother. Over the years, the older son's mocking tone and speech would even affect the entire family. As his father, I occasionally chastised our older son to speak 'respect and love' towards his family, especially his younger brother. The older son would go along with the correction for a time, but there was still the undercurrent of resentment.

I could remember the day's events that changed our family's lives as If they were happening in real-time, precisely and vividly. Oh, how I wished that the Creator of the universe would allow us to go back in time and do things differently. But alas, He only gives us this one opportunity to live for today and anticipate how we will live tomorrow, but yesterday has transpired and is the one thing we cannot change.

It was an early start to the day; it was the day to bring the offerings to the Lord God. My wife and I were getting around preparing to travel with our two sons, who were gathering the offerings that would be presented. We could hear the younger son calling and corralling the sheep that would be offered. The younger son had indeed chosen the best of the best to present to the Lord God. The Creator will be well pleased. We hadn't seen the older son yet, so I called out for him. The older son responded that he would meet us at the place of the offering to go on ahead.

At the place of the offering, the family gathered around the area where the offerings would be presented; we could sense the presence of the Lord God, we could see the cloud of covering lingering over the area, and we could almost hear and feel the breath of the Lord God. We all removed our sandals as we were standing on holy ground. As the younger son corralled the sheep and staked them in place, he began preparing them to be offered. While he was doing this, the older son arrived, bringing his offering of crops, and began preparing them for the offering to present to the Lord God.

The younger son would be the first to present his offering and begin the gruesome task of killing and slaughtering each animal. He slit the throat of the sheep and drained its blood, then he would carefully and thoroughly cut the fat around the internal organs of the lamb and bring it over to the large stone and lay the fat all out before the Lord God with extreme care and reverence onto the stone. He did this for an hour or so with all the lambs he brought until a substantial amount of fat was presented. When completed, the younger son, with humbleness and reverence, backed away from the offering, lay face down on the ground, prostrate before the Lord God. There was blood and carcasses all around the presentation of the offering, and the younger son was covered with the blood of the lambs also. He lay on the ground face down and waited for the Lord God to receive his offering. Several minutes passed, and we all began to wonder if the Lord God was pleased with the younger son's offering when suddenly a bright light flashed above the cloud. A pillar of fire flashed down, consumed the entire fat presentation, and then returned to the cloud.

The Lord God was pleased and had received the offering, Hallelujah! The younger son slowly stood and turned and faced the family. We could see tears in his eyes, the genuineness of his heart, and his love for the Lord God, and we could see his face and countenance glowing. He walked back over towards us while his older brother was walking out with his offering presentation; as they walked by each other, it seemed the older son intentionally bumped his shoulder into the younger son, interrupting the younger son's step, and seemed to scowl at the younger son. The younger son was still in awe and hardly noticed, but my wife and I looked at each other with concern.

The younger son arrived beside my wife and me, and we were so pleased and proud of our younger son that even though he was matted with the remnants of the sheep, each of us embraced him. We all then turned our attention to the older son while he presented his offering to the Lord God.

The older son also seemed to have brought the best of the best of his crops; I was very impressed. The older son's quantity was also more than he had ever brought before. It was apparent the older son had put a lot of thought and effort into preparing the offering to be presented to the Lord God. He had brought several containers of the grains of his crops, which were carefully processed and prepared. As the older son poured out each container of the grain onto the large stone, it created quite a large pile on top of the stone; once all of the grain was presented, the older son began pouring the oil from the olives all over the prepared grain, container after container. As he poured each container, he would take a staff and mix the oil into the grain. Once all the oil was poured out and thoroughly mixed into the grain, the older son poured out another set of containers, one by one, which was frankincense. As the older son mixed the frankincense into the grain, the aroma filled the entire area with an excellent and pleasing smell. It wasn't often that the older son provided such extravagance in his offering; he was truly giving the best presentation possible. For the final containers, the older son poured salt into the grain offering and again thoroughly mixed it in, which stirred up the aroma even more. When finished, the older son was pleased and confident with his offering presentation, which was performed excellently and elegantly, and he seemed proud of his efforts. He outstretched both his hands and performed a circle before the offering, giving the family a quick look of satisfaction, and then, with an abundance of confidence, he lay prostrate on the ground before the Lord God in anticipation of the Lord God receiving his offering.

The cloud hovered over the place of the offering, and we all held our breath, waiting for the response of the Lord, sure that He would be pleased with the selection, processing, and excellence of presentation. Seconds went by, then minutes, and more than a few minutes. The older son continued to lay prostrate on the ground, waiting for what seemed like an eternity. Finally, we could see movement in the cloud, and you could see and feel the beginning of the wind gently turning, and we all came to the same conclusion: this is it! The Lord God is about to receive the offering. But instead, something else happened. The cloud and presence of the Lord disappeared, and all was noticeably quiet and still.

The Lord God had rejected the offering....

We all just stood there, dumbfounded. The presentation was beautiful, as the aroma of the spices was still in the air. Such care was put into the older son's offering. Why didn't the Lord God receive the offering? The older son was still lying on the ground, but his head was up, looking around to determine what was happening. He could see that his offering was still on the stone, but the cloud and presence had departed. He then looked at us to see if there was any difference from our perspective. He could tell we were just as confused as he was; our younger son just shrugged his shoulders. The older son, obviously agitated, forcefully planted his head back into the ground.

The older son slowly got up from his prone position, and you could see that his head was still down. He was looking at the ground, dumbfounded, frustrated, and angry. He looked back over to us, and half lifted his hands in exasperation. The younger son began walking over to his older brother to comfort him, but when the older brother noticed him walking towards him, he held his hand up to him to signal that he didn't want his sympathy or pity. He stood there with his head down, shaking back and forth, brooding.

After a while, we all walked over to where he was. His mother went to put her arm around him, but he forcibly shrugged her off and walked a few steps away from us, furious. We had never seen him so unconstrained in his displeasure. His face was so contorted and twisted, tears streaming down his face. His countenance seemed downcast and strained simultaneously, and his whole body vibrated with an animosity that we had never seen before.

The younger son tried to calm him, "Brother, your presentation was beautiful, like nothing I have ever witnessed; the aroma is so..."

"NO!" the older son burst out. "NO... NO... NO...!" "I don't want to hear your pity! Especially from you!" he directed toward his younger brother.

"Son!" I interjected.

"I know, Father, don't speak to your favorite son that way!! I mean, he is precious; he is favored! Even the Lord God favors him, accepting that disgusting, smelly slaughter over the enticing, sweet smell of my offering."

He went over to the carcasses, now beginning to draw insects and reek of blood and flesh. He took in a deep smell through his nostrils and tauntingly, with his hands wafting in the fragrance, stated, "Mmmm, smell that magnificent smell of fresh meat still on the bone," he took in another deep smell, "the deep, rich odor of lambs blood." He tilted his head, leaned closer to the carcasses, pointed his finger in the air, and stated, "Do I smell a hint of intestines, possibly mixed with bile?"

"Yes," he continued mockingly, "I can see why the Lord God chose this delectable fare over my inviting mixture of sweet-smelling grains, olive oil, and mixed spices with an aroma so appealing that the air just bursts with flavor!" He went over and forcibly kicked all of the offering of grain off the stone, yelling at the top of his lungs!

We all just stood there, not sure what to do or say. We couldn't answer why the Lord God didn't accept his offering.

I then heard the familiar sound of the Lord God entering the place of offering. We all faced where we could sense the presence of the Lord God and bowed our heads.

Then we could hear the voice of the Lord God saying to the older son, "Why are you angry? Why is your face downcast? If you do what is right, will you not be accepted?"

We all stood there in the presence of the Lord God while he was correcting the older son. We then understood why the older son's offering wasn't accepted, and the younger son was. It was a matter of the heart. The younger son's offering was from a place of humility, reverence, and gratitude. But the older son was of pride and spectacle. We remembered when the older son enviously bumped into the younger son and glared at him when he brought his offering. It was all so clear now.

The older son's face and countenance were still disfigured in anger when the Lord God spoke again to him, "But if you do not do what is right, sin is crouching at your door; it desires to have you, but you must rule over it." Then, the Lord God's presence departed.

After a moment, I told my older son, "Son, you must reconcile. You must search your heart and do what is right as God instructed. Reconcile your pride, reconcile your envy towards your brother. Don't let sin have you!"

"Yes, father," the older son consented but could still sense some reluctance in his tone.

"Your mother and I will head back to the dwelling; you and your brother gather the lamb meat and grain and prepare for storage," I said.

"Yes, Abba," both sons said in unison.

While the parents were leaving, the younger son asked his older brother, "I will begin gathering the meat from the lambs while you gather the grain?"

The older son just shook his head and turned and began half-heartedly scraping up the grain to put it back into the containers. The younger son began to section the best cuts of meat expertly and efficiently from the carcasses. The older brother, was finished before, the younger brother and wandered over to help him finish before the sun went down. He picked up a sharpened flint stone for sacrificing the lambs and placed it in his pouch.

He looked over at his younger brother, who was diligently cutting up the lamb meat and placing it into a large sled to transport it back to the dwelling to prepare to store for their sustenance for the next several days and weeks. The older brother's heart and demeanor towards his younger brother were growing colder and colder, and his jealousy and hate for him was complete. He made up his mind and called for his younger brother.

"Let's go over to the field. I want to discuss what happened with each of our offerings and how the Lord God was so favorable to your presentation."

His younger brother acknowledged, put down his cutting tool, wiped the blood from his hands, and began to follow his older brother to the field. The older brother was waiting and seemed to be in deep thought when the younger brother arrived.

"Brother, I am here. What do you want to discuss?"

The older brother had his back to him, arms crossed in front of him with one hand holding his chin. He was obviously in deep thought and didn't turn around or respond for a minute or two.

"Brother?" The younger brother beckoned.

The older brother finally responded, "Well, little brother, I want to understand how the Lord God received your offering so well." The older brother turned to face the younger brother; who was still downcast but then seemed to brighten as he began talking with him. "Your skill with killing and then slaughtering and extracting the best of the fat portions to offer to the Lord God is incredible. How do you kill the lamb so quickly to where there seems to be no struggle? It almost seems that the lamb doesn't even feel it?"

The younger brother was not expecting the older brother to be so interested in offering the lambs, he never seemed to care before. But maybe since the Lord God had rejected his offering and the Lord God corrected the older brother, he genuinely wanted to revisit his methods and motivation.

"Well," the younger brother began, "I want to ensure that the lamb is killed as compassionately as possible."

"Hmmm," the older brother feigned interest as he crossed his arms again and put his hand on his chin as if in deep thought.

"So I first ensure that the flint tool is as sharp as it can be so that it will cut as quickly, deeply, and thoroughly as possible, then I soothe the lamb, pull its chin up to expose his entire neck, and then from one side to the other I cut its throat as cleanly and forcibly as possible to ensure I cut its breathing tube and its arteries completely. Then, the lamb will bleed out and die very quickly and not suffer too much.

"So you're saying," the older brother clarified, "that to ensure that the lamb dies with the most efficiency, compassion, and with minimal suffering, you must expose his neck and cut forcefully?" The older brother demonstrated this with a chopping and sawing motion.

"Not exactly," the younger brother corrected, "It's not a forceful chopping motion; it is a smooth, forceful slicing motion from one side of the neck as deeply as possible to the other in one smooth motion."

"Oh, I see," said the older brother and made a motion seeming to go backward across the imaginary sheep's neck.

"Not exactly," the younger brother corrected again, a little amused. "You have to go the other direction." Then demonstrated holding the chin of the imaginary sheep and making the slicing motion. "You hold the lamb's chin with your left hand, the flint in your right hand, and reach across and cut from left to right."

"Now I get it," the older brother responded with enthusiastic understanding, mimicking the motions of the younger brother.

"Exactly!" the younger brother confirmed.

"Let me try one more time," the older brother got behind his younger brother, "you pretend to be the lamb. So I grab it by the chin," he grasped his brother's chin, "then I, in one smooth motion, slice from left to right like this?" he drew an imaginary line across his brother's neck from left to right with his finger. The younger brother nodded his head up and down to affirm.

"Once more," the older brother prodded.

He grasped the younger brother by the chin, but this time he reached into his pouch and pulled out the flint-cutting tool, came across his brother's neck, and, with one swift, forceful motion, slit his brother's throat from ear to ear.

The younger brother fell to the ground on his hands and knees, eyes wide with shock and confusion, trying to cry out but was not able to as his throat was destroyed, blood gushing out onto the ground, and in seconds, the younger brother was dead.

My wife and I had just reached our dwelling and put our stuff away. I began hearing the sound of something crying out. I looked around the dwelling and saw nothing there. I went outside and looked around but saw nothing there, but I could still hear the sound of crying out. I asked my wife, "Do you hear that?"

"Here what?" she responded.

"That crying sound," I answered.

"I don't hear anything," she replied.

"Hmm," I said, "maybe it's one of the sheep; I'll check on them."

I walked over to the sheep pens, but they were all quiet. I could still hear the cry; it would come and go, soft then louder, and I couldn't zero in on where it was coming from. I'll see if the boys hear it when they return; they should be back anytime now. So I went back to the dwelling. When I arrived, my wife was preparing food for all of us for when the boys returned.

I saw the older son coming down the road, dragging the meat and grain that would be processed and stored. I didn't see the younger son; he must have been lagging. I went out to help my son drag the provisions. As I helped, I asked my son, "Where is your brother?" No response. A few minutes passed, and as we arrived and dropped off the provisions, I asked again, "Where is your brother?"

He shrugged his shoulders, "Am I my brother's keeper?" he responded.

I could see that he was still irritated from having his offering rejected, so he and his brother must have argued and decided to give each other some space to cool off. I then asked him, "Do you hear that crying sound? I have been hearing it ever since I got home."

He looked over me, shrugged his shoulders, and said, "I don't hear anything." He was still upset, so I figured that while putting away the provisions, I would wait a few minutes longer for the younger son and then go check on him if he didn't come soon.

The older son was finished a few minutes later, so I asked him, "Should we go check on your brother?" His response was not what I was expecting, and I could sense that he was still furious and was almost quaking with fury.

"If you want to go find your son, go yourself! Am I my brother's keeper?" he snapped back. He then turned and walked away and got a few feet from me, and we both felt a familiar presence coming into the area. The Lord God was here. My son and I took off our sandals and bowed before the Lord. The Lord asked my son, "Where is your brother, Abel?"

My son, haughtily, responded, "I don't know, am I my brother's keeper?

"Son!" I scolded; why was he being so disrespectful to the Lord God of the universe?

The Lord then said, "What have you done?"

I looked at my son and wondered why the Lord asked him this. I was puzzled.

The Lord went on, "Listen!"

I could hear the crying sound becoming more evident and louder, "What is that?" I thought to myself.

"Your brother's blood cries out to me from the ground," the Lord explained.

"What?" I exclaimed! I looked over at my son and asked, "What does the Lord mean that your brother's blood cries out from the ground? What does that mean, Cain? What have you done?" Panic was overtaking me.

My wife heard us as I was now yelling at my son, and she came running down to where we were. She realized the Lord was here and ran over to me. "What is going on?" she asked.

"The Lord asks Cain where his brother is and that his blood is crying out from the ground," I explained, emotion overtaking me.

My wife begins to sob and asks Cain, "Cain, what have you done?"

Cain's face is contorted, and he is shaking all over, tears of anger rolling down his face.

I held my wife in my arms, and we both fell to our knees in grief, realizing that Abel was no longer with us.

The Lord then announces to Cain, "Now you are under a curse and driven from the ground, which opened its mouth to receive your brother's blood from your hand. When you work the ground, it will no longer yield its crops for you. You will be a restless wanderer on the earth."

"Cain, what have you done?" I asked.

He looked over at me and began to tremble all over.

My wife couldn't stop wailing and crying. "My son, my sweet son..."

Cain cried out, "My punishment is more than I can bear! Today, You are driving me from the land, and I will be hidden from Your presence; I will be a restless wanderer on the earth, and whoever finds me will kill me!'

"Not so," the Lord replied, "anyone who kills Cain will suffer vengeance seven times over." The Lord then put a mark on Cain so that no one who found him would kill him. Then, the Lord left.

I continued to hold my wife, who was sobbing uncontrollably as we watched in silence as Cain looked over at us, turned, and walked away from us forever.

That was many years ago, but the event still affects my wife and me today. We lost two sons that day. I was so angry with Cain for a long time; I couldn't understand what could make anyone so enraged that they would kill someone. This has never happened before; a human has never killed another human.

How far have we fallen since getting expelled from the garden? I can't help but feel that I am responsible for Cain doing what he did. I mean, I didn't raise him to be vengeful, jealous, angry, or a murderer, but I can see the same similarities from the fall of Cain that my wife and I experienced from the fall in the garden. I can see the generational curse passed down from our generation to our children's generation and how they are reaping the cascading consequences of our regretful acts.

When the Lord didn't accept Cain's offering, the Lord came and asked Cain, "Why are you angry?" I remember when the Lord asked me a similar question in the garden. It reminded me of when the diabolical serpent that we had loved and accepted, along with all of the creatures the Lord God had created, had approached my wife and twisted the words of the Lord God.

The serpent instilled doubtful thoughts of what the Lord God said and what He meant. The Lord God created a divine order that the serpent had disrupted by approaching my wife first. The divine order was established that the Lord God was first and pre-eminent in all things, and then dominion was given to me (Adam) as the first created human. I was directly given dominion over all the beasts of the field, the birds of the air, and the sea fish to be fruitful and multiply. He gave every plant and tree to eat from but then commanded that we, from the tree of the knowledge of good and evil, do not partake, for when we do, we shall surely die. My wife would be the next in the divine order, created in my image and from my flesh and bone. Then, it would be our offspring when they came, and then all other creations.

When the serpent approached my wife and began misconstruing what God said, the serpent was disrupting that divine order; the order should have been to come to me first. I heard their conversation, and I should have infused myself and ensured that the Lord's commands and intentions were clearly understood and followed. I remember hearing the serpent ask my wife, "Did God say?" The serpent continued to deceive and convince her that God would surely not let us die, and wouldn't it benefit us to be like God, knowing the difference between good and evil? He was so convincing and unassuming that neither my wife nor I felt any apprehension in his conversation. When she began to look over the fruit of the tree, she was entranced with its beauty, which was pleasing to the eye. She even started to feel the texture of the tree's leaves and how smooth the fruit was, smelling the fragrance of the fruit. At some point, when I was not watching; she had picked some fruit from the tree and took a bite.

I immediately felt a dimensional shift and could tell everything was different. I looked at my wife; she had the fruit in her hand, and I could see her chewing. She was giddy as if she were captivated by the effects of the fruit. How delicious it was, how pleasing it was, and how liberating it made her feel; she felt that she could see and understand on an entirely different level; she was so enthralled and ecstatic with it that she wanted me to eat also to see and experience what she was experiencing.

For the first time, though, I felt sorrow. I knew that my wife had disrupted the order of creation by disobeying the command of the Lord God. Her appearance was now wholly different; her body was exposed and without covering. I could see that the glory of the Lord was now off of her. My sorrow was a strong feeling deep in my soul that I was going to lose my best friend, my soulmate, my help mate, my bone of my bone, and flesh of my flesh. The feeling of losing her was overwhelming and heart-wrenching, and I wanted to do anything that I could to fix what had just happened. For a second, I looked around and then caught the eye of the serpent; it was smiling at me with a crafty smile and motioned its head towards the fruit in my wife's hand. I knew then that if I were not to lose my wife, I would have to sacrifice what the Lord God had entrusted to me: to be in His likeness, to represent and reflect His glory to all creation, to have dominion, and to righteously rule and reign over His creation. I would have to eat the fruit so I wouldn't lose my wife. So I chose to eat the fruit so that she would not die alone; I would die with my bride.

As soon as I took a bite, immediately everything changed. It was like a veil had been lifted from my eyes and my ability to see and discern was remarkably heightened. I could now clearly see that the serpent had deceived and tricked us; its intentions were evil. I felt like I had lost something. I felt my body exposed for all of creation to see and it embarrassed me, and I felt ashamed. I could tell my wife was now going through the same experience, and we were both now standing in the Lord God's creation, completely exposed and naked, without

His glory to cover us. When I looked at my wife, I could no longer see the Lord's likeness, essence, or glory. We were now stark and bare, and our physical character and identity were flawed and corrupted. We were no longer who we were; we were something less, diminished, and in a lower state of what we were created to be. We could sense it and so could the rest of creation.

My wife and I were panicky and trying to process our mistake. Why did we listen to the serpent? Why were we so easily tricked? Why would we so easily disobey the command of the Lord God? The One who loves us so dearly, and Who we love and cherish with such adoration, connection, reverence, joy, and endearment, that whenever we are in His presence, as when He comes into the garden in the cool of the day, we run to Him with such anticipation and delight that we fawn over His every word. When His gaze is upon us, we feel such love, value, and affirmation in His eyes that nothing else in creation matters. When He speaks approval, acceptance, and favor over us, we overflow with His love, and we excitedly and enthusiastically convey that love to all of the rest of creation. But, for the first time, my wife and I feared that when He looks at us now, in our state, will His gaze be that of disappointment, embarrassment, and shame? When He looks at us now, will we be detestable in His sight? How could He not? For we are detestable in our sight. My eyes began to water up, and an overwhelming emotion began to overtake me. I could see that my wife also began to sob.

My wife then looked at me and apprehensively asked, “What do we do now? All creation is scrutinizing us; I can feel its eyes upon us. What will the Lord God think when He sees us? How can we ever face Him? He told us we will die when we eat of the tree of knowledge of good and evil. Do you think He will be so angry with us that He will destroy us? I don’t want to die; I don't want to see the disappointment in His eyes. Should we run, should we hide, should we escape?"

Fear gripped me! I began to chastise her, "Why did you eat the fruit? Why did you listen to the serpent? Why did you disobey the command of the Lord? Did you not think that there wouldn't be consequences if we disobeyed Him? Look at us! We are pathetic; I barely recognize you; you are naked! We are naked! Everything good has been stripped away; we are atrocious! How can we face the Lord God now? We cannot let Him see us like this!"

In trepidation I began to survey our surroundings searching and hoping for an answer, again I caught the crafty serpent looking at us with a demeaning expression in seeming amusement and it sarcastically stated, "If I were in the repulsive state you are in I would cover myself, so that my appalling appearance couldn't be seen. Maybe those fig leaves will hide your abhorrent spectacle!" The serpent irritated me, but I couldn't disagree, so my wife and I began pulling the leaves off the fig tree and some vines growing up the tree and began sewing the figs together into a covering. We tried the coverings on and hoped our corrupted appearance would be less noticeable.

I was adjusting my wife's covering when we heard a familiar sound. The Lord God is walking in the garden! We looked at each other in terror! "He's coming! What do we do? He can't see us like this!" she pleaded.

"Quick!" I said, "Let's run into the forest and hide amongst the trees; with the fig coverings we have on, we can blend in, and maybe He won't be able to see us!" So we ran into the thickest part of the forest, crouched down, and hid ourselves in the trees and vegetation. I could hear Him getting closer. I pulled my wife closer, and we held our breath, hoping the Lord would pass us by. He walked near to us and then walked past us. I thought, "Maybe the Lord will keep going, and we won't have to face Him." As I thought that he had stopped.

My breath caught, and my wife and I looked into each other's eyes, terrified. Then I heard His voice; it sounded like thunder in my ears.

"Adam, where are you?"

I tried to stay quiet with the chance that He would think we were somewhere else and maybe move on... but I could feel He knew where we were. After a minute or so, I finally stood up. My wife was still clinging to me and trying to stay hidden. I pulled her up beside me and tentatively, fearfully, we walked out into His presence. Shame and guilt overwhelmed me. I began to tremble and couldn't look into His face; I just wanted to take off running and never stop!

I was quivering so much that I could barely speak; my wife fell to her knees and buried her face in her hands, still sobbing. I couldn't look up, so I stared at the ground and attempted to answer, "I... heard... heard you in the garden... I was afraid... I... I was naked... so.. so... I hid."

There was a pause; it seemed like an eternity. I quickly glanced up and saw the sorrow that engulfed the Lord's face and cut me to the heart. I fell to my knees emotion and tears overtaking me. He then responded, in a still small voice, "Who told you that you were naked?" I couldn't answer; I was so overwhelmed with shame and the feeling that I had disappointed my Lord. He asked more sternly, "Have you eaten from the tree I commanded you not to eat from?"

I didn't know what to say; I was so flustered that I couldn't think straight, so I blurted out, "The woman you put here with me... SHE GAVE ME SOME FRUIT FROM THE TREE AND... AND... I ATE IT!!!"

My wife abruptly stood up and looked at me with a surprised and angry look, then looked all around in a trembling panic. The Lord then asked her, "What have you done?"

She was wringing her hands together, swaying back and forth, and desperately looking away from the Lord. Her eye caught the serpent, lazily lounging a little ways off and observing the scenario with amusement, and pointed at the serpent and yelled, "The... the serpent... deceived me! And... And... I... I ate!"

I could feel the gaze of the Lord turning from us and directly to the crafty serpent. The smile on the serpent's face melted away and it bowed with its face to the ground as the Lord's focus was squarely upon him. The Lord then spoke to the serpent in a voice of thunder, "Because you have done this," He paused and then continued, "Cursed are you above all livestock and all the wild animals! You will crawl on your belly and eat dust all the days of your life! And I will put enmity between you and the woman and between your offspring and hers; he will crush your head, and you will strike his heel."

The serpent was terrified by the voice of the Lord, buffeting it with the pronouncement of the curse; with every word of judgment that the Lord spoke over the serpent, we could see the serpent transforming right before our eyes. It was becoming exactly what the Lord pronounced it to be. When the Lord was finished, the serpent was only a slender, slimy figure of what it once was. It tried to speak, but the only thing coming forth from it was a forked tongue and a hissing sound. It then slithered away into the grass of the forest. Witnessing this once-beautiful creature transformed into the squirming, wriggling, hissing serpent was terrifying. We became terrified, was the Lord going to do to us what He did to the serpent?

The Lord then turned His gaze onto the woman. He then pronounced to her, "I will make your pains in childbearing very severe; with painful labor, you will give birth to children. Your desire will be for your husband, who will rule over you."

He then turned to me and stated, "Because you listened to your wife and ate fruit from the tree about which I commanded you, 'You must not eat from it,' Cursed is the ground because of you." through painful toil you will eat from it all the days of your life. I will produce thorns and thistles for you, and you will eat the plants of the field. By the sweat of your brow, you will eat your food until you return to the ground, since from it you were taken; for dust, you are, and to dust, you will return. "

We were a little relieved. The Lord God punished us for disobeying His command to not eat the fruit of the particular tree, but He didn't destroy us on sight or change us into some grotesque creature like He did the serpent. Based on the curses He pronounced, we weren't to die immediately, and we would be able to survive and live for a while longer. He did tell the woman that she would bear children, and He did tell me that I would eat the plants of the field. So, we still have some life left, but He also said that from dust, we came, and to dust, we will return; we will die at some point. He also mentioned to the serpent that the Lord would put malice between the serpent's offspring and the offspring of the woman, that he would bruise his heel of our lineage and it would crush the head of the serpent. So, could there be redemption in the future? The Lord God must have a plan? Since the Lord foretold that the woman would bear children, I named her Eve- for she will be the mother of all humankind.

The Lord then explained that our garments of figs would not be sufficient for covering our sins and that our transgression would have to be covered with a price. He then took an animal and slayed it, took its skin, and made garments for us. The animal had to sacrifice its life as payment for covering our nakedness so that we would not be ashamed to stand before God.

Then the LORD God said, "Behold, the man has become like one of Us, to know good and evil. And now, lest he put out his hand and take also of the tree of life, eat, and live forever." Then the LORD God took us to the garden's edge and put us out of the garden of Eden. Once outside the garden, the Lord God placed cherubim at the east of the garden of Eden, along with a flaming sword that turned every way to guard the way to the Tree of Life.

Being outside of the garden was another dimensional shift. The peace and serenity of the garden was shattered once we were banished to the wilderness. All creation was now corrupted, flawed, with a propensity for wickedness. The beasts we adored now seemed more ferocious and strangers to us. Another shift felt was that we could no longer feel the presence of the Lord. Would the Lord ever be near to us again? Is this the death, that the Lord told us we would experience, separated from His presence, glory, or comfort?

As I remember that event, I can see the correlation between our sin experience and Cain's experience. I can see that our fall and sin in the garden were passed down to our children. The evidence of this was through the questions the Lord asked me and the questions He asked Cain, which were the same in structure.

"Adam, where are you?" / "Cain, why are you angry?"

"Who told you that you were naked?" / "Where is your brother Abel?"

"Have you eaten from the tree?" / "What have you done?"

I also can see how the punishments and curses follow a similar template. When the Lord punished me, He pronounced by:

- Cursing the ground: The ground now would bear thorns and thistles. Because of me, there is a curse upon all creation. After the curse, the ground still produced good fruit for sustenance, but thorns and thistles more easily came and were a burden that constantly attempted to choke out the fruit.
- In toil you shall eat of it: I had worked in the garden of Eden before the curse, but it was with joy and ease.

Now, my work has a cursed element, with struggle and exhaustion part of work from the sweat of my brow.

- Dust you are, and to dust you shall return: The final curse upon me assured me there would be an end to my toil and labor and that it would not end with *deliverance* but would end in *death*.
- I was driven out from Eden: I was given dominion as the overseer of the garden and all the beasts, birds, and fish. But now I am banished.

Cain's curse, similar but amplified from my original curse:

- He was driven from the ground: His punishment was also a curse of the ground, but going to another level. No longer would it even produce crops for him.
- He will be a restless wanderer: Cain would never find a home on all the earth. As I was banished from Eden and never to return, Cain would never be able to settle himself on the earth; we never saw Cain again.

I can see how the Lord covered our sins:

- For me and Eve, it was the death and shed blood of an animal and its skin that covered our nakedness, shame, and guilt.
- For Cain, the Lord put a mark on him so that anyone who found Cain would not kill him.

As I process these two events that have entirely defined my family and me, I am sad and regret that we are in a fallen, sinful state. Not only do I have to deal with the consequences of our rebellion, but because of my wife and my rebellion, has now been passed down to our sons. I am thankful that the Lord has also been gracious to us by not being as drastic in His judgment as He could be. In each case, He has given a level of rescue and grace from our sinful condition, demonstrating that the Lord will continue to grant this rescue and grace from generation to generation. Thinking back to the Lord's declaration that the offspring of the woman will bring redemption back to man by bruising his heel on the head of the serpent, I worry that now that we have lost both of our sons, both of our offspring, how will this declaration come to pass? I guess I will have to trust by faith that the Lord has a plan and will work all things for our good.

The evening was coming, and I returned to my dwelling, where my wife had prepared our meal. My wife sets the table as I come inside and wash off the sweat and dirt of today's labors. I can see a spring in her step, and her countenance is more joyful than it has been for quite some time.

I tell my wife, "I am glad to see you seem in a better mood today."

"Mmm hmm," she responds.

"Has something happened to bring this cheer?" I asked.

"Maybe," she replied.

"Am I to assume you may let me in on this?" I queried again.

"Yes," she stated again.

"Ok," I responded in amused surrender, realizing I wouldn't know until she was ready to tell me.

As we sit down, and bless the food the Creator has provided us, my wife dishes out our portions. She sits back, looking at me with a smile and a few seconds later says...

"I am with child!"

Chapter 4

Show Me Your Glory!

After all of these thousands of years, we can see that we are still stuck in the same curse, the same predicament. We are NOT reflecting back His glory as He intended. Unless something disrupts the status quo, the future generations will also NOT be reflecting His glory as intended. Through all of these thousands of years until now, is there evidence that it is possible that our reflect-ability can be restored to its intended state?

Exodus 33:12-23

> *Moses said to the Lord, "You have been telling me, 'Lead these people,' but you have not let me know whom you will send with me. You have said, 'I know you by name and you have found favor with me.' If you are pleased with me, teach me Your ways so I may know You and continue to find favor with You. Remember that this nation is Your people."*
>
> *The Lord replied, "My presence will go with you, and I will give you rest."*

Then Moses said to Him, "If Your Presence does not go with us, do not send us up from here. How will anyone know that You are pleased with me and with your people unless You go with us? What else will distinguish me and Your people from all the other people on the face of the earth?"

And the Lord said to Moses, "I will do the very thing you have asked, because I am pleased with you, and I know you by name." Then Moses said, "Now show me your glory." And the Lord said, "I will cause all My goodness to pass in front of you, and I will proclaim my name, the Lord (Yahweh), in your presence. I will have mercy on whom I will have mercy, and I will have compassion on whom I will have compassion. But," He said, "you cannot see My face, for no one may see Me and live."

Then the Lord said, "There is a place near me where you may stand on a rock. When my glory passes by, I will put you in a cleft in the rock and cover you with my hand until I have passed by. Then I will remove my hand and you will see My back, but My face must not be seen."

Exodus 34: 29-35

When Moses came down from Mount Sinai with the two tablets of the covenant law in his hands, he was not aware that his face was radiant because he had spoken with the Lord. When Aaron and all the Israelites saw Moses, his face was radiant, and they were afraid to come near him. But Moses called to them; so Aaron and all the leaders of the community came back to him, and he spoke to them. Afterward all the Israelites came near him, and he gave them all the commands the Lord had given him on Mount Sinai.

When Moses finished speaking to them, he put a veil over his face. But whenever he entered the Lord's presence to speak with Him, he removed the veil until he came out. And when he came out and told the Israelites what he had been commanded, they saw his face was radiant. Then Moses would put the veil back over his face until he went to speak to the Lord.

We see that Moses has reestablished a measure of what Adam had in the garden. Of course, Moses is of the lineage of the fallen state of man. He, therefore, could not receive the full measure of the Lord God's glory as Adam had, or Moses would have died, but this scripture does show that Moses had found favor enough in the Lord that when he asked to see the Lord God's glory, the Lord conditionally granted his request. So, looking at this, we need to understand the context of this scripture in the storyline of the Exodus so that we can ascertain a few things:

- Through a burning bush, the Lord God called Moses out of the wilderness to lead the nation of Israel out of the land and bondage of Egypt, to go through the wilderness, the desert, and to the promised land across the Jordan River. As Moses answers this call, he then:
- Moses confronted Pharaoh many times, who refused to release Israel, and the Lord God brought ten plagues onto Egypt to bring about the release of the Hebrews, to which Pharaoh finally relents.
- Moses leads the Israelites out of Egypt, getting as far as the Red Sea. Pharaoh changes his mind and pursues Israel to recapture them.
- Moses receives power from the Lord God and parts the Red Sea, allowing the Hebrews to pass through the Red Sea. and once all of the Hebrews were through, closed the waters on the Egyptians who were in the bed of the Red Sea chasing after the Hebrews, defeating their enemies by drowning them once and for all.

- Moses begins leading the Hebrews through the desert. After three days of traveling and finding no water, when they reached Marah, the water was bitter; the Lord God instructed Moses to cast a particular piece of wood in the water to make it drinkable.
- The Hebrews complained of no food, so the Lord God rained down Manna and Quail from heaven.
- They complained again of no water, and Moses, through the Lord God, provided water from a rock.
- They arrived at Mount Sinai, where the Lord God led Moses to have the people consecrate themselves, and the Lord God came down to speak directly to the people in a cloud of smoke and fire. (The Lord God had to veil, shield His glory from them through the cloud of smoke, lest they perish.) And spoke the commandments and laws that the Lord God was giving them in order for them to follow Him through his divine requirements.
- Then, the Lord God called Moses to come up to the mountain for 40 days so that the Lord God could inscribe the commandments onto a stone and explain fully to Moses how the Hebrews would implement and hold to the commands.
- Moses comes down off of the mountain to find that the Hebrews had made a golden calf to worship and was so enraged with the people that Moses threw the tablets and broke them to pieces and ultimately called for who is for the Lord to come to him and then instructed those that opposed Moses and were unrepentant for their sin, about 3000 to be destroyed.
- Moses went back up to Mount Sanai again for 40 days to speak with the Lord and to inscribe a second set of commandments.

So now that we have the context of where we are in the storyline, we revisit the scriptures of Exodus 33:12. The Hebrew people have just sinned against the Lord. Moses has taken his tent outside the camp and established it as the tent of meeting with the Lord God and is contending for the Lord not to desert the Hebrews for their habitual resisting against Him and complaining of their circumstances, their continual doubt concerning the method of their deliverance, and blatantly sinning against the Lord by building and worshipping a golden calf. Moses has been called to lead these people and doesn't want the Lord God to abandon him while fulfilling this mission. Also, Moses deeply desires to grow closer to the Lord personally.

We see that whenever Moses would go into the Tent of Meeting,

> *The Lord would speak to Moses face to face, as one speaks to a friend.*
> *Exodus 33:12-23*

In their conversation, Moses tells the Lord God that he doesn't want to continue this mission without Him. In essence, Moses is reminding the Lord what He had told Moses-that the He knows Moses by name and has found favor in Moses, and Moses wants this partnership and close friendship to continue.

Moses entreats to the Lord God that to merely travel without His presence and to arrive at the promised land would be nothing special outside of fulfilling the covenant to the Hebrew's forefathers Abraham, Isaac, and Jacob, which would confirm that the Lord God will not go back on His promises. Still, it wasn't enough for the nation of Israel would make it to the Promised Land, which would be nothing special without the unique presence of the LORD. Moses pressed God on this point- would the Lord God's presence be with them?

The Lord confirms His relationship with Moses and agrees, "My Presence will go with you," which translates to "My Face will travel with you." This gives us some insight in what is meant when Moses met with God face to face (Exodus 32:11). The Presence of God implies rest and peace in life. This was an essential and necessary gift from God to Moses and the nation of Israel.

"If Your Presence does not go with us, do not bring us," we see that Moses continued his persistent way of petitioning with the Lord. Moses knew that nothing the LORD could give them would make them truly different from the other nations. Only the strong presence of the LORD Himself could do that. Moses wanted something for Israel that would show that they were not like all the other nations and what makes Israel unique could only be their God's powerful presence. Israel's relationship with God made them different from all other nations. God's PRESENCE among them is what made them different. It was important for Israel to know this themselves, but it was also crucial for the other nations to know this as a testament.

The Lord granted the strong intervention of Moses, and the Lord promised to restore His relationship with Israel. Moses won a personal favor from God when he asked for the unique presence of God to remain with Israel as they journeyed to the Promised Land (Exodus 33:12-17). He also won confirmation of the promise from God and an affirmation of a close personal relationship with himself. Yet Moses was still not satisfied. He wanted to see His glory.

Perhaps Moses, when making such a bold and brave request, may have ventured beyond what would be allowed for him to experience, yet the Lord God was still pleased with Moses and his desire to know the Lord in more significant and profound way. This hunger for more of the Lord God –is a mark of genuine revival and restoration of a relationship. Whatever Moses had already experienced with God, he now wanted more. Then the Lord God said,

> *"I will make all My goodness pass before you, and I will proclaim the name of the LORD (Yahweh) before you. I will be gracious to whom I will be gracious, and I will have compassion on whom I will have compassion." But," He said, "You cannot see My face, for no man shall see Me and live." The Lord God said, "I will make all My goodness pass before you."*

Moses requested the glory of God, and God agreed to show Moses His goodness. The Lord's glory is His goodness. When Moses beheld the glory of God, His first understanding was that God was good. If we never get that revelation, that understanding that God is good, we will never know much about Him. When the Lord God revealed His glory to Moses, it wasn't His justice that He revealed to Moses; it wasn't His power; it wasn't His wrath against sin. All those are genuine characteristics of God's divine nature, but when the Lord manifests Himself to Moses, He displayed His goodness, which is synonymous with His Glory, Hallelujah!

> *"Here is a place by Me, and you shall stand on the rock..."*

God was to unveil Himself to Moses in an extraordinary way. The Lord prepared the event carefully, giving Moses a specific place to stand.

> *"When my glory passes by, I will put you in a cleft in the rock and cover you with my hand until I have passed*

> *by. Then I will remove my hand, and you will see My back, but My face must not be seen."*

The Lord God had to protect Moses from the full force of His glory, particularly since Moses couldn't see His Face. So, this seems to be a quandary of sorts... The Lord God states that spoke to Moses 'Face-to-face' as a friend. Still, in this statement, He tells Moses that there is one stipulation: Moses may not see His face, for no one may see His face and live, and Moses may only see the back side of the Lord God as He passes by.

When the Lord God states that He has talked with Moses face to face, it is in metaphorical terms that we can find in the statement from Numbers 12:6-8 is an understanding of how the Lord delineated His speaking to Moses with how He spoke to other prophets; Moses heard clearly and plainly, while other prophets heard in dreams and visions.

> *6 He said, "Listen to my words: "When there is a prophet among you, I, the Lord, reveal myself to them in visions, I speak to them in dreams. 7 But this is not true of my servant Moses; he is faithful in all my house. 8 With him I speak face to face, clearly and not in riddles; he sees the form of the Lord."*

The Lord God Himself is explaining His special relationship and bond with Moses. This most likely refers to a figurative expression, meaning free and open fellowship rather than a literal face-to-face encounter. The phrase also demonstrates this, *"and he sees the form of the LORD."* This is likely what Moses saw of God with his physical eyes – only the form of the LORD, nothing specific or material because he could not see the LORD's face and live. The 'form' is the most likely of visual representations, pictures, or images of earthly and heavenly beings, a shadow. (Exodus 20:4). In the book of (Job 4:16). Job saw someone's form but could not identify the person from it.

This clarity of revelation from God made Moses unique. Moses alone was the only person out of all the Hebrews with him who could approach the holy mountain and gaze at the Divine Personhood of Jehovah, causing Moses' face to radiate following these encounters. This speaks of an unprecedented level of intimacy between God and Moses.

Why was Moses allowed this intimacy and access to the Lord God on a conversational basis as a friend, along with special access to see God's glory?

The calling the Lord God placed on Moses. It was because God needed a man with the capacity and the desire to get close to and to learn, to know, to understand the things and nature of the Lord God to be a vessel of revelation, instruction, humility, and obedience as a leader for the nation of Israel through this remarkable time of the Exodus.

- Moses was a humble man. Number 12:3 states, *"Moses was a very humble man, more humble than anyone else on the face of the earth."* The Lord God places great value on the trait of humility – those who are genuinely others-centered and who genuinely have no desire to seek their interests, to exalt themselves, to put their self-centered needs above their calling, mission, purpose, destiny, and ultimately above their relationship with the Lord God – this character trait grants access to personal communion with God.
- According to the Lord God, *"Moses is faithful in all My house."* Moses' walk of righteousness, demonstrated in over forty years in obscure service to God in the most minor things, revealed the faithful heart that God saw in Moses.

- Moses won a personal favor from God when he asked for the unique presence of God to go with Israel on the way to the Promised Land (Exodus 33:12-17). He also won confirmation of the promise from God and an affirmation of a close personal relationship with himself. Yet Moses was still not satisfied. He wanted to see His glory more in his personal relationship with God. With special protections, God rewarded Moses' desire to see His glory as much as humanly possible due to our fallen state. This demonstrates that God rewards the seeking, yearning, enthusiastic heart.

We also should have this same level of earnest desire to experience God this deeply. The apostle Paul invites every Christian to a special, glorious intimacy with God. This relational and transforming power is not the property of just a few privileged Christians. It is no longer for just the most dedicated and earnest who seek the Lord God's glory, such as Moses, but through Jesus Christ and our redemption and restoration through Him, it can now belong to all who desire and seek it, to everyone who has an unveiled face. So, how do we get an unveiled face?

> *But we all, with unveiled faces, beholding the glory of the Lord in a mirror, are being transformed into the same image from glory to glory, just as by the Spirit of the Lord.2 Corinthians 3:18 But whenever anyone turns to the Lord, the veil is taken away.*
> *2 Corinthians3:16.*

When we, as in a mirror, view the glory of God, We can see the glory of God, but we cannot see His glory perfectly. Paul says, *"We can see the glory of the Lord, but we can't see it perfectly yet."* As we observe His glory, we are transformed. God will transform our lives from the inside out. Though the old covenant had glory, it could never transform lives through the law. God uses the new covenant to transform us.

So we ask ourselves, "How can I change?" Or "How can I see His glory, as Moses did?"

The best and most enduring change comes into our lives through our being transformed by our time spent with God. There are other ways we can change, such as shame, willfulness, or coercion, but none of these methods bring change that is as deep and lasting as the transformation that comes through the Spirit of God as we spend time in the presence of the Lord. Moses gained favor and was considered a FRIEND of God because he **earnestly spent time with the Lord God.**

Yet, it also requires us to be beholding. The word- beholding- means more than just a casual look; it means to study and intently search and gaze upon carefully. We all have something to behold and study in the Lord God. As we gaze into His image, we are changed into that same image. When we spend time beholding the glory of the Lord God's grace, peace, and righteousness, we will see a transforming growth in ourselves of love, grace, peace, and righteousness. His mirror is not only a mirror that shows us what we are, but more importantly, it reflects to us what we will BECOME, and what we will become is based on our perspective of what we behold.

Thankfully, we don't have to be bound to a faulty image of ourselves or a skewed image of God. We can be transformed into His image when we behold the form of God and His Goodness, His grace, His Mercy, His Love, and His Truth. This is God's grand strategy for our deliverance,

> *for whom He foreknew, He also predestined to be conformed to the image of His Son.*
> *Romans 8:29.*

This work of transformation is a process. While being transformed, we experience this transformation in phases to varying degrees. The work the Lord God is doing in us will be ongoing to mold us into the vessel, the image that He will need for the mission, purpose, and destiny He has for us. The work of transformation is an ongoing progression from glory to glory.

This access to God and His transforming presence is ours through accepting the new covenant that was established through Jesus dying on the cross, shedding His blood, and paying the price to redeem us from sin and restore us to what was lost- our originally intended created identity as children and coheirs with Him.

We are also given the SPIRIT of the Lord through the new covenant. Therefore, this work of transformation is God's work IN us, which transpires through the Spirit of God, not by the will or effort of man. We don't achieve or earn spiritual transformation by beholding the glory of the Lord in a mirror without the Holy Spirit, which also renews our minds and transforms our lives. We need to put ourselves in a place of surrender, obedience, and communion with His Spirit, connecting with our spirit, allowing us to experience His glory, and then to reflect and shine His glory THROUGH us. That is how we are effective and impactful for the mission He has assigned us and to be able to serve, worship, and glorify Him!

Next, we will look at more hindrances that we must overcome, by letting the Holy Spirit renew our minds and transform our lives to become the created image that reflects His glory as Moses was able to.

Chapter 5

Our Skewed Belief System

Anyone who has attempted to live out their walk with the Lord for a reasonable amount of time will tell you that they have seen many alter calls and people accepting and believing in Jesus for conversion. Still, just as many aren't accessing the abundant life available. A misconception many have is that getting converted to be a Christ follower is crossing the finish line- but is actually just the beginning of the process. Time and again, many of us have experienced an altar-call conversion and then have been left stuck in a limited understanding of who we are in Him and failed to receive and live out the complete salvation, mission, and purpose that Jesus is calling us to- short-circuiting the promises of God in our lives.

Not often are the ways and things of Jesus this one dimensional, limited, unilateral or singular in purpose. When most say they believe in God, they usually are not referring to that they think and are ready to receive everything God has and intends for us (we are not as ambitious as Moses when asking to see His glory), but that we are getting our ticket to the "here by-and-by." For example, we can say that we believe that God is a healer but still do not receive healing. Although we may believe in healing, we may not think that it is for us, or maybe even that we brought the sickness on ourselves through poor decisions or how we live, and that we may even deserve our condition. So, although we may profess that we believe in healing, our Belief System nullifies us from receiving healing.

We have a contradiction of belief systems that are working against each other. On one hand, we may have witnessed the Lord healing someone, but on the other hand, we have not been healed ourselves. We may believe the Lord has healing for you, but for me, it is too hard for me to believe because of my guilt or shame or inadequate self-worth. We believe He can, but question, "Will He do it for me?" This faulty belief system allows us to believe that the Lord can open doors of opportunities, but still wonder, are those opportunities for me?

The quandary of this belief system leaves many of God's promises and opportunities for us sitting on the table because we won't allow ourselves to reach out and take them. So, we pray for the Lord to bless us, to change us, to heal us, to grow closer to us, but through our faulty belief system, we self-sabotage our way back down to our default belief system, never really receiving or realizing or claiming the answered prayer the Lord has given us.

These faulty belief systems, in varying degrees, can hinder or delay all that God has for us. Our skewed belief systems may not always be readily noticeable or come with warning tags identifying them, and we may not realize or recognize that this exists in our lives. Most of us are unaware that we are living by corrupted belief systems. Through our skewed perspectives, we ask God to bring peace into our homes, even though we continue creating strife. We ask Him to bless us financially, but we need to make sound money decisions. We are praying for a wayward child to come home with one hand but pushing them away with the other.

Faulty belief systems can cause us to cancel out our requests in answered prayer. Often, when we pray for something and when the Lord answers our prayer, we don't feel comfortable receiving the answered prayer, or the prayer comes in a way we weren't expecting. We inadvertently turn away from it, ignore it, or walk right by it because it doesn't fit our perspective of what we expected it to be. We will often reject the answered prayer and return to what is comfortable even though what is comfortable is not what we desire; it is what we are familiar with. We are more comfortable with what we are familiar with rather than the unfamiliarity of the promise, the victory, and the answered prayer God provides us.

We have been conditioned to live on the level of our belief system of familiarity. So, when the Lord gives us a promise or asks us to operate in a manner that we are not familiar with, we have a gravitational pull that will draw us back to comfort, dysfunction, and familiarity over victory. For instance, if we feel familiar and comfortable in poverty, we will end up staying there, and every time the Lord brings us out of poverty, we get uncomfortable with its unfamiliarity and will do things consciously or sub-consciously that will draw us back to being poor again and again, because that is our belief system. It's not that we don't want better, dream about better, yearn for better, but when better comes, it looks funny or tastes funny. The manna that God sent the Hebrews in the desert tasted funny. They wanted the leaks and onions from Egypt, not because they tasted better, but because they tasted familiar. This all ties to a system of beliefs that are a basket full of contradictions. We believe the Lord has so much more for us, but we won't let ourselves believe we are deserving or worthy to receive from Him.

This is similar to the story of the man who came to Jesus to heal his son. Jesus, along with Peter, James, and John, were coming down where Jesus was transfigured on the mount with the three disciples as witnesses who observed how a light shown from heaven over Jesus so brightly that His clothes were shimmering. Moses and Elijah appeared beside Jesus and were talking with Him. After this event, Jesus and the disciples descended the mount and they were discussing what they had just witnessed, and as they reached where they had left, they came upon a scene where the other disciples were arguing with the crowd and amongst themselves.

> *When they returned to the other disciples, they saw a large crowd surrounding them, and some teachers of religious law were arguing with them. When the crowd saw Jesus, they were overwhelmed with awe, (he had just come down from being transfigured on the Mountain) and ran to greet Him. "What is all this arguing about?" Jesus asked. One of the men in the crowd spoke up and said, "Teacher, I brought my son so you could heal him. He is possessed by an evil spirit that won't let him talk. And whenever this spirit seizes him, it throws him violently to the ground. Then he foams at the mouth, grinds his teeth, and becomes rigid. So I asked your disciples to cast out the evil spirit, but they couldn't do it."*
>
> *Mark 9:16- 18 (NIV)*

At some point, it became apparent that the disciples could not deliver the boy, and that's when the skewed, flawed, faulty faith and belief of everyone there was on full display; of the disciples, the son's Father, the crowd, and the religious elect, all arguing with each other, giving their opinions as to why this task wasn't working, and demonstrating that their skewed beliefs would not allow the miracle to happen.

The religious teachers in the crowd may have been challenging: who do these disciples think they are to presume they have the power and authority to cast out demons? They have no formal training concerning Jewish law; they have no pedigree or status, they are fisherman, merchants, tax collectors, and the like; it's no wonder they couldn't cast out this demon. They should be ashamed of themselves for leading this poor Father along; they do not have the credentials or ability to perform this task.

The disciples were probably also arguing with the crowd, in particular with the teachers of religious law, that they had seen their Rabbi do this type of miracle many times and were sent out in twos to perform all sorts of miracles, including casting out demons. They may have even argued that this demon is like no other, maybe it is too powerful, and maybe if the crowd wasn't distracting the disciples, perhaps the disciples could focus more and give the proper amount of intensity and diligence necessary to match the demon's determination.

The disciples possibly argued amongst themselves, stating that Andrew hadn't properly commanded the demon in the correct sequence. Perhaps they accused Phillip of trying to cast the demon out by trying to baptize the boy in the water the demon threw him in since Phillip was originally a disciple of John the Baptist. Maybe they accused Matthew of trying to charge the demon taxes for illegally residing in the boy and, therefore, had no alternative but to come out of him; after all, overdue taxes were a serious offense.

This is what Jesus walked into when He came down from the mount.

> *Jesus said to them, "You faithless people! How long must I be with you? How long must I put up with you? Bring the boy to me." So, they brought the boy. But when the evil spirit saw Jesus, it threw the child into a violent convulsion, and he fell to the ground, writhing and foaming at the mouth.*
>
> *Mark 9:19 (NIV)*

I'm sure the disciples and crowd looked at Jesus at this point and thought, "See, this is what he did to us; we couldn't do anything either..."

> *"How long has this been happening?" Jesus asked the boy's Father. He replied, "Since he was a little boy. The spirit often throws him into the fire or into water, trying to kill him. Have mercy on us if you can." "What do you mean, 'If I can'?" Jesus asked. "Anything is possible if a person believes." The Father instantly cried out, "I do believe, but help me overcome my unbelief!" When Jesus saw that the crowd of onlookers was growing, He rebuked the evil spirit. "Listen, you spirit that makes this boy unable to hear and speak," he said, "I command you to come out of this child and never enter him again!" Then the spirit screamed and threw the boy into another violent convulsion and left him. The boy appeared to be dead. A murmur ran through the crowd as people said, "He's dead." But Jesus took him by the hand and helped him to his feet, and he stood up. Afterward, when Jesus was alone in the house with His disciples, they asked him, "Why couldn't we cast out that evil spirit?" Jesus replied, "This kind can be cast out only by prayer."*
> *Mark 9: 21-29 (NIV)*

Again, this story is a basket full of contradictory beliefs! The Father, the disciples, and the crowd living out contradictory and flawed beliefs.

For the Father, who is trying to get his son healed of this evil spirit, he even displays his contradictions by stating to Jesus, "Have mercy on us if You can." The Father must have believed that Jesus could heal his son, for he had brought him to where Jesus was to have his son healed. At first, he couldn't find Jesus, so he asked his disciples, who were there waiting for Jesus to come back down from the Mountain to heal his son, but they weren't able to heal him.

This father has probably had many instances of healers, doctors, and soothsayers trying to heal his son over the years, all without success, and then, even when he asked Jesus' disciples to try to heal, there was no luck there either. You can say that he believed that Jesus could heal, based on all the other reports of miracles and healings, but his conditioning and thought process was, can or will He heal his son? The Father demonstrates that it is possible to believe and still have unbelief.

By the time Jesus' arrived, the son's Father finally asked Jesus to heal his son, but then stated,

> *"if you can."*

Jesus responds to him,

> *"What do you mean, 'If I can?"*

I don't think Jesus was scolding him in this case. I believe that Jesus was empathizing with a lost sheep that had lost his way in HOW to believe and is leading His lost sheep back to the fold by lovingly speaking to him, then imparting to him,

> *"Anything is possible if a person believes."*

The Father then responds through this impartation and revelation by declaring,

> *"I do believe, but help me overcome my unbelief!"*

This man is acutely aware of the contradictions he is living with daily. The consequences of his contradictions are so apparent that they manifest in his son. His son has become the fruit of his contradictions,

> *"Often he casts him into the fire, and often he casts him into the water,"*

Two elements should cancel out the other; the water should extinguish the fire. The Father had become so familiar with his contradictions that he considered them normal, so much so that they have now been handed down to his son. But once Jesus calls out the Father's contradictions and is made aware of his contradictory belief system, the Father now understands that he needs help overcoming his unbelief! How many of us believe that Jesus can do anything and everything that He says He can, but still have unbelief when it comes to receiving from Him for ourselves and our situation?

Let us all cry out,

> *"Lord, I believe, but help me overcome my unbelief!"*

We can also see these flawed belief systems in the crowd.

Our flawed belief systems can be both environmental and genetic. We can believe on the level of what we are surrounded with. When certain groups or individuals surround us, we usually think, behave, and believe on the level of the people we are surrounded by. Their ideologies are contagious; they reward us when we present ourselves in a certain way, but when we go outside the group norms, we are categorized as acting funny, out of the line, unfamiliar, or strange. Often, to fit in and not disclose our ambitions, we will dumb down or mute our desires not to stand out. We have become so conditioned by the culture we are in, that often; we are even trying to bring God down to our standards of conformity, ways of thinking, and believing. We try to get God to subscribe and function according to our beliefs, agenda, and way of life.

Our culture affects everything about us: the way we dress, what we do, who we interact with, and other various influences and traditions. For instance, we have a church culture, a work or career culture, and a media, entertainment, and celebrity culture. There are different cities, area codes, and regions that all have a different influence on us that, depending on our environment or who we are around, can determine how it affects our overall beliefs and thought processes. Our culture has so infused itself into us that it affects our cognition and ability to thoroughly think through situations or circumstances. We may have prohibiting perceptions concerning issues such as age, whether we are too young or old, our social status is inadequate, or we don't have the proper education or experience. This thinking limits our ability to progress or advance in many areas. Our limiting beliefs have sidetracked our ability to accept accolades or blessings, and these conflicting beliefs kill dreams. It is difficult to educate or elevate those who have these contradictory beliefs because of the intense indoctrination of our skewed belief system. We have been trapped in these flawed systems for years, which have become a system of desperation and feeling inadequate. We need to recognize that we are under a dysfunctional belief system that has been thrust upon us, that has and is conditioning us, and dictates everything we do.

We see this flawed belief system in the disciples when the Father asked them to heal the boy, but they could not. When the Father explains to Jesus that His disciples couldn't heal him, Jesus calls out their flawed belief system.

Jesus said to them,

> *"You faithless people! How long must I be with you? How long must I put up with you? Bring the boy to me."*
> *Mark 9:19 (NIV)*

The Amplified version states,

> *"O unbelieving generation (without any faith)! How long shall I (have to do) with you? How long am I to bear with you?"*
> *Mark 9:19 (AMP)*

Jesus was obviously frustrated that a flawed belief system still plagued the disciples, who could not cast out this evil spirit. Even with the fact that they have been following Jesus for some time now, watching him perform miracles, even sending them out in twos with authority to perform miracles successfully themselves as a practice run, some of which was the casting out of demons, and now they are faced with this situation and are not able to prevail. Why is this?

In Matthew's account of this story, Jesus tells His disciples clearly why they couldn't drive the spirit out,

> *"Because you have so little faith." Matthew 17:20 (NIV)*

Why did Jesus say that? He could have told them that it was because of the type of demon possession, that it was too strong for them, and only Jesus could cast it out. Still, Jesus expected them to cast it out and be operating at a higher level of faith and understanding by this point in their journey with Him.

Jesus goes on to tell them,

> *"If you have faith the size of a mustard seed, you can say to this mountain, 'Move from here to there,' and it will move. Nothing will be impossible for you."*
> *Matthew 17:20 (NIV)*

So, on one hand, Jesus tells His disciples that they couldn't cast the demon out because of their LITTLE FAITH, but on the other, He tells them that all they need is to have mustard seed size faith, one of the smallest seeds there are. Is Jesus Himself being contradictory? Not at all. We see here that Jesus is pointing out their skewed faith, their skewed belief system. The disciples suffer from being a product of a worldly, fleshly, carnal, cultural faith that they grew up with. They were operating by sight, and they saw the magnitude of how the demon controlled the boy and threw him to the ground, the fire, or the water, even in the face of their attempts to cast it out. I'm sure it shook their confidence when it didn't obey. They probably made several attempts, using different approaches, tones, and emphases, but to no avail. They may even have handed the task off to one another, thinking, "Maybe you can give it a whirl?"

Why do the disciples, at this point, still have this faulty faith/belief system? Why was Jesus, during the various stages of the disciples' journey following Him for three years, often challenging and calling out their weak faith? Is something inherently wrong with them that they cannot even have the faith as a mustard seed? Is there something about the way they perceive, think, and are unable to comprehend that Jesus was so diligently calling to their attention and explaining and re-explaining to get them to grasp why He was here and what He was trying to accomplish? Was there a veil over them that skewed or, at times, blinded their ability to see clearly and prevented them from being able to operate on the level that Jesus was expecting? As we examine our own lives and ourselves, do we see some of the same issues with understanding the things of God and what He expects of us the disciples were plagued with?

Where does this skewed belief system come from? Why are we humans so afflicted by this condition? If even the disciples walking with Jesus daily for three years could not overcome it, how can we?

Jesus answered his disciples by saying,

> *"This kind can only come out by nothing but prayer and fasting."*
> *Mark 9:29 (NIV)*

Jesus is giving us a fantastic and profound principle and revelation here, but we usually mistake what He means by what the words "*This kind*" refer to.

Most often, the understanding of the reference is that this casting out of this type of possession can only be delivered by prayer and fasting. This may be true and not incorrect, but through careful study of Jesus' ministry, we also find that very rarely does Jesus exalt, magnify, or acknowledge the power of the demonic realm. By and large, Jesus operates in the position that they have to exalt, magnify, and acknowledge Him. The demons are subject to His authority, not the other way around. So Jesus expects that when He has to address a demonic presence, they will have to fear and obey Him. For example, when Jesus landed on the shores of the Gadarenes, the Demoniac came running down and fell at His feet and inquired,

> *"What have You to do with me, Jesus, Son of the Most High God?"*
> *Mark 5:7 (NIV)*

The demons recognized Who He was and their subjugation to Him. So for Jesus, the demons, along with their oppression and strongholds –were what He came to **Expose, destroy, heal, and replace**. He intended to restore the man from possession and the gentile region of the Gadarenes from its oppression in order to further His mission and ministry in the gentile region; it was just a formality for Him to remove them from the situation. He simply had to command the spirits to come out, and they had to obey.

Due to this almost formality of Jesus' authority over the demonic realm, I believe that Jesus expected his disciples, and in turn- for us as his current day disciples- to operate in this same template and authority, as He calls us to follow Him.

However, I feel there is a deeper meaning and understanding that Jesus refers to in the statement of **"this kind."** There is more to the story of this statement than just dealing with the demonic realm. I believe that the "kind" that Jesus refers to is also our faith and belief system from which we operate.

Jesus is, in essence, calling us from our faulty, skewed, dysfunctional, world-conditioned, living by sight, sensual, self-centered belief system into the mustard seed, Kingdom-minded, Kairos, all things are possible belief system that moves mountains (spiritual strongholds) and that "This Kind," "This flawed Belief System" can only come out by prayer and fasting.

This follows with the calling of Jesus to deny ourselves to die to ourselves, to pick up our cross and to follow Him, to step from the fallen world dimension and step into the Kingdom of heaven realm. To renew our minds and transform our lives. He is calling us to become His disciples, his representatives here on this earth, to bring light into the darkness, to make disciples of all the nations. He is telling us that in our current state, with our tiny, skewed, faulty, weak faith, it is not possible. But, with God, ALL things are possible to him who believes, not with our faulty, insufficient "little" faith, but with the mustard seed, Kingdom, and spiritual faith that we must be transformed into through prayer and fasting.

Jesus, during His time here on earth, was often pulling away from the disciples and the crowds to pray and fast, usually all night, often for days at a time, even to the annoyance of His disciples. He did this to recalibrate, realign, and ensure that He and the Father were in one accord, connected, and of the same mind before stepping out to the next steps of His ministry. He did this to be able to operate from the Mustard Seed dimension but also as an example for us to learn and follow.

So some questions for us. How can we ensure that we follow the example that Jesus demonstrated? How can we ensure that we are aligned and understand God's will? How do we begin to operate in the mustard seed Kingdom dimension and belief system rather than the skewed and faulty worldly belief system we grew up with?

Chapter 6

I Am Willing!

There are many defining moments that we, the devil, and the world have infused in our lives. Some defining moments we bring upon ourselves, like the story of the prodigal son, who demanded and squandered his inheritance in riotous living, and as the money ran out and famine came upon the land, he lost everything, his family, his friends, his dignity and ended up tending pigs. Then there are defining moments that can be thrust upon us, through no fault of our own and through no control of our own, that completely disrupt and side-track our lives so that we no longer recognize who we were created and intended to be. Such is the case of this next story...

A man had had his whole life turned upside down during the time of Jesus' ministry. This man lived near Galilee. He had contracted leprosy, a horribly infectious, contagious, and debilitating disease that, during this period, would have indicted this sufferer to a life of isolation for the rest of his days, ostracized from his entire family and community, banished him outside of his village to live a life of solitary loneliness and abandonment from any contact, communication, or interaction with anyone.

Not only did he have to endure isolation, but due to contracting leprosy, he had to go out of his way to make himself easily identifiable as a leper whenever he happened to encounter travelers. He was required to wear shabby torn clothing and declare by yelling "UNCLEAN" to anyone who came near him to warn them away. Not only was he banished and ostracized from human contact, but he was also subject to horrific ridicule, beatings, and even potentially death in certain instances if he infringed on these regulations. Often, many who suffered this terrible agonizing disease and isolation went insane or died from depression, suicide, or eventually died a horrible death from the disease itself.

From the doctrinal laws and proclamations in Leviticus 13:45-46, it pronounced that,

> *"ANYONE WITH SUCH A DEFILING DISEASE MUST WEAR TORN CLOTHES, LET THEIR HAIR BE UNKEMPT, COVER THE LOWER PART OF THEIR FACE AND CRY OUT, 'UNCLEAN! UNCLEAN!' AS LONG AS THEY HAVE THE DISEASE, THEY REMAIN UNCLEAN. THEY MUST LIVE ALONE; THEY MUST LIVE OUTSIDE THE CAMP."*

This was a man who, during this first century, was brought up in Judaism from birth. His entire culture lived and breathed their religion, and now, because of this condition that was thrust upon him, through no fault of his own, he is having everything stripped from him that defined who he was!

As if his situation was not bad enough, the priests would not only deem him physically unclean, but they would even deem him spiritually unclean. This meant that this man was officially considered "UNWORTHY" even to worship or praise God. This man had an advanced case of leprosy, so he most likely had been suffering from it for years. He endured years of physical pain and disfigurement, years of banishment and isolation from his family and friends, from any single person on the known earth. He was forbidden even to serve and worship his God. Unworthy almost doesn't describe the condition this man was in. This condition had so disrupted this man's life that it had total control over him, so much so that he was unrecognizable physically and spiritually. It had so defined him that the Bible only referred to him as "The Leper."

Leprosy even took away his name...

Such was this man's life when Jesus of Nazareth came to Galilee.

So, we see that Jesus was,

> *"traveling through the region of Galilee, preaching in the synagogues and casting out demons."*
> *Mark 1:39 (NIV)*

This assumes that Jesus was in the area for a good period, perhaps days. The Leper probably heard the buzz and excitement in the voices of the crowds and snippets of conversations from those traveling to and from where Jesus was as they were following Jesus around, listening to His teachings and preaching, along with performing miracles of healing and casting out demons, and maybe the Leper even attempted to see and hear for himself from afar.

As the Leper hears of these amazing things that Jesus was doing, he wonders if he dared to allow himself any shred of hope, if Jesus could even consider him. The Leper is, after all, a pariah to his society; he is not allowed to be near anyone, especially this fantastic miracle worker sent from God. What makes him think that he could even consider approaching the Rabbi as a lowly, despicable, disease-ridden outcast? Even if he could convince himself to muster up the courage, no one would let him get anywhere near the Rabbi. He could be stoned to death for even attempting to get near him. The

Rabbi Himself may even order he be put to death for violating the Levitical ordinances.

So, the Leper continued to observe from afar and watched as a man was healed; how amazing! Then, before he can take his eyes off the man who is now dancing around celebrating and showing his family and friends, Jesus heals another and then another one. It was almost like he was walking through the crowd and just reaching out, and whoever He touched, whenever he touched them, they were instantly and completely healed! How utterly marvelous! This man must be the Son of God! How else would He be able to perform these miracles?

As the Leper thought this, he heard a terrible guttural screeching as Jesus cast a demon out of a woman that the Leper recognized. She would sometimes visit the Leper outside the village in his camp. She wasn't afraid of his leprosy and didn't seem to catch it; she was not in her right mind, and often, the Leper was very afraid of her. The demons inside of her would, at times, come to the surface of her consciousness and attack him or even other wild animals and terrorize the surrounding villages.

Everyone knew this woman, and nearly everyone avoided her. The Leper appreciated her company, though, no matter how crazy she would get, even when the demons manifested. He was so lonely. Any company from anyone was better than nothing. He felt a tinge of guilt, though; he could see that the woman was healed entirely and was obviously of her right mind, and he felt happy for her but was also sad. Over the years, he became more and more lonely. For a while, there used to be other lepers cast out of their communities, and they used to gather together and create their own little community, but over time, they had all gone away. They either couldn't bear the loneliness or the pain and suffering and would commit suicide or die off due to the effects of the leprosy itself. He was the only one left, and now that this woman has been healed, he won't have her to keep him company anymore, either.

If only Jesus could heal him.

The Leper reminded himself what the priests had told him and even his family when he first contracted leprosy lo those many years ago, that this was a life sentence.

There is no cure for leprosy, and there is not one single documented healing or miracle of a Hebrew leper being healed over thousands of years. Do not hope that you will be saved; there is no hope. So, as Jesus is healing everyone around him of every kind of sickness or disease, could He heal even leprosy? The Leper thought, "Is there a sickness that even Jesus can't heal?" He fell asleep for the night, trying not to let any glimmer of hope in. He couldn't afford to be let down again.

He woke to a procession moving near his encampment. He wondered who would be going through this area. He got up and around and maneuvered himself to the edge of a ravine covered with willows he used many times as a lookout point. He could safely observe the comings and goings between the villages without being seen; his clothing and shabby appearance blended perfectly to camouflage him from any passerby.

As he watched the group passing through, he saw a familiar figure and knew immediately that it was Jesus; they must be leaving town. The Leper's heart begins to race at the sight of Jesus and the thoughts of all the miracles and joy he heard throughout the night. If only there were hope for him. If only the mighty Rabbi could heal even leprosy.

Some people are placed on this earth to live and die no more. Such was his fate. He would watch Jesus pass by until he was out of sight; then, he would go back to his camp and wait to die. What else was there? What else could he possibly have hope for?

Tears began streaming down his face as he watched Jesus pass by and was about to pass around a bend out of sight when a teardrop fell from the Leper's face and hit the ground. In that instant, Jesus halted the entire procession and turned to face where the Leper was standing. The Leper froze and held his breath with all his might. The Rabbi was staring right through his disciples and directly at him; it felt like Jesus could see him.

The Leper began sobbing even more, to the point that it was everything he could do to hold it in. He dared not break from his cover; if the disciples saw him, they would surely confront him, possibly beat him, and maybe even stone him for even being in the same proximity as their Rabbi. So he just stood there, immobile, sobbing, hand over his mouth and nose, trying to keep from making a sound.

The disciples noticed Jesus looking into the ravine and questioned their Rabbi, "Master, did you see something in the ravine, maybe a wild animal?" Jesus stood there for a moment, not responding, looking directly into the eyes of the Leper. The Leper wondered how he could see me. I am well hidden, several feet, at least 20 feet away from the group, but somehow, he knew in his soul that Jesus could see him.

The disciple repeated, "Rabbi?"

Jesus stared even more intently into the Leper's eyes; the Leper silently began shaking his head slowly, in a back-and-forth motion, indicating no.

Jesus, with tears in his own eyes, began slowly nodding his head up and down, seemingly indicating- yes. The disciples were at a loss; they could see their Rabbi nodding his head up and down, with tears in his eyes, towards the ravine, and were growing concerned that Jesus was seeing something terrible in the ravine that was bringing him to tears. One of the disciples took it upon himself to determine what has upset his Rabbi and began moving slowly, cautiously towards the ravine with his hand on his sword. In contrast, the rest of the disciples set up a defensive circle around their master.

The Leper continued to swing his head back and forth slowly. Jesus readjusted his nod to form a beckoning gesture, and at this point, with the disciple prepared to enter the ravine. Jesus nodding for him to come out- the Leper came running out of the ravine and fell on the ground near the feet of Jesus, in the middle of the circle of disciples.

The disciples all jumped back, startled at the sight of the figure that had just rushed out of the ravine and was now on his knees with his face in his hands, obviously distraught and audibly sobbing, just in front of Jesus.

"LEPER! LEPER!" The disciples began yelling, "IT'S A LEPER, MASTER STAND BACK! LEPER, MOVE AWAY FROM THE RABBI! MASTER, DO NOT COME NEAR; LEPER, MOVE AWAY FROM THE RABBI!"

The disciple who was about to enter the ravine drew his sword and addressed the Leper, "LEPER, FINAL WARNING! MOVE AWAY FROM THE RABBI!" The disciple raised his sword, ready to strike, when a voice rang out, "SIMON!" Then, with a gentler voice, Jesus directed his disciple to put away his sword.

The disciples continued to try to warn their Rabbi and stood in between the Leper and Jesus, many of them with their tunics over their mouths and noses pleading, "RABBI, IT'S A LEPER, I BEG YOU TO MOVE AWAY, LEPER MOVE AWAY FROM THE RABBI!"

Jesus approached each disciple, put a hand on them, and directed each one away from in-between Himself and the Leper. One by one, they reluctantly obeyed their Rabbi and moved away to the side. Jesus approached Simon, still defiantly standing between the Leper and his Rabbi. Jesus placed a loving hand on his disciple's shoulder and whispered into his ear; the disciple gave Jesus one last pleading look and then moved over to where the other disciples stood, holding their tunics over their faces.

Jesus looked down on the Leper, who still had his face in his hands and was still sobbing uncontrollably.

Without looking up, the Leper could feel the gaze of Jesus up on him, and in between sobs, he kept stating, "I am unclean... I am not holy... I am unworthy... I should not be here. I am a leper... I am unclean... I am unworthy..." Jesus stooped down on one knee before the Leper and stretched his hand out to the Leper.

The disciples all began to rush forward and warned Jesus, "NO MASTER, DON'T TOUCH HIM!"

Jesus, with his hand still stretched to the Leper, held his other hand out to the disciples to silence them and give them a knowing look of warning not to interfere again.

Jesus turned his gaze back towards the Leper again. The Leper was looking through his fingers into the eyes of Jesus; there was caring and love in those eyes like he had never seen before, and it cut the Leper to the core. He began sobbing again and repeating, "I am unclean, I am unholy, I am unworthy..."

Jesus just continued to gaze at him and hold out His hand.

The Leper realized that Jesus would continue waiting on him and was at a loss as to what to do next. Finally, after some moments, with Jesus still on one knee, hand outstretched, the Leper tentatively stated through sobs and tears, in an almost imperceptible voice, begging Him, "Lord... if you are willing.... You can heal me... and make me... clean."

Jesus, moved with compassion, tears streaming down his face, told the Leper, "I am willing."

The Leper fell to the ground in a crumpled mass. This Jesus has just acknowledged that He is not only able but is willing to heal a leper, a wretch, a pariah, a nobody- this Leper, this wretch, this pariah, this nobody. He is taking time to heal him. The Leper continues to sob, continues to blubber, his thoughts race to when he first was indicted with leprosy, how he was not only physically banished but spiritually banished, away from all human contact, with no hope of ever recovering, no hope of ever being restored, no hope of ever turning to God or have God have mercy on him, because he was deemed spiritually unworthy even to worship God. If Jesus could speak the words, it would be enough. If He just spoke the words, the worlds were created by speaking, so if He just spoke, the Leper could be healed. It would be enough to heal Him if Jesus just spoke the words...

Then he heard it...

Jesus spoke, in His still small voice, "Be healed."

But then, something happened to the Leper that he was not expecting, and he couldn't believe it as it was happening; Jesus reached out and touched him! When he felt Jesus' hand upon him, it was like a shockwave that ran through his entire body, with electricity and power running from head to toe!

Jesus touched him! A leper! An unclean, unholy, unworthy less than human being! Jesus touched him!

The Leper was so shocked by another human being touching him that, for a second, he forgot all about being healed! He was being touched! He hadn't been touched in years!

As the Leper realized Jesus was touching him, terror struck him, "RABBI," he warned, "nothing clean shall touch anything unclean! If the clean touches the unclean, the clean becomes unclean! LORD, NO! Speaking is enough; Your word is enough!"

Then Leper could sense a voice in his spirit, "It is true that in this world, if the clean touches the unclean, then the clean becomes defiled and is now unclean, but I say to you that if the Son of Man who is clean and pure, touches anything unclean, then that which is unclean, then it becomes clean." Then, the leprosy left that man instantly, and he was completely healed!

The Leper looked at his skin, hands, and arms; they were spotless! Completely healed.

"Hallelujah!" the Leper proclaimed through tears of joy and disbelief.

The disciples gathered around to witness the amazing miracle. Leprosy the Rabbi can even heal leprosy. How amazing. One of the disciples suggested that the Leper should do away with his shabby clothes.

"You are no longer a leper!" he stated, and the entire group, with tears of joy and amazement, celebrated with him. The disciples each gave him a clothing item for the Leper to change into.

The Leper, entirely overwhelmed by all the attention- he hadn't had that much attention in a very long time, began crying again and thanking Jesus repeatedly for this beautiful miracle. He thanked all the disciples for giving him new clothing; it had been a long time since he had worn nice clothing.

When things calmed, the Leper asked Jesus, "How can I ever repay you?"

Jesus just smiled at him and gave him these instructions, "See that you tell no one, but go your way, show yourself to the priest, and offer the gift that Moses commanded as a testimony to them."

The Leper thought, how amazing! Not only did Jesus completely heal him of leprosy, but He also instructed him in the protocol to restore him to a citizen of society, back to his family, back to the right standing with his synagogue and the priests, so he can get back his name and no longer be called a leper, and ultimately and most of all... He can get back in right standing and with Adonai. He will be re-established as "Worthy" again, to be able to worship and praise God again. He will be restored in every way possible, physically, mentally, emotionally, and spiritually. He will be made whole. Oh, how amazing is this Jesus! He will have to revisit the doctrine of Moses writing in Leviticus 14 to gather the elements for the priests gift.

In this story of the Leper, we see Jesus's incredible power; He was able to heal even leprosy! How many of us think that the trials of life that have been thrust upon us damage us beyond repair? Has our skewed belief, like the Leper, convinced you that you are so far gone that even Jesus can't do anything about it. Have you told yourself over and over that you are unworthy even to consider salvation, redemption, or healing. Like the Leper, you are so convinced and sure that your condition is so chronic and incurable that you are going to let the opportunity of Jesus' presence pass you by. You can see others being delivered but feel there is no hope for you, that you are too far gone. Maybe, as with the Leper, you have been told your whole life by family, friends, and enemies that you are less than, beyond repair, that who you are and the things you have done have indicted you to your fate, don't expect help to be forgiven, accepted, or healed.

But like the Leper, Jesus can see YOU!

He can see behind the mask, the disguise, the camouflage, the condition, and the trauma that you endured. He can see the part of you that is redeemable even if no one else can, even if you can't. He is willing to stop everything to call you out of hiding, out of your shame, out of your incurable condition, and tell you,

"I am willing."

Don't let this moment pass you by; He is enough! You are enough! He thinks You are worth His time and effort. He believes that you are worth the cost that He paid on the cross to Expose, Destroy, Heal, and Replace all that you have lost and redeem you back to what He created you to be before the foundation of the world.

He is holding His hand to you if you will let him touch your life. Don't shrink back or pull away; allow Him to touch whatever defining moments you have, and let Him heal you mentally, physically, emotionally, and spiritually. He wants to restore you back to the Father, the Kingdom, and the Family. Something is missing when you aren't there. It's time to come home to Jesus.

Chapter 7

You Ask Amiss!

One of the most powerful tools we have as Christ's followers is prayer.

James 5:16 KJV

> *Confess your faults one to another, and pray one for another, that ye may be healed. The effectual fervent prayer of a righteous man availeth much.*

The effective, fervent prayer of a righteous man availeth much. The Greek word used for "righteous" in this Scripture is "dikaioó." The meaning of this Greek word from the Strong's Concordance is defined as:

> **Definition**: to show to be righteous, to declare righteous.
>
> **Usage:** I make righteous, defend the cause of, plead for the righteousness (innocence) of, acquit, justify; hence: regard as righteous.
>
> **Cognate:** 1344 dikaióō (from the dike, "right, judicial-approval") – properly approved, especially in a legal,

authoritative sense; to show what is right, i.e., conformed to a proper standard (i.e., "upright").

The believer is "made righteous/justified" (1344 /dikaióō) by the Lord, cleared of all charges (punishment) related to their sins. Moreover, they are justified (1344 /dikaióō, "made right, righteous") by God's grace each time they receive (obey) faith "God's inwrought persuasion" (cf. the -oō ending which conveys "to bring to/out")

The foundation of effectual, fervent prayers is based on the believer's righteousness (the right standing). The apostle John states, that if you ask anything in His name- the name of Jesus, He will do it. What keeps us then from a robust, powerful, practical prayer life?

I submit that through our self-centeredness, neediness, pitifulness, and victimhood, we are producing weak, ineffective, pitiful prayers that often won't get answered. A significant contributing factor to this self-centered state is that in the fall of the Garden, Adam became separated from love from the Lord God, and at once became in need of love. Adam, who was once part of the incorporation of love, now has been separated and is desperate for love! We, like Adam, were intended to be in His likeness: merciful, joyful, forgiving, joined in His love, but instead, we live and operate in the separation of and are now **opposing** His likeness- His love. We live protective, defensive, vengeful, angry, accusatory, and hurt. We cut people off before they can cut us off, and we separate ourselves from them, our loved ones, our friends, everyone, and everything that might challenge, hurt, disappoint, or betray us! We have become self-centered, self-focused, and needy because we have lost and been disconnected from the Source of all those things.

Another major contributor to our weak prayers- is our past. We have become like Lot's wife; we are stuck, frozen, looking back at what we can't let go of, never being able to focus on our future, destiny, and what we are being delivered from and into. Instead, we are stuck in our shame, our guilt, and our feeling of unworthiness. Our minds, emotions, and perspectives have been corrupted through our past bad experiences, and we live, breathe, and are identified by all the bad things that have happened to us that have defined us. We get so touched by life that when we hear a message, sermon, or word of victory or deliverance from our Lord God, we can't bring ourselves to acknowledge or respond because we harbor so many issues that we can't accept it. We have become so run over by life that we can no longer hear, receive, apply, or even rejoice in the new life Jesus has purchased for us. We can only push away, draw away from, shut out, and reject His encouragement because of all the past things that have accumulated and bogged us down! We can't even look up. We can only continue staring at the ground or our feet and say, "I can't do it..."

The Apostle Paul states:

> *Not that I have already attained, or am already perfected; but I press on, that I may lay hold of that for which Christ Jesus has also laid hold of me. Brethren, I do not count myself to have apprehended; but one thing I do,* ***forgetting those things which are behind and reaching forward to those things which are ahead,*** *I press toward the goal for the prize of the upward call of God in Christ Jesus"*
>
> *Philippians 3:12-14*

The apostle Paul knew the power of past deeds (defining moments) and how they can distract, deter, and stop us from living out the promise, the high calling, and the new life we have access to. Paul tells us that the "one thing" he does is forget the things behind him.

To break through the gravitational pull of our past and, consequently, our prayers that have not been answered, we have to recognize daily that through Jesus Christ dying on the cross, shedding His blood, and paying the price for our freedom, we have been delivered from everything that has held us back, that has kept us bound and enslaved us from our intended created identity. Looking back to our past defining moments diverts our focus from the Lord God and our future mission, purpose, and destiny and re-binds us back to our shame, guilt, hurts, and traumas, distracting and stalling us all over again.

This was the sin of the first generation of the Hebrews during the Exodus; they kept longing for and desiring to go back to Egypt, and ultimately, the whole first generation of Hebrews, except for Joshua and Caleb, were not allowed to enter into the promised land and were allowed to die off in the desert. They could not let go of Egypt to grab onto the promise!

This separated, self-centered, victimized state and its effects are highlighted in the book of James:

> *What leads to [the unending] quarrels and conflicts among you? Do they not come from your [hedonistic] desires that wage war in your [bodily] members [fighting for control over you]? 2 You are jealous and covet [what others have] and your lust goes unfulfilled; so you murder. You are envious and cannot obtain [the object of your envy]; so you fight and battle. You do not have because you do not ask [it of God]. 3 You ask [God for something] and do not receive it, because* **you ask amiss**, *with wrong motives [out of selfishness or with an unrighteous agenda], so that [when you get what you want] you may spend it on your [hedonistic] desires. 4 You adulteresses [disloyal sinners—flirting with the world and breaking your vow to God]! Do you not know that being the world's friend [that is, loving the things of the world] is being*

God's enemy? So whoever chooses to be a friend of the world makes himself an enemy of God. 5 Or do you think that the Scripture says to no purpose that the [human] spirit which He has made to dwell in us lusts with envy? 6 But He gives us more and more grace [through the power of the Holy Spirit to defy sin and live an obedient life that reflects both our faith and our gratitude for our salvation]. Therefore, it says, "God is opposed to the proud and haughty, but [continually] gives [the gift of] grace to the humble [who turn away from **self-righteousness**]." *7 So submit to [the authority of] God. Resist the devil [stand firm against him] and he will flee from you. 8 Come close to God [with a contrite heart] and He will come close to you. Wash your hands, you sinners; and purify your [unfaithful] hearts, you double-minded [people]. 9 Be miserable and grieve and weep [over your sin]. Let your [foolish] laughter be turned to mourning and your [reckless] joy to gloom. 10 Humble yourselves [with an attitude of repentance and insignificance] in the presence of the Lord, and He will exalt you [He will lift you up, He will give you purpose].*

James 4: 1-10 Amplified Version

The book of James is not for the faint of heart; he tells it like it is and calls us out!

James is calling out that our minds, emotions, and perspectives have been corrupted. We have become Christians for our selfish desires and well-being. We are Christians for our happiness, for our blessings, for our good health, and for us to prosper and be carefree. Therefore, all of our prayers have this undercurrent of selfishness driving them. James tells us that because of our corrupted motives and selfish desires, our prayers do not ask for the furthering His Kingdom or praying from a position of gratitude or a sense of worship. But we pray for our success, ambition, comfort, and being the "world's" friend. James states that being a friend and loving the things of this corrupted world is making us an enemy of God... Lord have mercy!

James also calls out that it's time for an intervention, a recalibration! Through our corruption, we are no longer friends of God but have become enemies of God. Our interaction and communication with the Lord God are on two different frequencies. We are using a frequency tuned in for the world, our carnal (fleshly) desires, and the things of this world, and only the world and the things of this world can hear and receive the transmission of the broadcast of our "out-of-tune" prayers. The Lord God is transmitting from the Kingdom of Heaven- on a higher frequency.

We must adjust our internal dial to align with His Kingdom's frequency, language, focus, and purpose.

He is transmitting, but because we are on the wrong frequency, we cannot hear and receive the frequency of God. So, there is a massive disconnect in the transmitting and receiving communication (our prayers) between the Kingdom of the world and the Kingdom of Heaven. Neither side is getting through.

We see this with Elijah as he hides in a cave, running from Jezebel, who wants to kill him.

> *11 The Lord said, "Go out and stand on the mountain in the presence of the Lord, for the Lord is about to pass by." Then a great and powerful wind tore the mountains apart and shattered the rocks before the Lord, but the Lord was not in the wind. After the wind there was an earthquake, but the Lord was not in the earthquake. 12 After the earthquake came a fire, but the Lord was not in the fire. And after the fire came a gentle whisper. 13*

When Elijah heard it, he pulled his cloak over his face and went out and stood at the mouth of the cave.

Then a voice said to him, "What are you doing here, Elijah?"

1 Kings 19:11-13

We see here in this event that the Lord God is conditioning and training Elijah to hear God on the heavenly frequency. God's language and frequency were not in the loud, boisterous things. He wasn't in the mighty wind, He wasn't in the earthquake, and the Lord wasn't in the fire. Those are the frequencies of the world of chaos, and the Lord isn't at that frequency.

When he had stilled himself enough, carved out the time, and got alone while in the cave, Elijah heard the frequency of God! In this case, it was a gentle whisper, and once Elijah heard it, he pulled the cloak over his face and went and stood at the mouth of the cave in the presence of the Lord.

And what did Elijah hear the still, small voice say? "What are you doing here, Elijah?"

The Lord God asks Elijah the same fundamental question He asked Adam in the Garden, "Where are you?"

In both cases, Adam and Elijah had become separated from the Source and turned internally away from the Source; they lost track of their original intention, so much so that they couldn't commune with the Father because they had lost the frequency!

Once we are in tune with the heavenly frequency as influential followers of Jesus who are aligned, settled in Him, and overflowing with His light, hope, and victory. We are not to operate as those praying seeking for answers; we are to be those who pray already **having** the Answer! We must shift our focus away from ourselves and back to Him.

We have fallen into the trap that our circumstances are overwhelming us, and our prayer, witness, relationship, and walk with God, suffer. Usually, when we fall into this trap, we are pleading for the Lord to fix our circumstances. When we don't see our circumstances being fixed, we will usually call one of our "prayer partners," who usually means well, but in most cases, the best that they can do is sympathize and empathize with us and our circumstances. Their prayers for us are also weak and pitiful, asking amiss prayers that have the reverse effect of deliverance and victory. Instead, they permit us and enable us to be hurt, to be victims, and to be okay with being stuck. We usually will hear them tell us, "Well brother, you know sometimes it's all in God's timing. We just need to have the patience of Job and persevere; we all go through trials, we just have to be strong and just get through it..." What they are stating is, well we prayed for you, but we don't know if He will answer or not, because we have never experienced our prayers answered either. They unintentionally empathize with our victimhood and project their own experiences onto us; this enables survival rather than victory and authority!

When we pray, it should be from the position of His faith, His ability, His authority, His provision, and His victory. Those are the prayers that are heard and answered! From this perspective, we are now in alignment, on the same frequency, and in communion! The key to having effective, fervent prayers is getting in alignment, right standing, and developing a personal relationship with Him. Hence, you know Him on an intimate level and not just knowing about Him. Our prayers must be from the foundation and position of communing and knowing Him. We need to develop our relationship with the Lord like a spouse. The only way to get to know Him on that level is by spending intentional, personal, intimate, memorable, one-on-one time with Him alone. We just learned in a previous chapter that this kind of behavior can only be manifested through prayer and fasting. To get to know Him like that, we must do what we did while pursuing our spouse. We need to begin to "date" the Lord. When we decided to marry our spouses, we got to know our spouses on a deep and personal level.

The key to developing a personal relationship with Him is by carving out and setting aside time to commune with Him one-on-one, just you and Him, and begin having conversations and interactions with Him regularly. If we only come to Him when we need Him or need something from Him, then we will never get to know Him. For most of us, getting alone in a room, spending time with Him, and just starting to communicate with, develop a relationship with, and converse with God can be awkward. Once we have finally carved out the space and the time and now are attempting to talk with Jesus, we go blank; we feel self-conscious, we feel unworthy, we feel like we have to muster up this grand prayer with this amazing, profound prayer "language" that is sophisticated and wise. That is not how we want to approach Him and not how He wants to be approached.

> *5. "And when you pray, do not be like the hypocrites, for they love to pray standing in the synagogues and on the street corners to be seen by others. Truly, I tell you, they have received their reward in full. 6 But when you pray, go into your room, close the door and pray to your Father, who is unseen. Then your Father, who sees what is done in secret, will reward you. 7 And when you pray, do not keep on babbling like pagans, for they think they will be heard because of their many words. 8 Do not be like them, for your Father knows what you need before you ask him."*
>
> *Matthew 6:5-15 NIV*

In Matthew, we see Jesus stating that we don't want to pray for our aggrandizement or based on our selfish needs. The Father knows what we need before we even ask Him, but when we pray, we go into our room, close the door, and pray to our unseen Father. Then, when He sees what we have done in secret, He will reward us. The reward is to get to know Him, get closer to Him, hear His voice, learn the Father's language and tone (frequency), and develop a close personal relationship with Him.

Where do we start the conversation?

We start where Jesus finished. On the cross. We begin where Jesus has accomplished and declared from the cross, "It is finished." We begin with the finished work of Christ, where He has paid the price for all of our sins, past, present, and future, and has restored us back to the right standing with the Father. We start where He has restored our created value, identity, mission, purpose, and destiny that was intended before we were born. We begin where He restored all that we lost. We start at the finished work of the cross. For heaven's sake, let's not start with our list of needs, wishes, and self-focus.

The best way to begin is by seeing ourselves, understanding ourselves, and allowing ourselves to be what He paid for and sees us as! This was all accomplished on the cross! Let's start on the right frequency so that we can get to know each other again.

The way a prayer like that would look is.

> Father, Lord Jesus, Holy Spirit, I want You to reveal Yourself to me. I want to know you as my Abba (my daddy), Savior, and Comforter.
>
> I thank You that you reveal this to me through speaking into my heart, reveal this to me through Your scriptures, and then manifest who You are inside of me.

Create in me a desire- a burning to know You so well that when You speak to me, I can hear You. That when You manifest Yourself, I can see You. When you confirm Yourself with me, I can acknowledge it. Father, I want to be so sensitive, perceptive, and aware of Your presence that it fills me with joy and confidence that You truly love me and know who You truly are!

Holy Spirit, I am so grateful that You have come into my life. I thank You for revealing to me today the heart of the Father and changing and transforming me into a child of my Father. I thank You that You are living in me, and I am becoming so much like You that when others see me, they see You! Thank You for Your presence, peace, and grace in me so I can see myself the way You see me. Now, I can see others the way You see them. Father, thanks again for revealing Yourself to me so I can know You!

"Father, I thank You that through Your Holy Spirit, I will make the most of every day, moment, and season to reflect You, to grow closer to You, and to love You, to be loved by You, and to be able to love others. I declare that every moment is precious, and every encounter is an opportunity to brag on You!

Jesus provided a tool for us to be able to commune- have communication, to participate in the finished work of the cross, and be able to continue in the ongoing finished work that He transacted on the cross, which allows us access to the Lord God, to the Father and His Holy Spirit filling us. By Jesus dying on the cross for us, for YOU, he has provided a bridge across the chasm of sin that has separated us. It has redeemed, paid the cost, and transacted us from the slavery of sin and the world back to our intended created identity, value, and purpose. In receiving this free gift and payment for our redemption and restoration, we have access to what He paid for! This tool, this bridge, this process is found in Matthew 26:26-28.

> *26 While they were eating, Jesus took bread, and when he had given thanks, he broke it and gave it to his disciples, saying, "Take and eat; this is my body." 27 Then he took a cup, and when he had given thanks, he gave it to them, saying, "Drink from it, all of you. 28 This is my blood of the covenant, which is poured out for many for the forgiveness of sins."*

If any of us has attended church or been a Christian for any amount of time, you have probably participated in the Lord's Supper or Communion. Communion has become such an institution within the church that it has become a ritual and tradition that the church and even we ourselves find that we go through the motions of partaking in the Lord's Supper without much thought, meditation, consideration, or the impact of what communion represents. But this can be a fantastic opportunity to remember Jesus and use it as a platform for an experience, an interaction with Him on such a personal level that we like Moses whenever we talk to Him or about Him, our faces light up! This tool of communion can contribute to building such "Faith" and "Love" in us that it will pull us out of the sensual, self-centered, corrupted, and skewed individual that sin, Satan, and the world have conditioned into.

Let's take a fresh look at how the Lord's supper, communion, can usher us into closer intimacy with our Father, our Savior, and our Comforter. We begin by making it a personal encounter.

A Communion with my Father!

Father,

As I enter this time of communion, interaction, and relationship with You, I want to linger in this time and not let it be another checked box. I want to use this time as a springboard into intimacy with You. I want to think about the things you have done for me...

How You have always been there for me, even when I wasn't always there for You.... how You remained faithful, and You make all things come together for My good!

Father,

I want to lean into understanding why You sent Your Son, Your only begotten Son, and also to understand WHY Jesus (Yeshua) would allow Himself to become the sacrifice, the payment, to redeem ME.

Why ME?

While Your Son was hanging on the cross, if I still myself enough- I can hear Him, in essence, speaking in that – still small voice- saying to me, between each gasp of breath,

(Your name here,)

"I love you..."

"I know WHO you are..."

"I know WHY you are here...."

"I have KNOWN you from the beginning..."

"I know WHY I created you..."

"I have an amazing PURPOSE for you..."

"You have great VALUE to Me..."

"KNOW...that the FATHER is pleased that I hang on this cross..."

"And pay this tremendously- costly price..."

"That through MY dying..."

"You can live... by My raising, YOU can be justified..."

"So I can take the lie off of YOU... and put THE TRUTH back into YOU..."

"And know... that You are... worth... every drop... of this... SACRIFICE..."

"YOUR life... is worth... every drop... of MY.... Blood..."

"IT IS FINISHED!!!"

The Bread

Father, as I take these elements...

I do so with the revelation that YOU want to restore what was lost!

You didn't do this because you pity or feel sorry for me.... but because I was fearfully and wonderfully made for so much more!

Thank you, JESUS (Yeshua) and Father God, that You never gave up on me. That YOU never condemned me for what I have become- due to the conditioning, the falseness, the separation from YOU, the isolation, bitterness, and hatefulness of this fallen world, but thank YOU that You came as a meek... humble.... Gentle... loving... Redeemer, to reunite us so that we can be a family again!

Father, as I take this bread that represents YOUR Son... YOUR one and only Son... and His body broken, for ME, that through HIS brokenness, I can see my brokenness restored. Jesus, YOU were broken so I can be healed!

So, I declare that as I take this bread- YOUR body- YOUR LIFE for mine, I give my LIFE to YOU!

His body is broken for me!

The Blood

Father, I confess...

It is truly humbling and overwhelming to know that YOUR Son shed His blood for Me... Lord Jesus, Your amazing, spotless, innocent blood... YOUR holy and spotless blood, from a holy and spotless lamb!

As I hold up this cup, I acknowledge and declare YOUR unbreakable covenant of restoring my Right Standing and Intimate relationship with the FATHER that YOUR blood- the tremendous price paid- has transacted for me.

Because of YOUR shed blood...

I can declare that I am no longer a slave to sin and the world! As YOU have given Your blood, I, in turn, give back to YOU my deceived and blinded and Veiled notion of my right to take offense... to be discouraged... to be disappointed...to be angry... to be self-centered... to be entitled... to be without joy and peace, from anything this world can offer, because I was never created for this fallen world... your blood has removed that from me!

Because of YOUR shed blood...

I can now put on what YOU died for... what YOU shed YOUR blood for... what YOU paid the PRICE for... which is:

- My created image and value...
- My right standing with the FATHER...
- A Child and heir to the KING...
- For the mission, purpose, and destiny you have set for me- before the foundation of the world- to represent, to reflect YOU to the world!

Father, I am so grateful that YOUR Son redeemed me.

Father, I declare that I am ALL IN...

I declare that nothing can separate me from YOUR LOVE!

That I am no longer MY own...

But that I am fully and gratefully YOURS!!!

IN JESUS MIGHTY NAME!
Amen, and hallelujah!

Another Communion prayer that I use for a deeper dive into intimacy.

Father,

I want to take a moment and think about the body of Jesus and how He came to the earth to take on flesh and dwell among us. That He set aside His deity and residence in heaven to come down into this fallen, corrupt, and evil world to be with us, to be with me, those of us whom You created in Your image and likeness, who have now become what we were never intended. Because of this fallen world, we have become such a disfigured, deformed, disgusting, and **unrecognizable** creature, that when You look at us, You can no longer see Yourself in us! But rather than looking at us in disgust, You look at us and weep because You now see us as a wayward, filthy, perverse, disenchanted lost sheep who has wandered away and has become lost and separated from the fold and is without a Shepherd.

I want to think about the price that Jesus had to pay to restore me back to my original intention, how he gave His flesh, surrendered His flesh to be scourged, and put Himself on the cross to die for me. I want to remember how His body was broken for me, battered, beaten, and bruised so that He became **unrecognizable**.

In Isaiah 52:14 it says,

14 Just as there were many who were appalled at him, his appearance was so disfigured beyond that of any human being, and his form marred beyond human likeness—

Father,

Help me understand that part of the price that needed to be paid- that as the first man and woman sinned in the Garden of Eden; they had so lost their image and likeness of the Father (the Glory of the Father) that they had become **unrecognizable**. They were so unrecognizable that the Father, when walking through the cool of the Garden and wanting to commune with them, couldn't see His image and likeness being reflected back, so he asked, "Where are You?"

You are even asking me now, "__(Your Name)___, where are you?"

Father,

Help me to understand that for my lost image to be restored, Your one and only Son, Jesus, Yeshua, had to become what we have become- a disgusting, disfigured creature so that He could take it away from us and destroy it on the cross!

Father,

I often wonder why the price to be paid had to be so brutal. How Jesus was beaten and whipped over and over and over and over and over until no part of Him could be identified as a man. That the innocent, spotless, blameless Son of God was so disgusting to look upon that we had to hide our face from Him and turn away from Him! Father, I now weep thinking about what Jesus went through for me!

Father,

Help me understand that the payment had to be so brutal because sin is so brutal! Sin is so impactful, destructive, and far-reaching that it extends its tentacles from generation to generation to generation up to me, and will be passed on to my descendants with no cure, hope, or remedy!

Except! The stripes that You have taken, and you giving your flesh!

The Bread

As I take this bread that represents Your body, I want to remember the price that needed to be paid with Your flesh.

- How you gave Your flesh, Your body. You surrendered to the chastisement and stripes.
- How Your body was broken for us.
- How You were beat beyond description, that You were unrecognizable.
- Isaiah 53 states that You were marred more than any of the sons of men.

> Jesus You were wounded for our transgressions and bruised for our iniquities. The chastisement for our peace was placed upon You, and then, by Your stripes we can be healed.
>
> His body was broken for us.

The Blood

Father,

Help me understand the power, impact, and scope of the shedding of Jesus' blood for my sins and for every sin that was ever committed by the entire human race- past, present, and future! As the God of yesterday, today, and forever more, the blood of Jesus is equivalent to that comprehensive breadth of Your omnipresence- your dimensional existence- The blood of Jesus can reach all time, space, and types of sin and redeem, destroy, cleanse, and heal! Thank You, Yeshua, that Your blood was shed for ALL of my past, present, and future sins! Hallelujah!

Father,

Help me to understand that as the bruising of the body of Your one and only Son was to take away the effects of sin, and now the shedding of His blood on the cross was to take away the sin! Help me also understand the purpose of putting Jesus on the cross and a pole.

Galatians 3:13-14 NIV

> *13 Christ redeemed us from the curse of the law by becoming a curse for us, for it is written: "Cursed is everyone who is hung on a pole." 14 He redeemed us in order that the blessing given to Abraham might come to the Gentiles through Christ Jesus, so that by faith we might receive the promise of the Spirit.*

By Jesus being cursed on the pole, on the cross, I now have the curse lifted off of me and put onto Him, and through the shedding of His blood, destroyed the bondage of it. It no longer has dominion over me! Now that sin, the curse, and slavery no longer have dominion over me, righteousness has now been transacted and has LEGAL AUTHORITY over me! Therefore, I have been, without equivocation, forgiven of all of my sins, and I can now come before the Father cleansed, righteous, and able to stand in His sight without shame or guilt!

Lord Jesus,

I stand in the presence of our Father, Who has been missing me... and I have so been missing Him, and can now say when He asks, (Your Name), where are you?" With tears of joy in my eyes, I can now say my head held high, without shame, guilt, or unworthiness, and with outstretched arms...

"My Father, my Abba, my Daddy... Here am I!"

The Father can now come, running to me, wrap His loving arms around me, kiss my face, head, and neck, and say,

Luke 15:22-24 NIV

> *22 'Quick! Bring the best robe and put it on him. Put a ring on his finger and sandals on his feet.*
>
> *Bring the fattened calf and kill it. Let's have a feast and celebrate. 24 For this Son of mine was dead and is alive again; he was lost and is found.'*

Thank you, Lord Jesus,

I can now rightly stand in the presence of the Father's glory, grace, mercy, goodness, power, authority, and love- fully restored and reconciled, in His sight! I now know that I can only do this because Your shed blood is on the mercy seat of the altar, in the holy tabernacle in heaven, and Your blood is speaking of greater peace, mercy, and grace through me and eternity. I can no longer be separated from the Father, and I will no longer be a slave, orphan, lost, or condemned.

Father, I am so grateful that YOUR Son redeemed me.

Father, I declare that I am ALL IN...

I declare that nothing can separate me from YOUR LOVE!

That I am no longer MY own...

But that I am fully and gratefully YOURS!!!

IN JESUS MIGHTY NAME!

Amen, and hallelujah!

The blood of Christ Shed for me!

Through our communion with the Lord God, we become more attuned to His love for us, His ways of interacting with us and knowing Him more. I challenge ourselves if we can get to such a point of knowing and communing with Him that it will develop such a faith in us to turn our focus away from our sensual- self-centeredness to becoming Kingdom-focused.

We need to ensure, though, that we are not just communing with Him just to be able to "FEEL" Him and let our ability to "Feel" Him be our gauge to determine if He is there for us- and if we don't feel Him, we are not sure if He is there or not. We need to get to the point of knowing that He is always there. He will never leave us or forsake us; it is us that does the leaving and forsaking.

We are called to be believers, and we don't want to get in the habit that we have to feel God's presence. He is right there with us always! We must know that He loves us, and we believe His love is always there- PERIOD! This scenario of feeling Him can be another emotional trap and roller coaster ride for us that will keep our focus on ourselves rather than Him.

Here are some examples of how we can change our frequency and perspective for our prayers from needy and pitiful to right standing and knowing.

Prayer for a wayward spouse.

Needy and pitiful.

Typically, this type of prayer is based on how our spouse's behaviors affect us. How they are hurting, offending, neglecting, or frustrating us. This will usually go along the lines of-

> "Lord, You need to come in and fix them. You know what they are doing, and how they treat me is wrong. Lord, You can see that they are not committed to this

> marriage, that they won't communicate, that they are only looking out for themselves, and I don't know how much longer I can take this. Lord, give me the strength and patience to deal with my spouse until You can turn them around."

Right standing and knowing.

We should see them for their potential when He is in them, from a place of mercy and love. To see them the way Jesus sees them and to see that if Jesus was in them and shining through them, they would not be focused on themselves. We should pray from the perspective that they have been made and called for so much more. To see them in a way that our heart cries out for them because they are wayward sheep in need of a shepherd.

> "Father, I lift my spouse to You out of my love and desire for them to align with You. Father, my heart cries for my spouse because they are dry cups that have been deceived or distracted, and they have lost sight of who they are in You and are functioning without You in their lives. Father, I know that when they are aligned with You and have You working on the inside of them, they will have their cups full to overflowing with Your Spirit and Your love in them, that they will no longer be lost sheep, and that they can have the capacity to love as You love. So, Father, I thank You that You pierce their heart with Your love so they can be reestablished back to the right standing with You, which will overflow into our marriage.
>
> Father, I also thank you for giving me the ability to demonstrate You and Your love to my spouse so that I can witness Your love, grace, and mercy for them."

Prayer for a wayward child.

As parents, when we see or experience something that our child is doing or going through that is not good; drugs, promiscuousness, skipping classes at school, or outright rebellion, our alarm system goes into red alert. We begin operating out of fear and worry. Few things will trigger us more than our children being off course. When our children are in the prodigal state, everything can and will be put on hold in our lives, careers, relationships, and even our walk with God. Because we operate out of fear and worry, how we interact with and treat our children comes from that fear. We treat them differently and even allow their waywardness to reflect our parenting-what did I do wrong, how could I have been a better parent, or why didn't I see this coming? We feel that we have failed to be a good parent and failed to anticipate or guide them away from their waywardness.

Our prayers reflect our fear and worry.

Not only that but when we have prayed for little Johnny, we are constantly watching and observing him with a very high scrutiny that is dysfunctional to see if the prayer is working. Johnny senses the scrutiny, is put off, and may become even more rebellious. This will trigger more earnest and desperate prayers from us, and then we watch Johnny even closer to see if the prayers are working, and the rift between us and Johnny grows further apart.

Through all of this, we are stuck in a dysfunctional, frantic insanity circle of apprehensive prayers, over-protective and clingy over watch, possibly challenging if the prayers are being heard since there is no evidence of improvement, then more intense, desperate prayers, feeling of helpless that nothing is working, that our faith may not be enough, that maybe we are being punished for our past sins. We may even be so hurt, discouraged, disenchanted, or deceived by this that we pull away from God, and we tell ourselves that until my child is fixed, I can't move on, stay engaged, seek His presence, or be His reflection, etc.

Needy and pitiful.

Our prayers for our children will usually be from the position of waywardness and the trouble they are in. We go to the Lord, praying from the position of the problem, desperation, and fear.

> "Lord, I don't know what has gotten into Johnny, but no matter what I say to him or how I approach him, he has become even more resistant and rebellious. Lord, I don't know where I went wrong. I pray that You stop Johnny from continuing in this mess he has gotten himself into. Lord, I don't know if I can live with this on my conscience if Johnny doesn't' change soon or ends up in jail, or worse, I don't know what I will do. Lord, I need You to fix this problem. I beg You to fix this problem; I am at a loss. I will do anything to get Johnny out of this mess! Lord, please, please, please! I beg you!"

Our children and family are the one area in which we are the most protective. It is the one thing that we will go to any extreme to protect, preserve, and defend. It can become a **defining moment** that can stall everything, put everything on hold, and affect our self-worth to the point where our focus is no longer on the Father. The devil knows the power of our family and, in particular, our children and their well-being, or lack thereof; he knows this can be a huge stumbling block for the most stalwart of Christ's followers. If the devil can wedge in and get our child into a mess, he can stall, skew, and alter OUR focus, our prayers, our walk, our connection, and the mission, purpose, and destiny- for possibly decades.

How do we, as Christ's followers, not fall into the trap of this insanity loop?

It is all based on where we have our focus. We don't take our eyes off the Lord God despite how difficult, painful, or as scary as the circumstance may be. We don't magnify the problem; we magnify the Answer. The story of the prodigal's rebellion was not because his Father was a lousy parent. Sometimes, our kids take a wrong turn, and our job is to be like OUR Father, the Lord God, and to be the anchor in the storm, to be consistent in our parenting and our faith walk, and to be a model to our children that we are steadfast despite the circumstances our children are in. We will not be able to do this in our power alone; we must be solid and steadfast in our relationship, trust, belief, and knowing the Father and in the power of His Holy Spirit working through us.

Before we can be good husbands, wives, and parents, we need to be settled, confident, steadfast, anchored, established, unchanging, unwavering, and ALL IN on Who God is, who we are in Him, and what our mission purpose and destiny are! If not, the storms and circumstances of life and our family will swallow us up along with our effectiveness for our family and, more importantly, for Him, and we will become impotent. If we are not solid in Him, then our prayers will be like trying to pull the Lord God through the eye of the needle of our family's hurts, betrayals, offenses, anger attacks, and dysfunction.

Our prayers for our family should come from the position of His faith, His authority, His ability, His provision, and His victory. Again, we are not praying and seeking answers; we pray having the ANSWER!

Right standing and knowing for little Johnny.

Father,

I thank You for Your heart, promise, and Spirit inside me. I thank You that I am becoming a loving parent through the modeling of Your Fathership over me. I thank You that I can present myself as a parent who brings faith, guidance, and love that goes beyond understanding to my children, to be able to show them that, like You, I am consistent, that I model Your attributes of being the same yesterday, today, and tomorrow because I reflect You!

Father,

I thank You for the gift of parenthood. I thank You for the gift of my children and the gift of being the steward over them. But I also thank You that the same Lord and Father who has been and is working in me is the same Lord and Father who is also working in my children. Therefore, I don't have to face this responsibility alone under my insufficient power.

Father,

I declare that through You, I don't have to let this situation with my child and the mess he is in matter more than Your Fathership and Lordship over me and my family. I thank You, Father, for Your investment in my children's lives. I declare that You predestined each of them before the foundation of the world and that there was a time for them to be born, and You intended their life to be in Your will, their destiny for You to watch over and to be fulfilled. I believe and declare that my children will not be lost, they will not be destroyed, and that they have a future and hope. They have a destiny to live long and well, be mighty in the land and the Kingdom, and find favor and honor among God and man!

I believe and trust that You will overflow and cover them with Your righteousness. I declare that each of my children is a child of the Most High God; therefore, they are not their own. I declare that I will rest in the comfort

> of Your Fatherly arms, holding, protecting, and guiding my children into their intended created identity and the mission, purpose, and destiny that You have before them. I declare that I have peace and comfort that my children are in good hands!

This type of prayer brings power, faith, direction, and alignment for redirecting your child and will give you peace to believe that the Lord God has got this! That you are not a fearful, fretting parent whose faith and walk have been tabled until your child is okay.

But you can rest in the knowing that the Father already desires the best for your child before you even have to ask and that if Your Father has done this for you and your life and walk with Him, He will do it for your child also! Hallelujah!

Our prayer life should be from the foundation and position of communing and knowing Him personally. Our prayers are not seeking an answer but that we have the Answer. We can pray this way for.

- Ourselves- to ensure we are solid, steadfast, and consistent and not let anything or anyone block our connection, alignment, and communion with Him.
- Our family
- Our church
- Our workplace
- Our city
- Our country
- The fallen world
- Revival

So whenever we get alone with Him, we can pray.

> Father,

I thank You for the work and revelation You are doing in me. I thank You that I am born again. I thank You for renewing my mind and transforming me into Your likeness. I thank You that my life will never be the same and that You have and will continue to change me into Your likeness. I thank You that Your truth has come inside of me, and Your truth is restoring me to what You designed me to be from the beginning! I thank You that stress, strife, and fear have no place in me. I thank You that when men see me, they see an overflowing cup that brings joy and life! Thank You for giving me the right to hold onto destiny for myself and my family.

I thank You and declare it all for Your great name and glory!

Here are some prayers my wife and I have developed through our communing with the Father to pray, which we have declared over our family. We pray these regularly over our family.

This prayer we developed using the template of the Lord's prayer that Jesus taught in Matthew 6:9-13

This, then, is how you should pray:

"'Our Father in heaven, hallowed be your name,

your Kingdom come, your will be done, on earth as it is in heaven.

Give us today our daily bread.

And forgive us our debts, as we also have forgiven our debtors.

And lead us not into temptation, but deliver us from the evil one.'

The Lord's Prayer over our family

Our Father in heaven, hallowed be thy name.

Lord, you are our Father- our "Daddy." As such, You are the head of our household and our family; as a family, we are precious in Your sight. We acknowledge Your Holy character: love, joy, peace, patience, kindness, goodness, gentleness, self-control, and faithfulness against such that there is no law, as our example to lead our family.

Your Kingdom Come, Your will be done on earth as it is in heaven.

Lord, we declare that, as a family, we will align ourselves to your Kingdom, which is entirely different from the Kingdom of the world and operates under different and pure principles. We recognize You as the King of Kings and Lord of Lords. As we align our family kingdom to Your Holy Kingdom, we will establish function from dysfunction, establish order from disorder, and establish the right hierarchy based on the principles of Your Kingdom, which will, in turn, create a flow and blessing of worship and align us to Your decree for a family structure.

Give us this day our daily bread.

Lord, as our family has specific needs, we will rely on You to provide for all our needs: physical, emotional, spiritual, relational, and mental. We will not rely on our power, but only as You can direct and provide for us. Lord, we know that You desire to provide more than we can ever ask or imagine, but by submitting our family needs to You, we will be satisfied with Your generous grace.

Forgive us our debts as we have also forgiven our debtors.

Lord, we now ask that You forgive our family of any debts/sins/transgressions against You. We recognize that You have a path set for us. You have called us and given our family a destiny, and we are asking for Your help so that our family doesn't stray from our place within Your Kingdom. Lord, we also forgive ourselves and each other for any offenses, seeds of bitterness, words spoken in anger, and hurt feelings that may not have been dealt with. As a family, we ask that we function from a spirit of forgiveness. We pray and forgive family members for personal and indirect offenses, treatments, mis-leadings, and lying to gain advantage. Give us the supernatural ability to discern, guard against, and, with your grace, prevent hurting each other and forgive quickly.

Lead us not into temptation.

Lord, as You are leading, guiding, and directing the steps of our family to be witnesses and messengers for You, we ask that You keep us from developing poor relationships, giving in to peer pressure, and speaking dishonor and hurtful words. We pray that we will be in the world but not of the world. We pray that our family will operate in a mindset of accountability, purity, and reverence to the family and, more importantly, to You and Your will.

And deliver us from the evil one.

Lord, our family is in constant spiritual warfare against a determined enemy that will never quit and uses subtlety and stealth to attack. The devil comes only to destroy, kill, and steal our family's health and wellness, our family relationship, and our family's relationship with You. But we also know that You are Lord over all! The enemy, no matter how determined, no matter how vicious, no matter how subtle, can ever stand against YOU! Lord, our family calls upon You to deliver us from this enemy. We pray for the ability to recognize when the enemy has infiltrated our family and to call on You on our behalf to defend and deliver us, not under our insufficient power, but in the mighty name of Jesus Christ! Father, teach our family to operate from a spirit of faith and not fear.

For Yours is the Kingdom and the power and the glory forever!

Another prayer that we developed.

Father,

I put on the whole armor of God- the helmet of salvation, the breastplate of righteousness, the girded waist of truth, the shod feet of the gospel of peace, the shield of faith, and the sword of the Spirit to stand against the evil of this world. I lift each family member to You, (Each member's name) and I pray favor, grace, and mercy over each one. I pray that You establish a hedge of protection around each one. I pray that You bless each one with Shalom- health, peace, and prosperity. I pray that You expose, destroy, heal, and replace all the defining moments in our lives.

Father,

We thank You for loving our family so much that You have reached down into the mirey clay of sin, and the world pulled each of us out and set our feet upon the Rock of Jesus.

I thank You for wiping the muck and mire from our faces and pulling the veils from our eyes so that we can see You clearly.

Father,

I thank You for sending Your Son, Jesus (Yeshua), to die on the cross for each of us to redeem and restore us all back to our intended created identities, missions, purposes, and destinies that You had for us from before we were born. I thank You that You have severed and cut through all the chains, hooks, and bondages of sin and addictions from this world: drug addictions, alcoholism, pornography, sex addictions, manipulation of others, witchcraft, sorcery, materialism, ego, self-centeredness, self-loathing, self-worth issues, and victimhood. We thank You that You have replaced all of these things with the fruits of the Spirit: love, joy, peace, patience, kindness, goodness, faithfulness, gentleness, and self-control against such there is no law and that we now live in right standing in Your sight, authority, victory, and peace as children and heirs to the King and no longer slaves to sin and the world!

Father,

I thank You for breaking generational curses that have been thrust upon our family and replacing them with generational blessings that will overflow and cascade down from generation to generation. I thank You for our legacy and descendants being mighty in the land and mighty in the Kingdom and for bringing many souls through them to the Kingdom! I thank You that You are teaching us all to be disciples, to live by faith and not fear, function and not dysfunction, that we listen for Your still small voice, and that we are good stewards of everything that You provide!

Father,

We honor, love, glorify, and worship You as the King of kings, Lord of lords, the Great I Am, the Ancient of Days, the Creator of the universe, King of the universe, but You are also the Good Father and the Good Shepherd who loved us first.

In Jesus' Mighty Name, we pray!

Amen!

Hopefully, you noticed that in all of these examples of prayers are in the position of right standing, of His victory, grace, mercy and redemption. I don't usually ask anything from our Father when I am praying. I don't come to Him with my list. Instead, I come in gratitude and declare who He is, who I am, and His mission, purpose, and destiny are for us. It is all for His great name and to glorify Him!

I come to him knowing that He already knows what I need. I don't have to ask! I can focus on communing with my Father, my Savior, and my Comforter the Holy Spirit. Our prayers should reflect Him inside of us that is so bright that He doesn't have to ask, "Where are you?" Because He can see His reflection coming back to Him. But also, through Him being inside us, we are like Moses when his face shines with the glory of His presence so that others can see Him in us! Hallelujah!

Then, when we come to Him with our petitions, we can go to Him knowing that if we ask anything in His name, He will do it because we aren't asking amiss! I will even go so far as to submit that we can be so in alignment, in knowing Him, and in frequency with Him, that we don't ask amiss because we only want what He wants, we only desire what He desires, and that our heart has become so in tune with the Father's heart that our petitions are His petitions.

Hallelujah!!!

Chapter 8

Come to Yourself!

Have you ever felt lost? Have you ever felt that who you are and how your life has progressed is at odds with how you had anticipated it? Have you ever thought that no matter what you do, how you plan, who you try to emulate, or what you strive for, it just seems to go differently than you thought it would? Whatever course you tried to take or accomplishments you have been attempting to achieve in life either doesn't work out or falls short of what you hoped to accomplish.

Have you ever wondered why I am this way? Have you ever found yourself wondering if God has made a mistake? Maybe He is too busy to notice you and the circle of insanity you live in. Does he have more important things to care for and people to look after? What is so special about you- that God would take the time to look down at your situation and intervene? Do you wonder if God even hears your prayers? Have you ever wondered if He is even real? Have you seen Him, felt Him, heard Him?

Have you ever thought,

"I am worth the Lord's time for Him to notice, love, or even bless me?"

Have you ever thought,

"After all I have been through and all that I have done, I don't feel worthy to allow God to help me."

As human beings living on this fallen earth since Adam and Eve, we have this innate desire to be accepted and blend in, but we also contend with the fear of never being enough, falling short, and trying to find ourselves in it all. Because of these two competing dynamics, we constantly strive to be enough and accepted by our family, culture, and place in this world. Achieving this will bring us satisfaction, value, and worth to our existence. The dichotomy is that through our desperate need to fit in and be accepted, we inherently drive ourselves to blend into the culture and society and reassure ourselves and society that we are one of them, ultimately leading to the reality of losing who we are. When we are constantly adapting to the culture, little by little, we are eroding our identity, our true self, the essence of who we are. Any time being one of "them" is more important than being you, your uniqueness, your inherent value, and your true purpose is becoming more and more hidden.

We have become so expert and adept at fitting in that we, along with our close family and friends, can no longer recognize who we are and only what we have become. It then begs the question from us, our loved ones, and even God...

- Where are you?
- What has happened to you?
- What have you allowed yourself to be transformed into that you have forgotten who you are?
- Where are you with your loving heart?
- With your unconditional giving heart?
- Your praying heart?
- Your worshiping heart?
- Have you begun imitating the culture so well that you are lost in the crowds and can no longer be seen?

- Have you realized that this transformation to the culture's standards comes with a price?

When will you realize that the things of this world, and trying to comply with its demands, will always come up short, will not satisfy, and will always cheat and dupe you? Have you allowed the masks, costumes, and garments of the culture and the ways of this world to be so "stuck" to you, so connected to you, so adhered to you that it's impossible to remove them without damaging, hurting, or traumatizing yourself?

Is it time to understand, restore, and preserve who you are at the core of yourself, even at the risk of protesting society's unwritten standards to be accepted, get along with, fit in, and go with their flow?

Is it time to come to "Yourself"?

In Luke 15: 11-22, Jesus tells the story of a family struggling with this issue.

> *11 Jesus continued: "There was a man who had two sons. 12 The younger one said to his father, 'Father, give me my share of the estate.' So he divided his property between them.13 "Not long after that, the younger son got together all he had, set off for a distant country and there squandered his wealth in wild living. 14 After he had spent everything, there was a severe famine in that whole country, and he began to be in need. 15 So he went and hired himself out to a citizen of that country, who sent him to his fields to feed pigs. 16 He longed to fill his stomach with the pods that the pigs were eating, but no one gave him anything.17 "When he came to himself, he said, 'How many of my father's hired servants have food to spare, and here I am starving to death! 18 I will set out*

> *and go back to my father and say to him: Father, I have sinned against heaven and against you. 19 I am no longer worthy to be called your son; make me like one of your hired servants.' 20 So he got up and went to his father. "But while he was still a long way off, his father saw him and was filled with compassion for him; he ran to his son, threw his arms around him and kissed him.21 "The son said to him, 'Father, I have sinned against heaven and against you. I am no longer worthy to be called your son.' 22 "But the father said to his servants, 'Quick! Bring the best robe and put it on him. Put a ring on his finger and sandals on his feet. 23 Bring the fattened calf and kill it. Let's have a feast and celebrate. 24 For this son of mine was dead and is alive again; he was lost and is found.' So they began to celebrate.*

In the story of the Prodigal Son, Jesus describes how the son demanded his inheritance from the father- **he was asking amiss.** After receiving, then squandered it in riotous living, found himself in a state of humiliation and scandal. He was broke, friendless, starving, a shame to the family name. He finds himself in all places, as a Jewish citizen, tending the pig pens, the last place any respectable Jewish person would be.

As Jesus unfolds this parable of the prodigal son, He is engaging a crowd who has gathered to hear His words. The crowd that gathered is a mix of tax collectors and sinners, who aren't typically seen in, and in most cases, not allowed in the synagogues of Jesus' day because of their chosen lifestyle. They are usually not interested in gathering around, let alone listening to some rabbi. They were the crowd that if you were a proper church attender, you would most likely avoid them, steer clear of them so that you wouldn't be seen as one of them, or made fun of by them, or they may even be hostile towards you. You would be in the "IN" crowd. You wouldn't necessarily want to be seen with these uppity, self-righteous, judgmental Pharisees who are always looking down their noses at you, always pointing out to you, "You can't do that on the sabbath..." "It is not lawful to consort with gentiles..." "you can eat bacon with your eggs...."

On the other hand, another element of the crowd that came to hear Jesus, was the churchgoers. You would fit more into the culture of being less free-spirited, less independent, and less able to live the life you choose, and have stronger inhibitions towards alcohol, promiscuousness, and using foul language and would strive to be living your life to honor the Lord God.

Another portion of the crowd that had also been drawn to listen to Jesus was the Pharisees. The Pharisees were there to catch Jesus in His words, to catch Him performing miracles, particularly on the sabbath, and to catch Him doing anything that would violate their perceived standards of righteousness, their interpretations of Jewish law and traditions, which Jesus did quite frequently, they wanted to catch Him to discredit him.

So here we are again at another crossroads; this time, it is of two primary cultures, lifestyles, and people types that have all come to hear the words of Jesus, who has gained for Himself quite a following and has become a form of celebrity at this point in His ministry. At this crossroads of culture and people types, Jesus is about to **Expose-Destroy-Heal-Replace** all the norms, skewed belief systems, judgementalism, and perspectives of religious worthiness all with one story!

We pick back up the story:

Through defining moments and events in his life, the younger son was conditioned and molded into a rebellious young man lashing out at his family and himself. He had become such a person of rebellion and resistance that he couldn't wait to leave home- you could say he hated his home. He wanted to get away from his country; he must have hated his country, to get away from his heritage, to get away from his religious traditions and values that to him must have seemed so restrictive. To get away from his older brother, who probably badgered him at every turn, and ultimately his father. His father was the patriarch, head of the family, overseer, provider, protector, and symbol representing everything the Prodigal had come to hate about his life. He hated the symbol of the father so much that he had gotten to the point where he wished that the father was dead. Then he could finally get his inheritance and get away from this miserable forsaken place- the environment- the family estate, which has become so oppressive, burdensome, and toxic that at times, just breathing this repulsive air over the years has polluted his very soul to where he has become so unbearable to be around, that his family must have been avoiding him as much as he avoided them.

How many tense conversations and arguments had he and his father had over the years? How must the father have tried to convince his son to see that he had been preparing this estate, this inheritance for him and his brother and their future children? This village, this estate, was part of their lineage built up by their father, grandfather, and great-grandfather, which was not easily gained and was to be in their family's legacy for generations to come. The Lord had blessed them with such abundance and considerable land, crops, and cattle that they needed hired servants to help maintain and manage their property, which eventually developed into an estate and a village. The family, even the hired servants, and the villagers all wanted for nothing, and this abundance was a testimony to Adonai, His goodness and love for them, and His plans and purposes for this family to be instrumental in expanding the Lord God's Kingdom- what an honor!

Over time, this all must have come to a boiling point. The Prodigal had had enough and couldn't take it any longer. Something had to give! So he arrogantly and insolently broached the father and demanded his inheritance, his portion of this cursed estate, this land that he loathed with every step upon it he took, and every breath of foul air he choked down, basically implying that he couldn't wait until his father died! That he had to have it now!

The father must have reached a point of futility with his son—the arguments, the toil, the heartbreaking, hurtful things that have been said. The animosity was so constant and so intense that no one wanted to engage with each other. The older brother and probably even some of those close to the family advised the father to give in, let him go, and stop the madness that was oppressing them all through the hateful rebellion of this son who would not relent.

At some point, for the father, the pain had to have gotten too much, and he had to decide to preserve the well-being of the overall estate and turn loose and let his son go. How the father must have anguished. Where was his little "ben"- his little son, who would follow him around asking thousands of questions, wanting to do everything that the father would do, say everything that the father would say, see everything the way the father saw? They were so close that they were the same person, a spitting image of each other, and inseparable from anyone watching them. They were so close that the older brother would get jealous and walk away from the conversations and games they would be playing. He would try to return later when the younger brother was sleeping or playing with the other children in the village to get his father's attention, appreciation, and acknowledgment. The father loved both sons, but his younger son had seemed to have stolen his heart. He was sure the older son felt slighted, but everything else seemed to fade away whenever the father was with the younger son; he was the apple of his eye.

The younger son also seemed to find favor everywhere he went. All the villagers would coddle and cater to him. As a toddler and young boy, he had an infectious personality; he was so inquisitive and humorous that everyone would stop to see what he would do next. They also noticed and acknowledged his older brother, who was so thoughtful and always polite and helpful with everyone and was appreciated- but the younger son would eventually return to the forefront of their focus with his antics that had everyone marveling and in stitches with laughter. They often commented that the younger brother reminded them so much of his father. They would notice later that the older son would wander back to the homestead, leaving them infatuated with the younger son.

As the two boys grew into young men, the animosity and jealousy that grew in the older brother began to cause a rift between the two brothers. Even as adults, they were often seen arguing, and the older brother constantly tormented his younger brother while performing their duties, which usually consisted of negotiating business and entertaining friends and business partners, including the synagogue community. The older brother had become an expert in all of the day-to-day activities of the estate. He was well respected as an organizer, problem solver, and administrator for ensuring that the village/estate continued to be profitable and sustainable for years. The father was so impressed with the older son's abilities that he eventually turned over the entire estate's affairs to him. He was delighted with how smoothly and proficiently the older son operated the estate for the family's legacy and Adonai's purposes.

At every possible opportunity, the older son would use his well-deserved good standing within the family and community to lord it over his younger brother. For the older son, all of the years as children growing up and the younger brother receiving all the adoration, attention, favoritism, and accolades for just being his silly little humorous, engaging, entertaining self, to which everyone, and especially father, would fawn over his every performance, at the expense of the older son who was more diligent than free-spirited. The older son's emotions soared to see the tables turn so entirely in his favor!

Now, because of the older son's diligence, studiousness, and competent management of the estate, he received all of the focus, accolades, and adoration of the community, especially his father's acknowledgment. The tables had so turned that the older son had seen his father reprimanding his younger brother for not being as diligent or having the desire to maintain the estate to the level required, and the father took the administration of the duties that the younger son was responsible for and turned them over to the older son. The older son was secretly overjoyed to see the wide rift between his father and his younger brother. It was about time that the older son was recognized for the value he brought to the family, the estate, and ultimately to Adonai. Indeed, Adonai also must be pleased with him, being such a good steward of all that father and, in turn, Adonai had entrusted to him. Look at how blessed and favored he was. Of course, Adonai was pleased with him!

The older son could see that his younger brother was no longer favored and was rebelling against everyone, including his father and Adonai. The older son felt a twinge of compassion and a little conviction for his younger brother's state, but isn't he getting what he deserves? Had he been more serious and careful with learning the family business, wouldn't he have been more successful and happier? The older son felt justified and not ashamed of his accomplishments. The younger brother would have to reap what he had sowed; humor and entertainment were not enough, and now he is suffering the consequences of his carefree lifestyle. Besides, was the older son his brother's keeper? It would be best for the father, the village, the estate, and especially the older son if the father would give the younger son his portion of the estate as he asked. Besides, if the father does give the younger son his inheritance, then the older son would also ensure that he received his portion, then he could make the remaining estate so successful despite splitting it up into lesser parts, and compared with the way the younger son would poorly manage his portion, surely father would see that the older son was so much more valuable than, the younger.

The father, after an agonizing night with no sleep and seeking Adonai for guidance, had decided to grant the request of his younger son. Part of the decision-making process was not only the distribution of the estate. Since he was splitting the estate and had his oldest son managing it, it would be prudent to distribute the appropriate portions to each son. Distributing the portions to his sons before the proper time bothered him, but the callousness and insolence of his younger son broke his heart the most. Did his younger son care so little for him that he wished he were dead? The family had stated this very opinion to the father many times leading up to this.

The father was distressed and tormented over how to proceed. He called for his two sons to be present for one last attempt to dissuade his younger son from doing this thing. As the conversation began, it was evident that the younger son was no longer listening to any counsel.

"My son," the father pleaded. "If you have any love, respect, or courtesy in your heart for me, for this family, do not do this thing. Not only are you disrespecting me and this family, but you are disrespecting Adonai Himself!"

"Father!" the younger son responded. "Any respect, perceived love, caring for you, this family left me long ago! I demand my portion and to be separated from the curse that this family has brought upon me! I require my portion of the estate so that I may live my own life, on my terms, with no interference from anyone, especially you, father!"

The father could barely sit and listen to his younger son ripping his heart from his chest. How could his treasured son become this uncaring, unloving person dripping with such contempt and rage, so much so that he was willing to remove himself from his family altogether? It is not understandable! Tears flowed from his eyes; he hid his face in his hands and sobbed.

His older son stepped in and rebuked the younger son, "How can you speak to our father this way, disrespect him, cutting his heart out?! Adonai should strike you down for your insolence! You are not worthy of being called his son! Father disown him! He is not worthy of your covering!"

The younger son was prepared for confrontation and lashed back at his brother, "Oh, you are so perfect! You, with your high and mighty attitude, constantly sucking up to father, wanting to be the perfect son, 'Father, look, I have negotiated a new deal that will make us even more profitable... Father, look, the rabbis at the synagogue have named me the official provider of the animals for sacrifice... father, did you know your younger son fell asleep again? The sheepfold has wandered off, and one is still lost, so we cannot take them to the market, but don't worry, Father, I sent out our more dependable hired servants to find the lost sheep that your wasteful younger son couldn't so that we have a hundredfold again to take to market. Aren't you proud of your older son father? You should take that responsibility from your prodigal and give it to me, the older, more responsible, skirt-following, suck-up son, and let your younger son tend chickens or doves or something of less value...' How dignified of you!"

"Curse you and your scoundrel attitude! Father, give him his portion, rend your clothes, and declare this Prodigal forever disowned; he is not worthy of this family! I will take the remaining portion and make it much more abundant than the whole; our legacy will be intact!" The older son responded in disgust.

"Enough! Enough!" the father pleaded from his covered face, now drenched with tears. "I have decided..." After a long pause and an awkward silence, the father began, "After careful and thoughtful consideration, I have decided to grant your request. I will divide the estate portions for each of you according to the traditions. The older son will receive the double portion, and the younger son will receive the lesser portion. You will each be separate from each other in the administration of your portions, and each portion will stand, or fall based on how it is administered, with no requirements for one another to be wholly separate. May Adonai bless each one of you."

The father persisted before anyone could interrupt, "As to the declaration of the ceremony of disowning my son...," again another long pause. "I cannot bring myself to disown my younger son. I will continue to call you my son, and hopefully, someday, we can once again live as a family. May Adonai make it so."

Before anyone could speak, the father abruptly got up, left the tent they were meeting in, and returned to his dwelling, leaving the two sons looking after him.

The only thing that the Prodigal could think is, "Finally!"

On the other hand, the older son had a myriad of thoughts; one of them was also, "Finally!" but for different reasons. Finally, I can be rid of this pesky, carefree person that everyone loved for no reason other than just because of who he is! Ugh! But over the years, through strategic comments, the precise timing of pointing out his inabilities, and ensuring that little brother always knew his place, the older son felt that finally, he could take his rightful place as head of this estate, head of the village, and father finally will recognize the older son's actual ability, that to operate in this world, to be successful, is what should be valued. Now that this Prodigal has shamed everyone, no one will want to adore him.

The older son looked over at his younger brother and said, "Father, I may not have disowned you as his son, but make no mistake, I have forever disowned you as my brother. Your shame will follow you the rest of your life and will be talked about for generations to come." The older son then left the tent.

The younger son just stood there. He was still trying to figure out what to feel. He felt victorious, vindicated, and free, but he also felt a tinge of guilt and sorrow and wondered if this was the right thing. He felt sadness for his father, but no matter, it was time to strike out on his own, to live his own life with no rules, no judgment, no responsibility. This is what will make him happy.

The father anguished for days, weeks, and months over his younger son. His son, whom he cherished, had become someone he didn't recognize. His son had liquidated his entire share of the estate, sold everything, and left without a word for where Adonai only knows. The father supposed that his younger son would use the money gained from the sale of the estate to purchase himself a separate place and begin anew, away from his family whom the son had come to loathe. After months of his son being away, the father received news that his younger son had not purchased any land or established himself somewhere within their country but had moved out of their country and is now living in the land with the gentiles, in riotous, scandalous living, squandering all on whoever would accept his offering of prodigal living.

"Oh my son, who has forsaken me, how I longed to gather you to my bosom as hen gathers her chicks under her wings! Lo, but not so, you resist; you pull away like a rebellious lamb who wanders away! Adonai, Adonai, I implore you to create in my son a clean heart, pull the veil from his eyes, and reveal to him the love of his father and his family. Adonai, protect my son. I wholly surrender him to Your benevolent providence that You will build a hedge about him and protect him from disaster. I also implore that, if it be Your will, bring my son back to me. I trust that You can turn the hearts of all men, so I trust You will change my son's heart, and he will return home! Until that day, I vow to wait and believe that You will bring it to pass, no matter how long it takes. Adonai, I only ask that it will be before my eyes close from this world."

Over the next several months, the father was often aloof and would stand outside his dwelling and stare down the road that led out of the estate. Their homestead was perched on a knoll that allowed viewing in a complete circle of their entire estate. The father would stare out across the countryside for hours daily. His oldest son would occasionally visit his father when he would go out to conduct business, tend their flocks, monitor the crops, and tend to the estate's affairs. The eldest son was doing a marvelous job of ensuring the estate's success, even beyond what the father could have imagined was possible. Not only had his oldest son made up for the loss of the younger son's portion, but he had tripled the value of the estate.

Years had passed since his younger son left, and the older son was returning from checking on the flocks and stopped to see his father. As he approached the homestead, he saw his father sitting outside under a canopy, staring down the road. The older son thought, "How long will the old man sit and stare off into the distance? When is enough- enough? He has been sitting in the same spot day after day for years, looking off down the same road, ever since that Prodigal abandoned him. When will he ever get over him and realize that the Prodigal has forsaken all and will probably never return and doesn't deserve to return?"

"Shalom, Abba," the oldest son beckoned.

"Shalom, son." His father responded while still staring down the road. "Are the sheep secure?"

"Yes," the son acknowledged. "They have multiplied 10-fold in the last three years, very healthy, and new lambs are ready to be inspected by the priests for the coming sacrifices for the Passover and festivals."

"Praise Adonai, His blessings endure forever.' Said the father.

"Yes," said the son, "Praise Adonai."

"Father, tomorrow, do you want to come out with me, walk the fields, and see how the spring harvest is going? It would be good for you to get out and visit the hired servants and our friends. Your grandchildren will be out threshing wheat; you know how silly they can be."

The father smiled and responded, "Maybe later this week; tell the little ones I will come out later this week."

"What, you have so much to do?" the son asked sarcastically. "Sit and stare down the road some more? Nothing ever comes down this road from that direction; that is the road to the land of the Gentiles. Are you looking for a gentile to come strolling down the road to visit us Jews?" The older son quipped.

"Don't test me, son; you know very well what I seek," the father admonished.

"Yes, I know very well," the older son responded, shaking his head. "You are seeking your prodigal. Father, your son has abandoned, deserted, and brought shame and reproach upon our family and culture. By every right, you should disown him, take the reproach off of yourself, and wash your hands of him. After all, he didn't think twice about washing his hands of you and this family! Not only that, but he is shamefully living with and doing only Adonai knows what with those cursed gentiles! Why do you waste your time out here daily, waiting for him, hoping he will return? Face it, Father, we are dead to him, and he is dead to us!"

"Guard your tongue, son!!" the father chided. "Your brother will return one day. I have petitioned and believe Adonai will restore his right mind, and he will come back and seek restoration. That will be a glorious day and a glorious testimony of the providence of Adonai. You should take care to speak ill of your brother and speak against the providence of Adonai. I will never give up on your brother; he will return down that road one day, and what a relief and joy it will be to see my son, who was lost, returning to the fold. My heart will leap for joy, and my soul will sing with gladness!"

"Oh, father," the older son pitied, shaking his head. "That son of yours, if he comes back, will come back destitute, ruined, dishonored, and an outcast to this family! He may be your son, but I no longer call him my brother! I would as soon as see a gentile walking on that road than to see that son of yours returning to mock this family! Father, you have a family all around you who loves, honors and cares for you. Do you not see? Embrace us, bless us, let us honor you, love you, and care for you. Stop wasting valuable years and precious moments seeking what has forsaken you!"

"My son," the father responded with tears in his eyes. "I love all of my family. I love you, your wife, and your children; I love you all. But all includes all."

The older son scratched his head. "Father, what do you mean? All includes all?"

The father returned his gaze down the road again and, only after a moment, responded, "Son, all means all. Do you remember a few years ago when we had one of the leanest years of profit and needed to take the sheep to the market? I instructed you, boys, to watch the last hundred-fold of the flock carefully and diligently, for the market would only accept the hundred and not any less; a hundred-fold is what they would accept."

"Yes, Father, I remember; I also remember one wandered off, thanks to your prodigal," the older son stated.

The father continued, "When the one sheep wandered off, we couldn't go to market; there was a good chance some of us would be very hungry and in want. So, we had to find that one lost sheep at any cost. We all looked for days, you, your brother, your cousins, my brothers, the hired servants, we all searched for that lost sheep; many of us had given up ever finding it, and we would miss the market, and our season would be ruined. But do you remember what happened on that last day for the market?"

The older son smiled and shook his head knowingly.

The father smiled, too, "On the last day, your brother was so distraught and felt so responsible for losing that sheep that he went off by himself in the countryside in grief and shame. While he was out, a few hours later, he returned to the village, singing and dancing. Why was he singing and dancing? Do you remember?"

The older son shook his head, still smiling, "He had the lost sheep on his shoulders."

"That's right!" the father said, pointing to the sky. "Do you remember how he found the sheep?"

His older son just shook his head back and forth in disbelief, "He didn't; the sheep found him."

"That's right!" the father said, "Do you remember how the sheep found him?" The father asked, getting up from his seat with his finger still raised.

The son continued shaking his head in disbelief, "The sheep heard his voice."

"Ha, ha, ha," the father chuckled, "the sheep heard your brother singing a sonnet, singing to Adonai for Adonai to bring the sheep back! And lo, the providence of Adonai, while your brother was in grief, ashamed, feeling responsible for losing the sheep, off by himself singing to Adonai about his lost sheep, what was it that your brother heard, but the bleating of a sheep who is returning to the voice of the shepherd. THE SHEEP

RETURNED TO HIM! PRAISE ADONAI!" "Your brother could hardly believe his ears, could scarcely believe his eyes! The lost sheep was now found! So what did your brother do? Did he disown the sheep for shaming, abandoning, and forsaking the fold? No! Your brother ran down the road, met the sheep, took the sheep in his arms, put the sheep on his shoulders, and sang and danced back home! The hundred-fold was restored, just in time! The season and our estate were saved, praise Adonai! So what did we do after we took the hundredfold to market?" the father asked his son again.

"We celebrated," the older son responded.

"That's right!" the father said while grabbing his older son's arms and began to dance around in a circle with him. "We celebrated! We killed the fatted calf! We ate and were merry! And why, my son, did we celebrate?"

The older son answered, "Because the sheep was lost and now was found."

"Exactly!" his father exclaimed. After a pause, the father continued, "Your brother is now that lost sheep, my son, but more than a sheep, he is my son and your brother! So how much more will I seek, wait, and believe that Adonai will bring your lost brother home to the fold?"

The older son shook his head, unconvinced, and commented, "I don't know, father, I don't know."

"I do, son, I do," said the father, "all means all," and sat back down and fixed his gaze on the road to the land of the Gentiles.

After a few moments, the older son said, "I'll see you tomorrow, Father, when I return from the fields. Shalom."

"Shalom, my son," the father answered.

Oh, how strange life can be, thought the younger son. He had never felt so free when he left his father, older brother, and the estate. He had sold the entire portion of his estate and had a substantial fortune to go and do anything he wanted. He wanted to live without limits and boundaries from his family, culture, religion, and even God.

He found that to do the things he wanted to do, he would have to leave this region altogether. The Jewish culture wouldn't allow him to live without boundaries and limits. So he struck out for the land of the gentiles. Although this was not usually done and not accepted by a good Jewish boy to consort with gentiles, he learned that they were even more free-spirited than he was once he arrived in the far-off land. It wasn't long, and he had drawn a cadre of friends who were more than happy to accommodate the wild lifestyle he had craved.

With his fortune, he could fund their parties every night. They would sing and dance and frolic, and each night, there seemed to be more and more people joining in his parties, with so many women who were so attracted to him that he would have 4 or 5 hanging on his every word, encouraging him to drink, sing, dance, be merry. There were many nights that he couldn't even remember where he was, what he had done, and how he had awoken with several women who were all there with him. Each day and subsequent night was an endeavor to outdo the previous one. He and his friends would create new ways, new experiences, and new avenues to enhance each day with new drinks, new potions, and new hallucinogenic substances to create new experiences and atmospheres. The younger son began to feel like he was in a different dimension. His thinking, speech, and behavior would become so contorted that he no longer felt in control and no longer felt that he was himself. It was almost like a spirit had taken over his entire personality and being until he was no longer in control of his actions, speech, or behavior and no longer recognized who he was.

Every day would blur into the next, each day a new challenge to see how intoxicated, how drug-induced he could get

—each day involved a new orgy and vulgarity that would go further and deeper into debauchery so that nothing seemed out of bounds or off limits. There were days that he was sure that he hadn't even woken up or slept through several days, and when he finally did wake up, he didn't know where he was, who he was with, or what they had done. His new friends would offer him some wine, and it wasn't long before he was the life of the party again.

It was during one of these binges and subsequent prolonged periods of stuporous slumber that he slowly awakened and noticed that something was different. At first, he couldn't pinpoint why he felt so strange, and everything around him seemed out of kilter. It took several minutes to clear the fog in his brain and to be able to get up from his pallet that he had been asleep on, obviously for a few days. He had experienced these extended periods of blackouts before, and they were becoming normal, but for some reason, this one was different.

Then he realized what it was... he was alone.

Where was everyone, all of his friends? Was there a party they ran to, and because he passed out, they left without him? In his stupor, he wandered around his substantial dwelling. Why was he alone? He couldn't believe or accept that he was alone. The younger son couldn't remember a time that he had ever been alone. Even back at the estate, he was never alone. That was one of the things that he had an issue with. But now, this was a foreign experience for him that he couldn't get his mind and emotions to comprehend. He questioned again, "Why am I alone?"

It was mid-afternoon, and his throat was so dry that he couldn't swallow. He roamed the dwelling, looking for something to drink, preferably wine. Every vessel that he came across was empty. He also reeked; his body odor was overwhelming and disgusting. He had been out for a few days, and he smelled awful.

He continued roaming to find some water to freshen up a bit. But there was no water either. Well, he would have to go out to the city well and freshen up there, then he would go down to the city tavern to see if his friends were there and get a proper drink.

He rummaged around the dwelling, looking for his money pouch. It took him a while, but he finally found it. It was empty. That was unusual; his satchel had always been full. Since he sold all he had when his father gave him his portion of the estate a few years ago, he was a very wealthy man who had a never-ending stream of money to party with- for him and all of his friends.

Maybe since he passed out, one of his friends had been keeping the money for him so that it would be safe. They were probably at the tavern, so he determined he would stop by the village well, clean up, and head to the tavern.

He took a change of clothes with him and wandered to the city well. No one was there at this time of day due to the heat at midday, so he could clean himself up without worrying about anyone seeing him. He drew the water several times and thoroughly rinsed himself off. He changed into his extra clothes and tossed away the clothes he removed because they were offensive. Then he headed down to the tavern.

When he arrived, he entered and noticed that it was empty except for the keeper of the tavern and a lonely regular who would always beg for a drink from whoever would see him. The younger son made it a point to avert his gaze from him and went up to the bar.

"Hello, my friend," the younger son greeted the barkeep. "Can I get my usual?" he asked.

The barkeeper brought him a cup of red wine and said, "Six pence."

The younger son smiled and said, "I haven't got my money satchel; add it to my note."

The barkeeper pulled the cup back out of reach and stated, "Your note is significantly overdrawn and hasn't been paid for nearly a month now; I can't allow any more advance; I am going to need you to settle up."

"What?" the younger son exclaimed, a little taken aback. "I have always paid my debts to you with extra. Why is this hostility?"

"Look," the barkeeper explained, "Times are getting very tight, money is getting very tight, there is a famine breaking out across the region, and you and your friends have built up quite a bill due, more than I have ever allowed, but now I must have payment."

"I understand," the younger son replied. "As soon as I find my friends, I will settle our account."

"You can have your next drink when you can pay for it," the barkeeper responded.

A little taken aback, the younger son left to find his friends. As he was walking out, he walked by the man who would beg for drinks, who gave the younger son a knowing look. The younger son felt a sense of empathy for the beggar for just a second, then walked out of the tavern.

He walked all over town, to all the hot spots where he and his friends had partied, but no luck. He was becoming perplexed. He and his friends were always together; no matter how wild, how disgusting, no matter how depraved, they were committed and loyal to each other. For him not to be able to find them was very unusual. It was evening and getting dark, and he noticed he was thirsty and hungry.

He returned to his empty home by way of the village well to get some water, and when he arrived at his house, he found a few food items that hadn't spoiled yet and ate and drank his water. He craved some wine, though, but water would have to do. As he finished eating, he again thought, where were his

friends? This didn't make any sense. He would look for them again in the morning.

The next day, he began the search for his friends for the next several days but had yet to find them. What in the world is happening? Why can't he find them, and where have they gone to? He began asking some of the town's folk but had yet to learn anything. After a couple of weeks, the younger son realized his friends had abandoned him. He also discovered that he had no more money and wondered if that was why they abandoned him. No cash and no parties equals no friends. He also realized that no money meant no food and no drink. After a few days of living off his little food, he needed to figure out how to generate money to get some food. He also needed to pay off the note for the barkeep so that he could get his wine again. But how was he going to generate money? He didn't have any fundamental skills, but he did have a home and possessions. He could sell or barter some of his furnishings and household items for food.

So he began to take inventory of the things in his home that had value, and he could use to barter for food. So, he procured food over the next few weeks by bartering his household furnishings. However, the amount of food he gained compared to the value of his furnishings was not commensurate despite his haggling. Due to the famine, the amount of food he received was much less than he expected. He avoided the tavern to avoid the notice of the barkeep until he could find a way to pay off his debt.

One morning, he was taking the last household item to the market to trade for food, but there were no vendors when he arrived. The younger son stood there dumbfounded, not understanding why no one was selling food. A few other patrons also discussed why the market wasn't open, so the younger son went over to inquire what they knew.

"Where are all the vendors?" the younger son asked.

"There is no food!" one of them answered. "The famine has wiped out all the crops, and even the cattle are dying, starving. We will probably starve, too!"

The younger son walked away, a little shaken.

He just had not realized the extent or severity of the famine. Now, it wasn't a matter of whether you could afford food but that there wasn't any food to buy. Genuine fear began to settle into his heart for the first time. How can things get so bad that it's not even a matter of affording food but that there is no food? He had heard his father tell stories of how famines had broken out in the lands during the times of his ancestors, but those were just stories, and the younger son didn't think of those stories as something he would ever see or experience. But now he is experiencing the full effects of a famine and the realization that he could starve! While contemplating this, he was abruptly interrupted by someone yelling at him.

"There you are! You owe me over a month's fees! I want my payment now! If not, I will have you thrown into debtor's prison!" It was the barkeep. "How do you intend to settle your account? I cannot wait any longer!"

The younger son was caught off guard and wasn't sure how to respond and only muttered, "I will find a way..."

Before he could finish, the barkeep jerked the furniture item the younger son had brought to trade for food out of his hand and said, "We can start with this, and I want the rest by the end of this week, or I will have the constable snatch you up, and your next home will be in debtor's prison."

"How... uh... how much do I owe?" the younger son stammered.

"A hundred denarii!" the barkeep barked. "Four month's wages for a common man's work. I want it by the end of the week; it has been long enough!" he abruptly walked away.

A hundred denarii surprised the younger son. He would have never guessed that the note was this overdrawn. He was walking back to his home, thinking of how he would pay this bill by the end of the week. He had no money, and he had no income. Was he to end up in debtor's prison? As he was thinking this, he stopped in front of his home, and an idea came to him as he was staring at the front of his home.

At the end of the week, he had no choice. His home was worth much more than the note owed to the barkeep, but the younger son was out of time, and the last place he wanted to be was in a debtor's prison. So, he signed over the ownership of the home to the barkeep. The younger son sat outside of the tavern numb. He was broke, friendless, and now homeless. What was he to do now?

A few weeks passed, and the younger son was so hungry that his stomach was constantly aching. He had never felt hunger like this. It had been 15 days since he had eaten anything. He left the town and was now wandering from town to town, trying to find a way to make an income to buy any available food. But the famine was so severe that there was no food. He stumbled onto a home, a farm in the countryside, and decided to greet the occupants and see if he could work for any food they had.

As he approached the farm, he could smell and hear the presence of swine. So, these were pig farmers. Let's see if he could negotiate a way to get some food. He approached and hailed the occupants who were out working on a cart.

"Hello there!" the younger son greeted.

"Who are you?" the lead occupant asked.

"A hungry wanderer looking to earn a meal," the younger son replied. "If you could allow me to work for some food, it would be much appreciated."

"We don't have much food and not much work, or at least work anyone wants to do," the occupant responded.

"Any food and work would be welcome; I haven't eaten in weeks. I will do whatever chores needed to get some food," the younger son assured.

The lead occupant looked at the other two, who shrugged their shoulders. The lead occupant told the younger son, "Come over here then. I will show you the work, and then you decide if it will be worth it."

He led the younger son over to the pig stalls. The smell that assailed them was so strong and pungent that the younger son gagged in response; he had never smelled anything so revolting in all of his life.

"No one has cleaned these stalls in weeks," the occupant explained. "All of the laborers left due to the famine. So, the buildup of waste has not been tended to. If you can bear it, you can clean these stalls, and I will pay for you with food. We can slaughter one of the swine for you."

The younger son had conflicting thoughts going through his mind. He was a Jew; Jews had nothing to do with swine; they were deemed unclean by Jewish law, yet here is this Jew, considering cleaning the stalls of these filthy, smelly, unclean animals for a meal. Once he got his gag reflex under control, he responded. "Sir, I can do this chore, but I cannot eat one of these swine; it is against my culture. If you have another way to pay?"

"We have a few chickens left that we have been saving for ourselves," the occupant responded, "but if you are willing to do this chore, we can spare one for you as payment."

The younger son thought for a moment, felt his stomach grumble with hunger pains, and decided to clean the stalls for a chicken. "I agree," he told the occupant while stifling another gag.

A few hours later, with a cloth over his face and a rake in his hand, barefoot in the most disgusting, slimy filth he had ever experienced, the younger son was still far from being done.

The swine were immune to the filth they lived, wallowed, and rolled around in, covering themselves with it. The younger son could now understand why the Jews were forbidden to eat these repugnant creatures.

Evening was coming on, and he still needed to finish. He asked the occupant if he had a place to sleep and he would finish the chore the next day. The occupant took the younger son over to the small manger that had straw in it. He also showed him where the well was so that he could clean up some. The younger son tried cleaning off the best he could, but it seemed that no amount of water would get the slime and the smell off of him. He was so exhausted that he resolved to try to sleep for the night, finish this repulsive job, get his chicken, and be done.

The following day, the younger son awoke with the rooster's crowing. He groggily got up from the hay, still smelling of swine, and prepared to return to the pig stalls. His hunger pains were so intense that he caught himself and bent over, holding his stomach until they subsided. As the younger son walked back over to the stalls, the occupant gave him a bushel of slop and pods to give the swine to eat.

The younger son looked at the pods, and his hunger made him crave the possibility of eating the disgusting pods. The younger son climbed over the stall's fence with the pods, and as he was about to feed the swine, his hunger pains began again. The younger son even thought, what if I grab some pods and eat them myself?

The pigs rushed over for the pods, and one of them ran into the leg of the younger son, who lost his balance and fell backward into the slimy mess. The pods were scattered all through the stall. Not only was the slime on his legs but also on his clothes and hair. The younger son got up, frustrated, smelly, and starving, wanting to finish this terrible chore. He watched as the swine devoured the pods. "Great, more waste to come," he thought.

He spotted one of the pods stuck in the slime that the pigs hadn't yet found and reached down, picked up the slime-covered pod, wiped it off on his tunic, and looked at it for several seconds.

"You know," he thought, "if I can just imagine that this slimy pod was a pomegranate or a piece of his mother's tasty honey-covered baklava, I may just be able to eat this."

He stared at it for a few more seconds and started to bring it to his mouth, and the smell of the slime and the bitter smell of the pod caused his gag reflex again. When he finally managed to stop heaving, he saw one of the pigs staring at him as if thinking, "You going to eat that?" The younger son tossed the pod to the swine, who devoured it with gusto. The younger son stifled his urge to begin gagging again. He climbed out of the stalls to escape the stench and clear his head.

He went to sit down at a nearby workbench. "What am I doing?" he thought. "What have I done? Who am I? What have I become? Look how far I have fallen since leaving the estate. I was an heir with a legacy, and now I am a disgrace! How many of my father's servants have bread enough to spare, and I sit here and perish with hunger?

For the first time in a very long time, he felt shame. These last few years, even though he has lived the carefree life of adventure, of fulfilling all of his desires, drinking to his heart's content, imbibing in all sorts of substances, experiences, lusts, orgies, every perceived pleasure and debauchery imaginable that he thought would give him satisfaction, give him a sense of joy, give him a sense of freedom that he would never have been able to experience back at the estate with his father's and his brother's rules and oversight. Even though he did experience all these things, none of it was lasting, none of it fulfilled, none of it profited anything of value, and in the end, here he sat, no money after having much wealth, no home after having the largest most luxurious gentile home in the gentile township, no food, no future, NOTHING!!

The scripture from the Torah from King Solomon came to his mind; his father taught him many times: "Vanity of vanities says the preacher, vanity of vanities, all is vanity. What does a man profit from all striving in which he toils under the sun?" The younger son could see that he had followed the same folly of King Solomon, all the carousing, the female companionship, the excess in every sense, all leading to nothing. Unlike King Solomon, though, who was never destitute of his wealth, the younger son was sitting here entirely destitute, a Jewish man of all things, sitting on a gentile farm, covered in and smelling of swine, about to eat the swine's food! He had become his environment, a gentile, a swine, even less than the swine; at least they knew what they were and felt no shame. The more he thought about it, the more ashamed and disgraced he felt. If his father and brother could only see him now! Alas, he may never see them again, and probably wouldn't allow him back anyway.

He had already disgraced the family by demanding his portion of the inheritance before his father's time had come, basically telling his father, and the whole world for that matter, that he had wished he were dead, that he cared more for his father's possessions and inheritance than his father. The younger son remembered the look of grief on his father's face; he was so heartbroken. He also recalled how his reaction toward his father was so cold, so callous, that he didn't care and would have said and done anything to get his inheritance and leave his miserable life by any means.

"Oh, Abba," he thought. "I am so sorry." He buried his face in his hands and sobbed.

How could he have done that? His father never did anything to deserve that kind of treatment. The younger son knew that his father loved him, stood up for him, protected him, and provided for him; even when his father chastised or corrected him, he could see that it was out of love for him. Just his callous treatment towards his father when he left would be enough for his father to disown him and declare the younger son dead and never think of him again, but if his father only knew what he has done since he left, it would bring even greater shame on the family.

"I must go back to my father, though," he thought after regaining his composure. "I must go back and make amends; I must go back and let my father know I am sorry!"

But how?

He sat and thought until midafternoon and then decided, "I will arise and go to my father, and say to him, Father, I have sinned against heaven and before you, and I am no longer worthy to be called your son. Make me like one of your hired servants." I will appeal to my father to make me his hired servant, and I will put myself at the mercy of my father, and whatever he decides, let it be so. If he banishes me for being too shameful, so be it. I deserve no less. But if there is even the slightest chance, the slightest hope, the slightest mercy, he could make me one of his hired servants, even the lowest of the lowly servants, with the worst of all the chores, on the furthest outskirts of the estate, where he will never have to see me or speak to me, I will accept it gladly.

So he arose and began walking down the path of a several-day journey back to his father.

The father was in his usual position, staring down the road while sitting under the canopy. His attention was slightly distracted from time to time due to the older son positioning some of the hired servants to begin planting the fall crops near the homestead as the ground was fully rested after a year of no planting. His older son was out orchestrating the finishing of the last harvesting of the summer crops on the other side of the estate. He told the father that he would be back later in the evening to check on the progress of the planting.

Even though summer was ending, it was still hot. The servants were taking a break to draw water. The father was also yearning for a cup of water to quench his thirst, so he beckoned for one of the servants to bring him a cup. A few of the servants came over, bringing him some water, and sat with the father for a few minutes to visit and rest. The servants were talking amongst themselves; the father was only half listening. While the servants were visiting, they noticed that the father was slowly rising from his seat and staring intently down the road with his eyes squinted and his hand over his head, shading the sun. The father stepped outside the canopy for a better look down the road. He could see a speck of a silhouette of something on the road along the horizon line very far off.

Maybe it was a mirage from the sun generating heat waves, playing tricks on his eyes again. It was there one minute, then disappeared the next. The father stood there with his eyes squinted, hand on his forehead, watching to see if he could see it again. After a few seconds, he saw it again. There was definitely something on the road, but it was too far off to make out what it was. During this time of the day, with the heat, it was probably a lost animal. Maybe one of the sheep got out again. He kept looking as it disappeared again. The father wished his eyesight was as good as it used to be. While he was thinking this, he saw the object again; he stared and tried to determine if it was one of the sheep; it seemed to have stopped and was hunched over for several seconds, maybe grazing on something since this road was rarely used, it led to the country of the gentiles, there would be no reason for a gentile to come into Jewish territory or vice versa. Vegetation was growing over the road due to no traffic to keep it tramped down, so it was most likely an animal foraging. He watched to see if he could make it out to be one of the sheep when it raised back up.

He saw the figure rise, and his heart stopped! The figure stood upright, and it wasn't an animal! He could hardly believe his eyes and had trouble catching his breath. He stumbled backward a few steps, knocking over his stool and spilling his cup of water, startling his servants. The servants looked at the father, who was trying to catch his breath, holding his chest, and would not take his eyes off the road, and they became very concerned for their master and gathered around him to determine why he was in distress and determine how they could help him.

They were asking him many questions all at once, concerned he was having a health crisis. But the father was unable to speak; tears were running down his face, and his breathing was elevated. The father then became very anxious and began jumping up and down and around in a circle, half crying and seemingly half laughing, and the only sound he could make was like a baby crying, "AAAAH, uh, AAAAH, uh, AAAAH!!!!"

The servants were at a loss as to what was happening to their master: was he having a stroke, was he in pain, was he going crazy?

They could not tell what was wrong with him. As they watched this episode, he began pointing down the road and yelling again, "AAAAH, uh, AAAAH, uh, AAAAH!!!!"

The servants all turned around to see what the father was pointing at, fearing the worst. As they looked to where he was pointing, expecting a terrifying beast or calamity, they saw a distinct figure of a man stumbling down the road very far off. While they were staring at the figure, the father had somewhat gained his composure, tied his tunic around his waist with his legs exposed, and took off running through the servants down the road towards the figure of a man now yelling clearly and audibly, "IT'S MY SON! IT'S MY SON!"

This startled the servants again, and they stood there dumbfounded, confused, and not sure what was happening; their master was running down the road that led to the gentile country towards an unknown man yelling. They watched the father run for a few seconds and then began looking at each other in bewilderment, unsure what to do. Then, one of the servants began running down the road after the father. Still staring at each other, the rest of the servants shrugged their shoulders and started running down the road after the father.

The younger son was as exhausted as he had ever been in his entire life. He had been traveling for several days with barely anything to eat in weeks and knew he was starving to death. He was so weak that he could only walk for a few minutes at a time before weakness and exhaustion overtook him, and he had to stop and rest. It took double the time to return to the estate as it did to leave.

He had just stopped to rest again by kneeling on the road. He was in Jewish territory now, and he could tell the difference; all the vegetation was alive and lush around him, even growing in the middle of the road. The famine was behind him now, and he knew he was getting closer to the estate, and he began rehearsing the speech he had planned to give to his father when he arrived.

He started practicing it again, "Father, I have sinned against heaven and before you, and I am no longer worthy to be called your son. Make me like one of your hired servants." He would propose that his father make him the lowest of the lowly servants and post him on the outskirts of the estate so that the father would never have to speak to or see him...

His thoughts were interrupted by a strange sight that caught his eye further down the road. He saw a man running down the road towards him, with several more men a little way behind him chasing after him. What could be happening that these men were chasing after this man? Did he steal something?

The man was getting closer, and he could faintly hear him between gasps, "My son.... My son...."

The younger son's heart began to skip a beat and then started pounding in his chest. It was his father running to him. It was still quite a way off to the estate; he could barely make out the homestead on the knoll, and his father had run all this way. The younger son began to hyperventilate, and his mind started racing; why would his father be running to him? His father must be trying to stop him before he got onto the estate and brought shame to the family. The father must be so ashamed and angry with him that he was going to turn him away before anyone else saw him. Grief and shame started to wash over him, and he began to sob. Because of his physical exhaustion, he felt his knees buckle, and he fell into a kneeling position and sobbed uncontrollably. He was a fool to come here. The shame of facing his father was worse than if he had just starved with the Gentiles.

He could now hear his father's footsteps and panting still running towards him, and could still hear him wheezing, "My son.... My son...."

The younger son could not look at his father and hid his face in his hands, bent over, and continued to sob. When his father reached him, he was so out of breath that the younger son could barely hear his still, small voice whispering, "My son.... My son...."

When the father reached his son, he could barely breathe. He saw his son kneeling on the road, bent over with his face in his hands, sobbing, so much so that he could see his son's torso panting in and out. His son was filthy; his clothes were rags and covered in mud; his feet were as dark as the road; he had no sandals on; his hair looked like a filthy mud-caked lion's mane and his son was so thin it alarmed him.

The father fell on his son's neck, kissed him, pulled him in, and embraced him. "Oh my son, my son..." the father cried. "My son..." They both knelt on the ground, embracing each other, exhausted, in tears, and a state of shock. The servants came running up shortly after, out of breath, surveyed the situation, and determined their master was in no danger. Relieved, they bent over to catch their breath, and one of the servants dramatically fell on the ground on his back in exhaustion!

"My son," the father whispered, "My son, you are finally home..." and continued kissing his neck, hands, and forehead. The younger son just continued to cry, not able to look at his father. Finally, the father pulled his son's hands from his face. His son was unrecognizable. His face was as filthy as the rest of him except for the streaks from the tears. He had a full, unkempt, mangy beard, and his cheeks were so thin they looked sunken and sallow. The father calmed his son enough to say, "My son, welcome home."

The younger son began shaking his head weakly back and forth, and when he had composed himself, with help from his father, they stood to their feet; the younger son began to speak, "Father...." He began, but his throat was so dry he could barely talk. "Father..." he tried again, "I have..." he had to swallow to continue you on, "I have sinned... against heaven.... And against you..."

"My son," the father tried to interrupt, fresh tears beginning in his eyes again.

The younger son persisted, "Father... I have sinned against heaven and against you.... And am no longer worthy to be called your son...."

The father interrupted him by slapping his son on the back, putting his arm around him, standing beside him, and with enthusiasm, said to his servants, "Bring me the family ring and put it on his finger, bring the best robe, and sandals for his feet!" They walked back to the homestead, and as they arrived, the servants had the robe, the ring, and the sandals waiting for them. The father was so joyous that he snatched the robe and threw it around his son's shoulders, "There, that's better." He exclaimed. He then took his son's hand, placed the ring on his finger, and sat him on the stool. He had the servants give the younger son water to drink, and while his son drank, the father grabbed a larger basin of water and washed his son's feet, with his son protesting, but the father was determined and kept a firm grip. Then, when finished, he put the sandals on his son's feet. The hired servants stood around in their bare feet. As servants, they never had sandals to wear, but as family and masters of the kingdom, the family always wore sandals, the servants recognized, and the younger son also recognized that the father was ceremonially redeeming his son back to his place as son and heir.

His father stood, clapped his hands, and told the servants, "Bring the fatted calf here," he pointed at the fire pit he used for the great homestead meals, "Kill it and let us eat and be merry!" He grabbed his younger son's hands, lifted him to his feet, and started dancing around circles hand in hand with him and declared, "For this, my son who was dead and is alive again!!!! He was lost and now is found!"

And they all began to celebrate.

The celebration continued well into the evening and showed no signs of slowing down. The father had his servants and family gather and join the celebration with music, dancing, and feasting. The father's heart was so full of joy and relief over the one soul- his son, who came to himself, came home, repented, and is now safe and sound where he belonged; he wanted all of his estate to rejoice! The father danced all night long.

While the celebration continued, the younger son was still reeling. He had never expected the reception he received, never imagined that this would be the response. How could his father be so gracious, so forgiving, so generous? It goes beyond all understanding. The younger son had cleaned up the best he could, removing most of the muck and smell of swine and gentile territory from himself after much effort and scrubbing and rinsing. He had one of the servants cut and groom his hair and beard. With a fresh set of clothes, his robe and ring, and new sandals, he somewhat resembled a respectable son of a Jewish father again, now if he could see himself or even allow himself to become a son of his father and citizen of this estate again, he still saw himself as the Prodigal.

For his father, though, there was no question. He told his younger son earlier that evening when the son brought up this concern, "My son, you are and have always been my son. Nothing you have done, nowhere you have gone, can ever separate you from who you are- My son. You were born, my son. My blood runs through your veins, my spirit and personality have been infused with yours, and your likeness is the same as mine. This is because you are my son. Just because you threw a tantrum, disowned your family, your culture, who you are, and even though you ran away from us, stopped remembering us, and participated in Adonai knows what, does not disqualify you from being my son. My love for you will never fail; neither height, depth, principalities, powers, nor any created thing can separate my love for you!" The younger son teared up again, thinking over what his father had told him, and he would never forget these words. His father never gave up on him, never forsaken him, even though he deserved to be forgotten and forsaken, even when everyone else did, and justly so, his father never did; he unconditionally accepted and restored him to who he was before he fell into shame and iniquity. "Thank you, Father," the son cried, "and thank you, Adonai."

The older son was through for the day; it was evening, the sun was almost down, and the harvest was complete. He was walking back with his hired servants to the homestead to check on his father and the spring planting. As they drew closer to the homestead, they could smell food and hear music and singing one hired servant returning with him commented, "Your father is throwing a celebration. He must be celebrating you, his son, as a reward for all the hard work and diligence you show for the community and estate affairs!'

The older son wasn't sure what to think, but if his father were throwing a celebration, that would mean his spirits would be up. Maybe, finally, Father recognized all that the older son was doing to expand and prosper the estate, and with the harvest being so bountiful this year, a double portion when all of the other regions are in a state of famine, that father was to celebrate the older son's accomplishments. "It's about time," the older son thought, "that father woke up from his melancholy and acknowledged all of the good things the older son has contributed to making the estate successful."

"Let's go join the celebration!" The older son encouraged the servants.

When they arrived, the servants peeled off to find their families. The older son was looking for his father, and when he couldn't find him, he asked one of the servants in charge of the spring planting where his father was and why they were celebrating, secretly suspecting the reason.

The hired servant began explaining, "It is a miracle!"

"A miracle?" the older son asked, a little confused.

"Yes!" the servant continued. "Your brother has come!"

The older son was caught off guard, and his demeanor went from a smile to a look of confusion and then irritation. "What do you mean my brother has come?" he asked.

"Yes!" the servant responded enthusiastically, "Your brother has come, and because he has received him safe and sound, your father has killed the fatted calf! It is a miracle!"

The older son, finally realizing that the celebration wasn't for him after all but, of all things, for the return of a prodigal son who abandoned, disowned, shamed, and squandered everything for riotous living, is now back home, and his father has obviously forgiven all that this Prodigal has done to this family! Unbelievable!

The older son stalked off, visibly upset, leaving the servant alone.

After a while, the father noticed that the hired servants out in the harvesting fields were back and joined in the celebration but didn't see his older son. The father walked around the celebration, asking the servants if they had seen the older son. They responded that they had yet to since they had returned.

As he walked around looking for his older son, he saw the family and servants doting on the younger son as he animatedly acted out a story. The younger son had everyone in stitches, and you could hear the laughter as their attention was fixed on the younger son as he entertained them. The father beamed in pride and gratitude and thanked Adonai that he answered his prayer, that He would bring his son back home before the father's time on this earth was over.

After an extensive search for his older son, the father finally found him. "Oh, my son," the father greeted him.

"Father." the son responded matter-of-factly. The son was busy cleaning the harvesting tools and putting them away.

"Are you coming to the celebration?" asked the father excitedly. "Have you heard? Your brother is home safe and sound, the fold is complete, and the lost sheep is no longer lost!" The father was joyful and grabbed his older son's hands to dance around.

His older son abruptly and forcefully yanked his hands away from his father, walked to the other side of the dwelling, and continued cleaning the tools with his back to him.

The father was taken aback by his older son's response, and they both stood there quietly for a time before the father spoke again. "My son, please come to the celebration. Please understand that this is a joyous occasion that could only have been arranged by none other than Adonai Himself. Your brother has come to himself; he has come home, safe and sound; you should be..."

"I SHOULD BE WHAT??" the older son demanded. "I SHOULD BE GRATEFUL THAT THIS SON OF YOURS, THIS PRODIGAL, IS HOME AGAIN? "He runs off," the older son continues, "breaking your heart, squandering his portion of the estate, in a gentile country no less, shames this family, and then when he has finally hit rock bottom and nowhere and no one else to turn to, he dares to come back here, to show his face to all whom he has dishonored, and you just welcome him back with open arms, no compensation, no explanation, no atonement, no conditions, nothing! He can just come back, wearing the family robe, the family ring of authority, and the master's sandals, without so much as earning back his place, building trust, or reconciling his wrongs?"

"My son..." the father attempted, but the older son pressed on.

"Not only that," the older son persists, "but I come home, and the servants tell me you ran out to him. Why would you disgrace yourself that way? Your son should have crawled back to you and begged for your forgiveness!! You should have demanded that at a minimum, if at all, he should have been established as the lowest hired servant, not even an ordinary slave whom we consider to be like a member of the family, but the weakest of hired servants who could be dismissed at a day's notice. Then he is not one of the family at all, but he will have to earn his way back to family status, and if he pulls a stunt as he did before, we will dismiss and banish him forever, as we should and as he deserves! But instead, you go running to him, which is a disgrace to our customs; not only that, but the servants tell me that you tied your tunic and exposed your bare legs, which is also a disgrace to our custom, and then you fall on him and kiss and forgive him, give him a robe, a ring, and sandals, and then kill the fatted calf and celebrate this prodigal disgraceful conduct for all the world to see!!!!" the older son crescendos and then threw his hands up and spit on the ground in disgust and turned away.

"My son..." the father attempted again, but before he could continue, the son turned around and interrupted again.

"You know, father," he started with a low intensity of furious pressure, "Lo, these many years I have been serving you.... I never transgressed your commandment at any time... and yet," he paused to maintain control of his composure, "and yet, you never gave me a young goat, that I might make merry with my friends.... But as soon as this son of yours came.... Who has devoured your livelihood with harlots!!! You killed the fatted calf for him!!!"

The older son was finished and turned away, his head down, visibly disappointed, confused, and angry.

The father could see his older son's hurt and anger and understand why he felt the way he did. His older son was right; most other Jewish men would have done exactly what his older son had just explained and would have forever banished the dishonor the younger son had brought on this family.

But the father's heart and the younger son's heart met on that lonely road between the two kingdoms, the kingdom of the Gentiles, and the kingdom of Adonai and His people. Since the beginning of time, mankind has contended with this struggle. But the heart of the father longs for, yearns for, and will never cease to want the return of his lost child who has been delivered from the clutches of the cruel taskmaster of this worldly kingdom. The man, who is his younger son, whom the father ran out to meet on that lonesome road, was a man that, in his years of riot, was not himself. It was not the Prodigal who was the real man. The real man was the remorseful man he met on the road, not the Prodigal."

As he and his younger son walked back to the homestead, the younger son explained and attempted to convince his father that when he finally came to himself, he wasn't thinking of how to improve his conditions in the Gentile country; he wasn't blaming his father, his brother, his friends, his gentile landowner, or the pigs. He recognized his misery without dwelling on it and instead focused on his father. He explained to his father that he told himself, "I will arise and go to my father:" The father didn't hear his younger son say that he thought of his village or home- but of his father. The father recognized that when the son returned to his father, he also returned to the town and the estate, but his focus was primarily on returning to his father.

To the father, the younger son demonstrated true repentance. After his misery, the veil was pulled from the younger son's eyes, and he saw and thought completely differently about his father, which would flow down to how the younger son felt about himself, his home, and his family. The father recognized the change in his younger son and the transformation from when he was the Prodigal, who demanded the father "to give me!" but after his departing and subsequent wretchedness, his request now was, "Father, make me." This second request and obvious revelation and repentance brought unspeakable joy to the heart of the Father.

The father's heart now ached from the words of his older son. The father knew self-righteousness is typical for those holding on to bitterness. The older son was finally showing his bitterness to the father, but only after it had done its damage to his heart over these many years. The father felt sadness for his older son.

His older son was demonstrating how truly unappreciative of all he *did* have. The older son had his father's company every day and the blessing of home and family. His father's love was surrounding him constantly, and everything the father had was his. Yet, the father knew from his many years of experience that the boastful and the self-righteous always feel they are not treated as well as they deserve. The father acknowledged that the older son was obedient yet still far from his father's heart.

The father realized that not only did he lose one sheep, who wandered away from the fold, but he also had another lost sheep right here amongst the fold. The father silently prayed to Adonai, "Adonai, You have done it once and brought my younger son, who was lost in riotous and prodigal living but is now found and restored. Merciful Adonai, grant this old father one more request before my eyes close forever on this earth. Restore the heart of my older son to be full of love, joy, peace, patience, kindness, self-control, gentleness, goodness, and faithfulness, first to You and then towards his family."

The father told his older son, "My son, my dear child, you are always with me, and all that I have is yours." Then he continued, "It was right that we should make merry and be glad for your brother was dead.... and is alive again... and was lost.... and is found."

This is where Jesus ends the story.

As we review the story of the Prodigal, we can see the descent that transpired. The impact of his descent can be stated in this way:

- Through demanding his inheritance and demanding it out of order, out of protocol. In this culture, during this time, the inheritance isn't executed until the father has passed or the father decides to administer the inheritance early for his purposes, starting with the oldest son, who would also get the double portion. The father can also refuse to administer the inheritance to one or other of the children or even change the inheritance, write them out of the will, so to speak. The fact that the prodigal demanded his inheritance was counterculture and disrespectful to the father- In essence, the son was saying to the father that he wished he were dead! This sin was against the commandment to "Honor your father and mother."

- He liquidated his portion of the estate to use for wild living. This is an act of self-centeredness and narcissism. It was disrespectful to his father and his legacy for his children's inheritance, particularly in this time and culture. The inheritance was not intended for the current individual to do with whatever he fancied. But it was designed for him to take it, build upon it, and pass it on to the next generation, his children, his children's children, and so on to continue the legacy, to establish and launch his descendants into success, honor, and destiny for the works of the Lord for the succeeding generations. By liquidating his portion and going to another country for the riotous lifestyle and just squandering it, he was doing this at the expense of his future legacy, mission, purpose, and destiny that the Lord had for him and his descendants. How many **defining moments** has he condemned his future generations through this selfish act?
- With his money squandered along with the effects of the famine, the Prodigal was reduced to tending the swine and became so hungry that he was even considering eating the slop and pods the swine were feeding on. This was directly against the Levitical Laws for a Jew; you could say that the son has forsaken his heritage and identity and has become part of the environment he was in. It wasn't bad enough that he left his family, country, and culture to live with the Gentiles, but now he is breaking the commandments of God by tending the swine. He had stooped to the level that he was living in, ready to act and become the very culture that he was in. He looked

like his environment: the swine were muddy- the son was muddy, the swine smelled awful-the son smelled awful, the swine were feeding on slop and pods- and the son was considering feeding on the slop and pods. He was no longer recognizable as the son of a Jewish father but now was more recognizable as an unclean, filthy, smelly, starving, gluttonous Gentile swine.

- His choices were shameful to the family, estate, community, legacy, and the Kingdom. The Prodigal was sinning against his earthly father and legacy, to heaven, and ultimately to God. As with God's chosen people, set apart, sanctified, and justified for good works for representing the Father, the Prodigal's decision was against everything the Father intended and expected from him. He was willingly and intentionally going against the expectations of the Kingdom and principles of God.

As he was on his journey home, after mercifully and thankfully **"coming to himself,"** the younger son was practicing his speech for when he would plead his petition for the father to allow him back into the estate. The son came to himself and realized his fallen state, what he had become, and that it was no longer acceptable!

The Prodigal goes on to state,

> *"How many of my father's hired servants have bread enough and to spare, and I perish with hunger! I will arise, go to my father, and say, "Father, I have sinned against heaven and before you, and I am no longer worthy to be called your son. Make me like one of your hired servants"*
> *Luke 15:17, (NIV)*

It is essential to point out that it was in his misery that the prodigal son was finally able to think clearly, humble himself, and come to the point of repentance. How many of us aren't thinking clearly until we get to the end of rock bottom? To the fact that there are no longer any distractions or worldly desires to deceive us and leaves us unsatisfied and worse off than before. When we have reached such a dire need, whether physical, mental, or spiritual, it takes us to the point of getting so far down that looking up is the only way to see.

Through the descent into his miserable state, it could be determined that the Prodigal wasn't himself and had become another man, another person; he had lost the identity he was created for; he wasn't his true identity any longer. While in rebellion and disobedience, he was no longer himself and had become the opposite of who he was born to be!

Jesus uses this parable of the Prodigal to **Expose, Destroy, Heal, and Replace** the many personality types of the crowd that had gathered to listen to Him. His message to the tax collectors and sinners was similar to the Prodigal: repent and come home to the Father. The Prodigal's heart was to the father first, not his family or village, but for the father. This is how we need to come back to God when we have strayed– to come back to *the Father* FIRST and FOREMOST; before coming back to our earthly family, church, or even our Christian friends, our heart must be first to the Father.

The message to the religious leaders was also evident, like that of the older son: be happy when the lost are found when they repent and come home to the father. The older son failed because his heart was bitter against his younger brother and his father for accepting his brother back home. There was no grace or repentance. this became a perfect illustration of the religious leaders who were angry and condemning that Jesus consorted with tax collectors and sinners.

How many of us need to come to ourselves? How many of us need to realize that we have ventured so far away from who we are that we look more like the metaphorical swine of our environment and culture than as the son and daughter of our Father? How many of us must come to the revelation that in our Father's house- even the servants have enough bread to spare while we are perishing?

How many of us have realized that what we have become by trying to fit into this world, by allowing ourselves to be conditioned to what we were never intended to be, has brought us to the confession that we are no longer worthy of being called a son and daughter, and if the Father could make us like one of the servants, it would be enough and probably more than we deserve?

Questions to consider:

- What are the things in your culture, society, and environment that appeal to you and that you desire to achieve? What are you willing to lower your standards to conform to the norms of what it takes to be successful and fit in?
- Does who you are compete with or contradict society's "Unwritten Standards" of their acceptance of you? What about you doesn't jive with society's acceptance of you?
- What things have happened to you, whether you have brought it on yourself or has been thrust upon you, that you are so ashamed of- that you have to put on the masks, the costumes, the garments of your culture to hide what you don't want anyone else to see?
- What has happened and needs to surface so that the desire of being accepted outside of who you are is no longer acceptable? What needs to happen for you come to yourself, and go to your Father, and say... "Father, I have sinned against heaven. Before you?"
- What things have you hidden, repressed, or committed that cause you to consider yourself "Unworthy" to be

called a son or daughter, and if the Father could make you one of the hired servants?

- How do you think the Father would respond to you?

Chapter 9

Adoption- A Superior Form of Chosen!

We, as human beings in our fallen state, left to our own devices and abilities, are pitiful, corrupt victims who are constantly craving and searching for where we fit in this life. Even when we have most things going for us, a good family with mom and dad caring and providing for us, good friends, and even a promising career, life can be disrupted with a tragedy, layoff, death in the family, divorce, or even worse. We can get to the point that nothing is fair; what's the point, and why am I here?

Without our receiving Jesus the Messiah as Lord and Savior, we will always be in this category. Sometimes, even though we have accepted Jesus as our Lord and Savior and we are attempting to work out our faith, we can become disenfranchised and still feel that even though we are saved, we have no purpose, no sense of belonging, and no victory.

In this chapter, we will **Expose, Destroy, Heal, and Replace** a critical foundational principle into our hearts by getting crystal clear with.

- Who God is.
- Who we are and whose we are.
- And why we are here and our mission, purpose, and destiny.

To do this, we are going to go to the book of Ephesians to bring clarity into our lives, pull away the veils of deceit and distraction, and get a clear, hyper-focused view of the critical points that will get us in alignment with our created value and identity that the Lord God intended. Let's get started.

> *Paul, an apostle of Christ Jesus by the will of God, To God's holy people in Ephesus, the faithful in Christ Jesus:2 Grace and peace to you from God our Father and the Lord Jesus Christ. 3 Praise be to the God and Father of our Lord Jesus Christ, who has blessed us in the heavenly realms with every spiritual blessing in Christ.*
> *Ephesians 1:1-3 (NIV)*

Assuming you have read the many epistles (letters) that Paul the apostle had written, you are familiar with the many opening greetings of his epistles and may have developed a tendency to gloss over them. But we need to see these greetings not as perfunctory or common courtesies, but full of the essential characteristics of Who our Lord God is.

Paul's letter to the Ephesians greeting starts with giving- because our God is a giver. The first thing we see is that we are being given; "Grace and Peace from God our Father and the Lord Jesus Christ." God gives first, He loves first, He first loved us!

Paul goes on to explain that the Lord has also; “blessed us in the heavenly realms with every spiritual blessing.” God is imparting into our spirits through the Holy Spirit, who communicates all of God's spiritual treasures to men. The blessings we receive are spiritual. The Holy Spirit is the conduit of communication by which the blessings can reach our spirits, through Christ's ascension- which is the reason for our access into the heavenly places, which sin, previous to His ascension, has hindered us. What Paul is emphasizing here is before and while Christ was in the flesh here on earth, God's people could not activate their heavenly privileges as sons and daughters because the transaction of His sacrifice hasn’t been fulfilled yet. Now that He has ascended, our citizenship is in heaven, where our High Priest forever bestows His blessings. Our treasures are stored there, along with our desires, affections, hope, and inheritance. The access to the gift of the Spirit itself, the source of our "spiritual blessing" that Paul refers to, is by Jesus Christ having ascended where His blood has once and for all been placed on the mercy seat. Christ has become the center and source of all blessings from heavenly places; hallelujah!!! He has an infinite capacity to bless, any limit to His blessing is due to the lack of vessels (you and me) to fill or our capacity to receive. The Lord God is blessed in and of Himself and IS the blessing. Therefore, as we are created in His image, He desires to bless us and make us a blessing so that we can be a blessing and bless others.

> *4 For he chose us in him before the world's creation to be holy and blameless in his sight. In love 5 he] predestined us for adoption to sonship] through Jesus Christ, in accordance with his pleasure and will— 6 to the praise of his glorious grace, which he has freely given us in the One he loves.*
>
> *Ephesians 1:4-6 (NIV)*

The Lord God CHOSE us before the creation of the world. Before we were alive, before we breathed our first breath, and before we did anything, He chose us! That is amazing! If you have never considered yourself to be anyone important or to have any value or worth, this statement right here shatters any thinking of being "less than."

Why would the King of the Universe, the God of all creation, the Lord of lords, be thinking about, let alone choose us, if He didn't know we were worth it? Things and people that are considered worthless are not what is thought about, considered, or chosen. So, if the Lord God is thinking of us and has chosen us before the foundation of the world, what kind of value must we possess for that to happen?

We have to surrender what we have been conditioned into based on our backgrounds, environment, upbringing, thought processes, inadequacy, hurts, guilt, shame, the walls that we have built up to protect ourselves, and the masks we use to hide our shame to the Lord God so that our minds can be renewed, and lives transformed into what **the Lord says we are!**

He has declared us as His CHOSEN!

Who are we to argue with what God has declared? Who are we to question whether we are what He says we are? Why can't we see ourselves as what He declared us to be instead of seeing ourselves as guilty, worthless, less than, or shameful? As if Jesus dying on the cross, shedding His blood, and paying the price to redeem us wasn't enough? We need to get into **accordance** with and **become** what He has declared us to be before the creation of the world, chosen, blameless in His sight, predestined for adoption! We need to receive and allow the understanding THAT WE ARE WHO HE SAYS WE ARE!

PERIOD!!!!

What the Lord has declared as clean and right before His sight, let us not declare it otherwise!

> *9 About noon the following day as they were on their journey and approaching the city, Peter went up on the roof to pray. 10 He became hungry and wanted something to eat, and while the meal was being prepared, he fell into a trance. 11 He saw heaven opened and something like a large sheet being let down to earth by its four corners. 12 It contained all kinds of four-footed animals, as well as reptiles and birds. 13 Then a voice told him, "Get up, Peter. Kill and eat." 14 "Surely not, Lord!" Peter replied. "I have never eaten anything impure or unclean." 15 The voice spoke to him a second time, "Do not call anything impure that God has made clean."*
>
> *Acts 10:9-15 (NIV)*

The price Jesus has paid makes us clean; let us not call ourselves unclean!

IT IS TIME FOR US TO RECEIVE AND BELIEVE THE FULL REVELATION OF WHO HE SAYS WE ARE!

The Lord God chose us before the creation of the world to be holy and blameless in His sight. Through the blood of His Son, He intends that we should be holy, and without blame, before him in love; He did not choose because we are holy, but so that we might partake of the sanctification of the Spirit; that we might be sanctified by him here on earth, and then we can be without fault and blame, both in this life and ultimately in the life to come. The intention and desire for us from before the earth was created were to be in His presence; for us to be in His presence, we have to be spotless; to be spotless, we have to accept the salvation of His Son through His blood and then allow ourselves to be sanctified by His Spirit, both while we are on this earth and then when we are ushered into His presence in heaven.

Be- Definition.

- To exist, to occupy, to live, a state of being.
- To belong, to attend, a fact.
- Used as a linking verb, a precursor- become, belong, befriend.

Come -Definition.

- To move towards, approach a destination.
- Movement, progress, to happen, to condition.
- Transitional, invitation,

Become-Definition..

- To grow into, change, be conditioned, and come into being.
- To be suitable is necessary to the dignity of the situation or responsibility.
- To mature, to be transformed into

In love, He predestined us for adoption to sonship through Jesus Christ in accordance with his pleasure and will. These two words, adoption, and accordance are such amazing forms of grace that have been bestowed on us as believers- that I could probably write an entire book for each word. I am not doing that now, but I want to look closely at each.

In this first chapter of Ephesians, Paul uses the word four times.

- In vs. 5- in accordance with His pleasure and will.

- In vs. 7- in accordance with the riches of God's grace.
- In vs. 9- of His will according to his good pleasure.
- In vs. 11- according to the plan of Him who works out everything in conformity with the purpose of His will

The definition for accordance or according derives from the root word **accord.**

- To be in accordance with, in alignment with, in harmony with, in agreement with.
- To grant or to bestow, to apply.
- Free will and partnership, to be alongside.

Adoption: Definition.

- The act of adopting, or state of being adopted, is the choice of acceptance of a child from another parent to be the same as one's child.
- The legal act of establishing a relationship between a parent and a child outside of the child's biological parent, thereby entrusting the designated adult with responsibility for raising the child:
- Admission to a more intimate relation: reception.
- The choice to make one's own, which initially was not, to be accepted.
- A legal decree establishing a relationship between adult and child, not of their bloodline; the adopted child has access to all claims afforded to a biological child (including the right to inherit).

Adoption is a special designation of **choseness.** Born children are children of their parents by birthright, but adopted children become part of a family by choice- the parents choose the child. The adoptive parent often possesses a higher level of intentionality, commitment, willingness, joy, and preference.

The current adoption process is very lengthy and arduous. Adoption has to be confirmed by a legal act! It is not to be a temporary choice or designation when a child is adopted. The process often requires submittals, screenings, and compatibility considerations. There can be distance or boundary barriers if adopting outside of your home country, extensive fees, mitigations, delays, lost opportunities such as the original parents changing their minds and deciding to keep their child, or the agencies involved have halted the process, along with many more considerations.

But even through this rigorous process, many parents are determined to do what it takes, regardless of the length of time, the excessive costs, the screenings, the distance, the legalities, delays, and often heartbreak. They **choose** to submit themselves to this process because they **desire** to have a child they can call their own and be part of their family.

In ancient Rome, during the time of the Apostle Paul, adoption had a robust significance. When parents gave birth to a biological child, they were allowed the option of disowning the child for a variety of reasons. There would often no longer be a desire or commitment for their child, nor was it guaranteed that their status in the family would be permanent.

Not so, however, for an adopted child. In ancient Rome, adopting a child meant:

- The parents desired and freely chose the child for adoption.
- The adopted child would be a permanent part of the family; parents couldn't disown a child they had adopted.

In Roman law, an adopted child receives a new identity. Previous agreements, responsibilities, and debts were erased.

The adoptive parents took on the new child's rights and obligations. Also, inheritance was an ongoing part of life, not something that began at death. Being adopted made the child an heir to their new father, joint-sharers in all his possessions, and wholly united to him.

"When the adoption was complete, it was final. The newly adopted child had all the rights of a biological son in his new family and lost all ties and obligations in his old family. They were a new person in the eyes of the law, with no connection to their past.

This is what the Lord God desires for us! He desires and will go through all the steps necessary to adopt us as His children. He gave His one and only Son to come to earth, live as a man, and die on the cross as a sacrifice to redeem and pay the price to *ADOPT* us from being slaves to this world and into being His sons and daughters as coheirs with Christ. We now have all the rights as a child and heir and have lost all ties and obligations to our past. We are a new person!

> *And since we are his children, we are his heirs. Together with Christ we are heirs of God's glory.*
> *Romans 8:17 (NLV)*

Let's look at two examples of this principle of adoption in the Bible. Caleb and Ruth, two Biblical characters that were initially outside the tribes of Israel but were adopted into the lineage particularly in the tribe of Judah of Israel through marriage- Marriage is also another form of adoption. Their stories show how God desires to adopt those willing to commit and follow Him wholeheartedly.

Caleb

Caleb was attributed to the tribe of Judah and best known as one of the twelve spies chosen on a mission to cross the Jordan River and survey the promised land of Canaan. He was a soldier, mighty in battle with supernatural strength even into his old age. At 85 years old, he was still fighting giants and the enemies of God. He was a settler; Caleb possessed and settled the hill country of Hebron in Canaan.

Secret Agent.

During the Exodus from Egypt, Caleb, along with eleven others, was to survey the promised land. When they returned forty days later, ten of the twelve spies gave a bad report. Even though the land had agricultural abundance and was flowing with milk and honey, they described the inhabitants and their fighting men as unconquerable and their cities as too fortified to be able to take the land of promise and convinced the Hebrews nation who had gathered to hear, to be fearful and unbelieving. The crowd was so distraught that they began protesting and wailing.

Caleb, along with Joshua, who was also one of the 12 spies sent, attempted to silence their rebellion and stated:

> *"We should go up and take possession of the land, for we can certainly do it"*
> *Numbers 13:30 (NIV)*

Based on their excellent report, Caleb and Joshua contended vigorously against the fear and unbelief of the ten spies. Still, the community chose to listen to the other spies and began to riot.

Caleb and Joshua rent their clothes in frustration and contend with the people,

> *"The land we passed through and explored is exceedingly good. If the LORD is pleased with us, he will lead us*

into that land flowing with milk and honey and give it to us. Only do not rebel against the LORD. And do not be afraid of the people of the land, because we will devour them. Their protection is gone, but the LORD is with us. Do not be afraid of them."

Num. 14:7-10, (NIV)

But the community's fear and unbelief had settled into the hardness of heart, and the community chose to stone Joshua, Aaron, Moses, and Caleb and go back to Egypt. In the midst of this rebellion the Lord's presence showed up, and he declared that the unfaithful generation would wander and perish in the wilderness until only the second generation was left. But Caleb and Joshua only from the first generation would survive and lead the second generation to enter the promised land.

A Fighter.

At the time for the Israelites to enter the land after the first generation had passed away, the Lord chose Joshua to lead them, who eventually designated the land to the tribes. Caleb, now 85 years old, was instrumental in being the leader of the tribe of Judah, and Judah led the rest of the tribes in battles to rid the land of the foreign inhabitants.

He convinced Joshua by demonstrating his diligence, belief, and purpose:

"You know what the LORD said to Moses the man of God at Kadesh Barnea about you and me. I was forty years old when Moses the servant of the LORD sent me from Kadesh Barnea to explore the land. And I brought him back a report according to my convictions, but my fellow Israelites who went up with me made the hearts of the people melt in fear. I, however, followed the LORD my God wholeheartedly. So on that day Moses swore to me, 'The land on which your feet have walked will be your

> *inheritance and that of your children forever, because you have followed the LORD my God wholeheartedly.' Now then, just as the LORD promised, he has kept me alive for forty-five years since the time he said this to Moses, while Israel moved about in the wilderness. So here I am today, eighty-five years old! I am still as strong today as the day Moses sent me out; I'm just as vigorous to go out to battle now as I was then. Now give me this hill country that the LORD promised me that day. You yourself heard then that the Anakites were there, and their cities were large and fortified, but, the LORD helping me, I will drive them out just as he said."*
>
> *(Josh. 14:6-15, NIV)*

Caleb went on to possess the mountains of Hebron and drove out the descendants of Anak, who were giants, extremely tall and adept fighters.

A Colonizer.

Caleb settled in the mountains around Hebron. (Josh: 21:12, NIV). Caleb also conquered Kiriath Sepher south and west of Hebron. Caleb offered a challenge to capture this city, and his daughter Aksah as a reward would marry the one who succeeded. Othniel was victorious and received Akash, the land, and springs of water (Josh. 15:18-19).

So we see that during the Exodus from Egypt, wandering in the desert, and possessing the promised land, Caleb was a significant leader of the tribe of Judah. What makes Caleb even more unique though, is that he was purported not to be an original descendant of Jacob, who was the father of the 12 sons that became the tribes of Israel; therefore, he was not a descendant of Judah, whose tribe he ultimately belonged to and became its leader.

Caleb's ancestral heritage stems from the Edomites through Esau, who was the twin brother of Jacob. Jacob stole the birthright and blessing of Isaac their father that was intended for Esau, who was considered the firstborn. Esau had a son named Eliphaz who had a son named Kenaz (Gen 36:11), who was a chief (Gen 36:15) and one possible ancestor of the Canaanite people group known as the Kenizzites (Gen 15:19), who may have been part of the mixed-multitude that joined Israel (Ex 12:38; Num 11:4). So Caleb was not part of the Israel nation per se, but from the lineage of Esau, Jacob's brother.

Caleb's clan were slaves in Egypt along with the nation of Israel and lived on the outskirts of Goshen, the city where the Israelites lived for 430 years during their captivity in Egypt. Many of the ten plagues brought upon Egypt didn't affect the Israelites or their village of Goshen. Caleb got his family to live in Goshen to protect them from the effects of the plagues. During that time, Caleb settled near and made alliances with the tribe of Judah to live amongst and under their covering.

As the Israelites left Egypt and wandered the Wilderness, Caleb was attuned to any opportunity to volunteer his services for the tribe of Judah. Caleb was always the first to fight in battle and distinguished himself as a fierce warrior. When it came time for Moses to send the 12 spies, Caleb was called upon by the Lord to represent Judah. Caleb also married Judah's available daughters (in those times, they commonly married multiple wives).

Caleb is called the Kenizzite and in Num 32:12 & Josh 14:6,14 and in Josh 15:13 it says that Caleb was given "a part AMONG the children of Judah." This indicates Judah had accepted Caleb, they had adopted him. Caleb's blessings and acceptance were not due to bloodlines or family connections to Judah, they resulted from his **choice** to wholly follow God and commit his loyalty to the tribe of Judah and the nation of Israel which led to his adoption and subsequent leadership of Judah by the tribe of Judah and the nation of Israel.

Ruth

The story of Ruth is found in the book titled after her name. Her story takes place in the times of the Judges, right after the Israelites have possessed the promised land and before the era of the Kings.

> *In the days when the judges ruled] there was a famine in the land. So a man from Bethlehem in Judah, together with his wife and two sons, went to live for a while in the country of Moab. 2 The man's name was Elimelek, his wife's name was Naomi, and the names of his two sons were Mahlon and Kilion. They were Ephraimite's from Bethlehem, Judah. And they went to Moab and lived there. 3 Now Elimelek, Naomi's husband, died, and she was left with her two sons. 4 They married Moabite women, one named Orpah and the other Ruth. After they had lived there about ten years, 5 both Mahlon and Kilion also died, and Naomi was left without her two sons and her husband.*
>
> *Ruth 1:1-5 (NIV)*

During the ten years of living in Moab due to the famine in Judah, Naomi's husband, dies and makes her a widow. Her two adult sons had married Moabite women, Oprah and Ruth, and they were now the providers for their wives and their mother, Naomi. The two sons also die; all three women are now widowed without providers in a time when women had no way of providing for themselves.

> *6 When Naomi heard in Moab that the Lord had come to the aid of his people by providing food for them, she and her daughters-in-law prepared to return home from*

there. 7 With her two daughters-in-law, she left the place where she had been living and set out on the road that would take them back to the land of Judah. 8 Then Naomi said to her two daughters-in-law, "Go back, each of you, to your mother's home. May the Lord show you kindness, as you have shown kindness to your dead husbands and to me. 9 May the Lord grant that each of you will find rest in the home of another husband." Then she kissed them goodbye, and they wept aloud 10 and said to her, "We will go back with you to your people." 11 But Naomi said, "Return home, my daughters. Why would you come with me? Am I going to have any more sons, who could become your husbands? 12 Return home, my daughters; I am too old to have another husband. Even if I thought there was still hope for me—even if I had a husband tonight and then gave birth to sons— 13 would you wait until they grew up? Would you remain unmarried for them? No, my daughters. It is more bitter for me than for you because the Lord's hand has turned against me!" 14 At this they wept aloud again. Then Orpah kissed her mother-in-law goodbye, but Ruth clung to her. 15 "Look," said Naomi, "your sister-in-law is going back to her people and her gods. Go back with her."

Ruth 1:6-15 (NIV)

Naomi is trying to think of her two daughters-in-law's best interests for their future and releasing them from her torment and their obligation to her. She tells them that she is going back to her land in Judah, with no prospects of ever being able to marry again, and that they should go back to their country and start over. This was a heart-rending moment for them all, for they had become very close, and it was not easy to separate.

Oprah, although sad, sees the logic in Naomi's request. Orpah and Ruth had stronger family ties in Moab than they did with Naomi and her land in Judah, so it made sense for them to stay in Moab. So Oprah departed. But Ruth refused to leave, and even though Naomi was persistent in trying to persuade Ruth, Ruth clung to Naomi even more.

> *16 But Ruth replied, "Don't urge me to leave you or to turn back from you. Where you go I will go, and where you stay I will stay. Your people will be my people and your God my God. 17 Where you die I will die, and there I will be buried. May the Lord deal with me, be it ever so severely, if even death separates you and me." 18 When Naomi realized that Ruth was determined to go with her, she stopped urging her.*
>
> *Ruth 1:16-18 (NIV)*

This is an unusual commitment on Ruth's part. She has been released to move on with her life in her own country, which she is familiar with, but she will not leave Naomi's side, so she convinces Naomi to allow her to go to Judah with her.

When they arrive in Judah, they go to Naomi's hometown of Bethlehem during the barley harvest time. As they settle into Bethlehem, Ruth tells Naomi she will glean behind the harvesters to get food for them. Naomi agrees. Ruth goes to a particular field, gets permission to glean, and gleans diligently all day. The owner of the field, Boaz, a wealthy man, comes to check on the progress of the harvesting and notices Ruth gleaning and inquires of her. The harvesters tell Boaz that this is Ruth, the Moabite who returned with Naomi. Boaz shows favor to Ruth for her commitment in caring for her mother-in-law and tells the harvesters to leave extra for Ruth.

When Ruth returned with the grains she had gleaned and explained whose field she had gleaned from, Naomi took courage and said that Boaz was a close relative of her late husband Elimelek and was considered a guardian-redeemer. A guardian-redeemer or relative redeemer was designated to sustain the interests of extended family members' needs, including providing an heir for a relative who had died, redeeming the land that a poor relative had sold outside the family, and redeeming and restoring the legacy.

So, Ruth returned to Boaz's field daily until the harvest was complete. On the last day, Ruth comes home to Naomi, and Naomi advises Ruth.

> *2 Now Boaz, with whose women you have worked, is a relative of ours. Tonight he will be winnowing barley on the threshing floor. 3 Wash, put on perfume, and get dressed in your best clothes. Then go down to the threshing floor, but don't let him know you are there until he has finished eating and drinking. 4 When he lies down, note the place where he is lying. Then go and uncover his feet and lie down. He will tell you what to do."*
>
> *Ruth 3:2-4 (NIV)*

In the culture of that day, this was understood as an act of respectful *submission*.

Boaz awakens startled, and Ruth requests that Boaz spread his robe over her as a symbolic act of espousal. Boaz agrees but has one more logistical detail that he must address. There was a close relative who had the first right to redeem. So Boaz makes the arrangements to meet with this close relative in the company of ten town elders at the town gate as witnesses to ensure a proper legal agreement and explains the situation to him. But the nearer relative did not have the willingness or resources to receive Ruth, giving Boaz the right to redeem her.

Boaz then officially and publicly receives the rights of the property of his brother Elimelek, which included the land,

Naomi, who also was redeemed into the covering of Boaz, and Ruth, who he made his wife. This act solidifies the legacy of Elimelek, Naomi and Ruth- who is now adopted through marriage from a Moabite to a Judean Israelite.

Boaz and Ruth eventually have a child and named him Obed. The lineage that Ruth has been adopted into leads to the legacy of King David and ultimately to the Messiah- Jesus (Yeshua) the Christ!

Here, we see David's genealogy.

> *18 This, then, is the family line of Perez:*
> *Perez was the father of Hezron,*
> *19 Hezron the father of Ram,*
> *Ram the father of Amminadab,*
> *20 Amminadab the father of Nahshon,*
> *Nahshon the father of Salmon,*
> *21 Salmon the father of Boaz,*
> *Boaz the father of Obed,*
> *22 Obed the father of Jesse,*
> *and Jesse the father of David.*
> *Ruth 4:18- 22 (NIV)*

Ruth's complete loyalty to the Israelite family, into which she was received by marriage, began with her total devotion to her mother-in-law. Ruth exemplifies that her blood lineage as a Moabite did not disqualify her participation in the Kingdom of God as a Judean Israelite, but instead through her conforming her life to the will of God and through obedience that comes from faith. Therefore, she has been redeemed from a Moabite to an Israelite, from a widow to married, from childless to a royal legacy, and from foreign gods to the God of Israel.

In these stories, Caleb and Ruth are two Biblical characters outside the tribes of Israel but are adopted through marriage. In both marriage and adoption,

- There is the act of choosing and being chosen.
- The person is chosen from one lineage and into a new lineage. From their old life and into their new life.
- The person is then under the covering of the new parent or husband.
- Both processes are confirmed through a legal act.
- They are now part of the family lineage and are in line as an heir to the family inheritance.

As believers in Christ, we fall into adoption and marriage. We were foreigners and outside His Kingdom, and as we learned in Ephesians, we are predestined and chosen for adoption to the family through Jesus Christ, and Christ is also the bridegroom to the Church- who He calls His bride.

> *Christ loved the church and gave himself up for her* 26 *to make her holy, cleansing her by the washing with water through the word,* 27 *and to present her to himself as a radiant church, without stain or wrinkle or any other blemish, but holy and blameless.*
> *Ephesians 5:25-27 (NIV)*

As His sons, daughters, coheirs, and *brides*, we have access to all Spiritual blessings.

- His grace and peace.
- Spotless and blameless in His sight through the cleansing of His blood.
- The redemption through his blood, the forgiveness of sins, in accordance with the riches of God's grace.

- All wisdom and understanding- He makes known to us the mystery of his will. We can have inside knowledge that can only be gotten by being part of the family. We have been initiated so that we can fully know and receive ongoing instruction and insight into the mysteries and revelations through our rite of passage as His adopted children, to be put into effect when the times reach fulfillment for our calling, mission, purpose destiny that He has for us!

And here is the promise, the covenant, the contract, and the legal ruling that seal the deal for justifying our adoption to Him as His children by our new identity, our belonging, and our choseness.

> *13 And you also were included in Christ when you heard the message of truth, the gospel of your salvation. When you believed, you were marked in him with a seal, the promised Holy Spirit, 14 who is a deposit guaranteeing our inheritance until the redemption of those who are God's possession—to the praise of his glory,*
> *Ephesians 1:13-14 (NIV)*

We were marked with a seal, the promised Holy Spirit! This is evidence; that we have His Spirit living in us. This guarantees our inheritance and that we are HIS children, Hallelujah!!! Nothing can revoke it; no one can revoke it. He will not revoke it; He will never forsake or leave us!

The burden of worrying whether we are enough is taken away! We have a legal decree from our Father bought and paid for by His one and only Son's sacrifice. We are desired, wanted, chosen, selected, loved, cherished, and valued. It is His good pleasure to adopt us, and the decree has been sealed with a guarantee through His Holy Spirit. Hallelujah!

We now have must **become** what we have been adopted into.

Chapter 10

Becoming!

When we experience significant changes, transitions, struggles, or troubles in our lives that overwhelm us entirely, especially when they seem to go on and on with no end in sight, we get to the point that we will usually ask,

"What do I do now?"

We expect an answer as to what we do we do to remedy the circumstances we find ourselves in. We, as human beings, naturally gravitate to doing something to progress past our undesirable circumstances. Everything about our world, society, and culture is about "doing" to solve problems. However, in many cases, "doing" may not be enough. Doing may get you to a level of relief or the perception of a reprieve from the struggles, but often, the reprieve will not be sustained. Many of our "doings" are frequently misguided, off-track, and fear-based in the stress of our circumstances. We "do" just to be doing. Our logic is, "Let's do something, and then hopefully, we somehow will do the right thing." The dichotomy of this, though, is that we are called Human **beings**, not human **doings**.

So if the question of, "What do we **do** now?" is not the right question for many of our circumstances, then what is the right question? In the story of Gideon and the Israelites in the book of Judges chapters 6-8, we see that it is the **becoming** of Gideon and the **becoming** of the Israelites when their victory is realized and their subsequent realignment back to the favor of the Lord. The Lord calls Gideon and Israel to **become** what they were called to and intended to be, what was lost in their disobedience, and back to right standing with the Lord. The story of Gideon is a story of becoming. The Lord God tends to give us the vision for the becoming, which will usually give us direction for the doing.

> *"The Israelites did evil in the eyes of the Lord, and for seven years he gave them into the hands of the Midianites. 2 Because the power of Midian was so oppressive, the Israelites prepared shelters for themselves in mountain clefts, caves, and strongholds. 3 Whenever the Israelites planted their crops, the Midianites, Amalekites, and other eastern peoples invaded the country. 4 They camped on the land and ruined the crops all the way to Gaza and did not spare a living thing for Israel, neither sheep nor cattle nor donkeys. 5 They came up with their livestock and their tents like swarms of locusts. It was impossible to count them or their camels; they invaded the land to ravage it. 6 Midian so impoverished the Israelites that they cried out to the Lord for help."*
>
> Judges 6:1-6

Inevitably, in our lives, most of us will have situations and circumstances that we find ourselves in through our own poor decisions or the poor decisions of our parents or grandparents. Through these decisions, we end up in a state of oppression, depression, or possession. We become enmeshed in a stronghold that we can't break free from, a lifestyle that dominates and robs us to the point that when the enemy invades, we fall back to our caves, hideouts, and shelters, whether physically or psychologically to protect, survive, and hold out until the threat has pulled away from us or at least has subsided.

During these times, we naturally regress into survival mode, which, depending on the type of circumstances, will entail hoarding, protecting, hiding, analyzing, reacting, and resorting to outbursts, rage, anger, depression, and isolation. Often, these natural reactions serve us well for a season and will usually diminish the circumstances and sustain us until the subsequent trauma, or series of problems, rears its ugly head again. Then, when the next attack comes, based on how we navigated through the last series of events, we respond even more aggressively: angrier, withdrawn, protective, and isolated, which may again get us through the current cycle, until the next time. This can be deemed as the insanity loop- doing the same thing repeatedly, expecting a different result.

This lifestyle can progress and crescendo to a state where our tactics eventually become so routine that we default to these behaviors as soon as any glimmer of trouble, perceived trouble, false starts, or triggers occur. We automatically progress down this path of survival, defensiveness, and protection, potentially without consciousness. We become so conditioned and familiar with this lifestyle that we think we are doing good when we have times of peace, even though we know that the enemy is lurking just over the horizon for the next season in our lives to plunder, sabotage, and destroy any and everything we have worked so hard to accomplish. We grow weary, frustrated, and exhausted reliving the circumstances over the seemingly endless days, weeks, months, or even years. We become so impoverished from the increased assaults of life and the enemy that we reach a breaking point. We have lost hope and become numb to it all, and we surrender to the realization that "this is our lot in life." But the enemy keeps coming and is now not just plundering, sabotaging, and destroying our livelihood but seems to be rubbing our faces in it, taunting us, and knocking us to our knees. We finally get to the point where we are beaten down, broken down, we are so low, so oppressed, so depressed, that there is nothing left for us to do but to cry out!

"WHAT DO I DO NOW?"

- "I have no answers!"
- "I am in a mess!"
- "I can't break this grip!"
- "I can't seem to pull through!"
- "I can't seem to stop the heartache, the thief, the system of oppression, the plundering!

"LORD, WHAT DO I DO NOW???"

This is the backdrop where we find Gideon and the Israelites in this story. They have been under the oppression of the Midianites, Amalekites, and other eastern peoples who invaded their country for the last seven years. The Israelites would plant their crops; the enemy would come at harvest time and camp on their land and steal and ruin their crops to Gaza, on the coast. The enemy was so numerous that when they would come into the land, the scripture describes their arrival as swarms of locusts, and it is impossible to count them or their camels. They were so ruthless that they did not spare a living thing for Israel, plant or animal, sheep, cattle, or donkeys. They would come to Israel during each harvest and impoverish them so entirely that after seven years, the Israelites cried out to the Lord.

In the next scene, we see that the Lord has heard their cry, and we see His response.

> *"7 When the Israelites cried out to the Lord because of Midian, 8 he sent them a prophet, who said, "This is what*

> *the Lord, the God of Israel, says: I brought you up out of Egypt, out of the land of slavery. 9 I rescued you from the hand of the Egyptians. And I delivered you from the hand of all your oppressors; I drove them out before you and gave you, their land. 10 I said to you, 'I am the Lord your God; do not worship the gods of the Amorites, in whose land you live.' But you have not listened to me."*
>
> Judges 6:7-10

The Lord is **Exposing** to the Israelites through the prophet how they have gotten to this state by telling them:

- The Lord brought you out of slavery.
- The Lord rescued you from the hands of the Egyptians.
- The Lord delivered you from all of their oppressors.
- Before Israel's arrival, the Lord drove out the people who possessed the promised land.
- The Lord gave the Israelites their enemy's land.
- The Lord instructed the Israelites not to worship the gods of the Amorites, in whose land they were living.
- The Israelites did not listen to the Lord and worshipped the gods of the Amorites.
- The Lord turned them over to their oppressors.

Based on the fact that the Israelites were crying out to the Lord suggests that they didn't know why they were being oppressed or for how long. The Israelites may have thought the problem was-that it was just a case of the Midianites being too strong. The Lord exposed to them that it was their disobedience that was keeping them oppressed. Through His prophet, the Lord gave the Israelites a roadmap showing them how they had wandered so far and the breadcrumbs for how to get back to right standing with Him. He is giving them the coordinates of how they became lost in the first place! It was not enough for the Lord to deliver the people from their circumstances but for them to understand the slippery slope into separation and oppression.

When we know the warning signs, the markers, the red flags, and the coordinates to how we ended up lost, separated, and oppressed, we can ensure that when these signs appear again, the alarms go off, our intuitive recognition kicks in, and we turn back before it's too late! The Lord wants to ensure that when He delivers the Israelites, they have the knowledge and directions to ensure that the deliverance sustains them and that they will hopefully not fall away again.

For more context, when the Lord had brought the Israelites out of the wilderness and had them cross over the Jordan and take possession of the promised land, the book of Judges provides the accounts and stories of Israel's repeated disobedience and their turning away from the One True God of Israel and worshipping false gods over and over again. Each time that Israel would turn away from the Lord God, the Lord would turn Israel over to their enemies to oppress them and get them to repent of their wicked ways. When the oppression would become too severe, prolonged, or oppressive, the people would cry out to the Lord. The Lord would hear their cry; then the Lord would send a prophet with a message for them. Once the prophet spoke to the people and they repented and turned from their wicked ways, the Lord would raise a deliverer (a Judge) to rescue them from their oppressors, vanquish their enemy, and restore Israel to right standing with their Lord God. Inevitably, though, whenever the Judge would die, Israel would revert back to their wicked ways and turn their faces from the One True God of Israel and back to worshipping the false gods. As we enter this story with Gideon, we are observing another one of these cycles.

Unbeknownst to Gideon, he was about to become the 5th of these Judges since Israel entered the promised land.

11 The angel of the Lord came and sat down under the oak in Ophrah that belonged to Joash the Abiezrite, where his son Gideon was threshing wheat in a winepress to keep it from the Midianites. 12 When the angel of the Lord appeared to Gideon, he said, "The Lord is with you, mighty warrior." 13 "Pardon me, my lord," Gideon replied, "but if the Lord is with us, why has all this happened to us? Where are all his wonders that our ancestors told us about when they said, 'Did not the Lord bring us up out of Egypt?' But now the Lord has abandoned us and given us into the hand of Midian." 14 The Lord turned to him and said, "Go in the strength you have and save Israel out of Midian's hand. Am I not sending you?" 15 "Pardon me, my lord," Gideon replied, "but how can I save Israel? My clan is the weakest in Manasseh, and I am the least in my family." 16 The Lord answered, "I will be with you, and you will strike down all the Midianites, leaving none alive."

Judges 6:11-16

The Angel of the Lord comes to Gideon while Gideon is threshing wheat in a wine press. When it comes to threshing wheat during the time of Gideon, the worst way you could thresh wheat is in a wine press. A wine press was a sunken place, a large hole in the ground. This was both cumbersome and humiliating. Threshing was performed in open spaces, typically on a hilltop, with a heavy grinding wheel or a heavy sled, and then winnowed so the breeze could blow away the chaff. Wheat was not usually threshed in a sunken place like a winepress. This was a place of privacy, for if the Midianites had caught Gideon threshing the wheat, they would have surely descended upon him and robbed him of his harvest.

How many of us have had to hide or cover up our harvest so that the enemy doesn't come to rob us?

So while Gideon is hiding, threshing his wheat in the most difficult way; humiliated, angry, exhausted, and frustrated, the Angel of the Lord appears. The Angel sits under an oak tree and observes Gideon performing a task out of order, in a dysfunctional manner, obviously hiding while performing his duties. So, what did the Angel say to Gideon?

"The Lord is with you, mighty man of valor."

As I read this scripture, I have to confess that is not what I expected the Angel to say. I would have expected the Angel to say more like, "What are you doing? Threshing wheat in a wine press, don't you know that's not where you are supposed to thresh wheat?" I would have expected more of a statement of the obvious from the Angel.

Gideon's response must have been along the lines of my thinking, for he said, "Pardon me, my Lord, but if the Lord is with us, why has all this happened to us? Where are all his wonders that our ancestors told us about when they said, 'Did not the Lord bring us up out of Egypt?' But now the Lord has abandoned us and given us into the hand of Midian." Gideon is skeptical; he doesn't acknowledge or respond to being addressed as a Mighty Man of Valor but responds to the Angel's greeting, "The Lord is with you."

How many of us have felt that the Lord has abandoned us and given us over to our enemy?

Gideon had recently heard the prophet's words about how the Lord brought them out of Egypt, sustained them through the desert, and gave them the promised land. Still, Gideon was reasoning about how the Lord could be with him while he was oppressed, losing his harvest year after year, and his people suffered. I'm sure Gideon was thinking, how can the Lord be with him while he is impoverished at the same time? Gideon did not recognize the person addressing him as an Angel of the Lord. The Angel didn't necessarily introduce Himself, so to Gideon, he may have recognized Him as another man, possibly another prophet, and therefore, did not understand what was transpiring.

Even though Gideon has not responded to what the Angel called him, let's not skip past this too quickly. The Angel calls him a "Mighty Man of Valor," and to any objective observer, there is no evidence to support this title. Gideon is not a soldier; he has not stood up to the enemy, shown no indication that he is a leader, or has the esteem of his tribe of Manasseh or his nation, the Israelites, or as someone who can stand against the Midianites. By all accounts, Gideon is no different than any other Israelites, afraid, beaten down, burnt out, and just trying to survive another year.

So then, why does the Angel call Gideon a "Mighty Man of Valor?"

It is a Kingdom of Heaven principle that is found throughout the scriptures. The Angel is not calling Gideon what he is; the Angel is giving Gideon a new vision of what He is calling Gideon too! The Angel is, in essence, saying that what I am about to do with you will **make** you a Might Man of Valor!

There is also a subtle nuance that can be easily glossed over... Gideon **IS** in a winepress, threshing wheat. Yes, it is not the proper way to thresh. Yes, it is humiliating. Yes, it seems pitiful. But there is another perspective here. Gideon is operating under the premise that regardless of the oppression around him, he is determined to protect his harvest and is determined that the enemy is not going to steal away his harvest. Through this courageous act of resistance against the opposition, the Angel is seeing a kernel of a grain of valor- the desire, drive, and perseverance to protect his harvest and the Angel feels that He can use these traits that Gideon is demonstrating to partner with. We can see this in the next set of verses.

> *14 The Lord turned to him and said, "Go in the strength you have and save Israel out of Midian's hand. Am I not sending you?"*
> *Judges 6:14*

I believe this statement of "Go in the strength you have" is, in part, a reference to this kernel of valor that the Angel sees in Gideon. The Angel also clarifies to Gideon that the Lord is here, that the Lord is planning to free His people, and that the Lord is calling on Gideon to fulfill this task. As Gideon is threshing his harvest, the Angel of the Lord is getting ready to use Gideon for the Lord's harvest- **to harvest the Israelites from the hands of the oppressor.** The Angel of the Lord also ensures that God is not Gideon's or Israel's enemy and that He wants to partner with Gideon and the Israelites to fight against a common enemy.

What hidden kernels (seeds) are planted inside each of us that the Lord wants to call forth? Seeds of valor, courage, joy, praise, words of knowledge, encouragement, leadership, prayer, or truth? What is the Lord getting ready to call us into, getting ready to activate? The Lord has a mission, purpose, and destiny for us while we are alive. It is not to survive until we go to the "Here by and by," but to be a conduit, a partner for His purposes to **Expose, Destroy, Heal, and Replace** what He intended from the beginning, to restore and redeem that which was lost, that which has been oppressed, that which has been stolen, and to bring us into His presence to walk alongside Him to re-possess, expand, and reign over His Kingdom of Heaven here on earth with victory and authority! Whew!

You may be thinking that is a little over my pay grade! The evidence of my past, flaws, shame, and guilt disqualifies me from such a high calling and responsibility! Gideon also has these reservations, and in verse 15, Gideon explains to the Angel,

> *"Pardon me, my lord," Gideon replied, "but how can I save Israel? My clan is the weakest in Manasseh, and I am the least in my family."*

Gideon could not see himself as someone who could do great things for God. He thought of himself as insignificant, from the most minor clan in his tribe, the least in his own family and the least in his own eyes. In this, Gideon was correct: *he* could not save Israel in and of himself. But an almighty God, who, as the prophet just recently spoke to Gideon and the Israelites, brought them out of Egypt, made a highway through the Red Sea, closed the waters over their enemy, sustained them through the desert, and then gave them the promised land, is also the same almighty God who could use a small and weak kernel (Gideon) to rescue Israel.

God doesn't call the qualified; he qualifies who He calls! Hallelujah!

The Angel responds to Gideon,

> *The Lord answered, "I will be with you, and you will strike down all the Midianites, leaving none alive."*
> *Judges 6:16 NIV*

I like the King James Version in this passage,

> *"Surely, I will be with you, and you shall defeat the Midianites as one man:"*
> *Judges 6:16 (KJV).*

The Angel's assurance to Gideon was not just to build up Gideon's self-confidence but to assure Gideon that God was indeed with him. The Angel was providing Gideon with the Lord's confidence and assurance. Like Gideon, knowing that God has sent us is essential, but it is even more important to know that He is with us.

Gideon is at a place, setting, and scenario where he is about to realize what the Lord has known about him all along. Gideon is about to step into a moment with God where he will get on the same page about who God is, who Gideon is, and what mission, purpose, and destiny He is calling Gideon into. He is about to step into another dimension of relationship and partnership through a move of God.

As Gideon has been threshing and protecting his harvest, the Lord is about to activate Gideon to partner with Him in threshing and protecting the Lord's harvest. But, before Gideon could operate publicly and lead the people of Israel from their oppression, Gideon needs to get in alignment with the Lord- he has to become.

Chapter 11

Partnership!

As we continue with the story of Gideon from Judges chapters 6-8, we learn that this is the beginning of the seventh year of the oppression the Israelites have experienced with the Midianites, the enemy of Israel. We learned that the Midianites would return to the land during each of the harvest times in vast numbers to pillage and plunder Israel's harvest of every living thing, both plant and animal, that they had worked so hard to produce. The Midianites would devour, rob, and destroy everything thoroughly and then leave the Israelites, their land in total ruin, destitute, and with no harvest until the following season.

We learned that due to the length and severity of the oppression and subsequent impoverishment, the Israelites cried out to the Lord. The Lord heard their cries and responded by sending a prophet to explain and remind them that their oppression was not due to the Midianites being too strong for them but that they were being oppressed due to their disobedience to God's command not to serve the false gods of the inhabitants in their region.

As we step back into this scene, it is at the beginning of another harvest time, and true to form, the oppressors begin to gather and set up their camps just over the horizon of Israel's territory to invade, pillage, and plunder their harvests once again. This time would be different, though. This time, Gideon is conversing with the Angel of the Lord and is about to be activated to deliver the Israelites out of the hands of their oppressors.

We listen in on the discussion between the Angel of the Lord and Gideon; there seems to be confusion as to the understanding of Who the Angel is, who Gideon is, and what the Angel is calling Gideon to do.

> *17 Gideon replied, "If now I have found favor in your eyes, give me a sign that it is really you talking to me. 18 Please do not go away until I come back and bring my offering and set it before you." And the Lord said, "I will wait until you return."19 Gideon went inside, prepared a young goat, and from an ephah of flour he made bread without yeast. Putting the meat in a basket and its broth in a pot, he brought them out and offered them to him under the oak.20 The Angel of God said to him, "Take the meat and the unleavened bread, place them on this rock, and pour out the broth." And Gideon did so. 21 Then the Angel of the Lord touched the meat and the unleavened bread with the tip of the staff that was in his hand. Fire flared from the rock, consuming the meat and the bread. And the Angel of the Lord disappeared. 22 When Gideon realized that it was the Angel of the Lord, he exclaimed, "Alas, Sovereign Lord! I have seen the Angel of the Lord face to face!"23 But the Lord said to him, "Peace! Do not be afraid. You are not going to die."24 So Gideon built an altar to the Lord there and called it The Lord Is Peace. To this day it stands in Ophrah of the Abiezrites.*
>
> Judges 6:17-24

Gideon wants to be sure he is receiving a word from the Lord, not just from anyone. He gets this strange message from a stranger who is talking, acting, and strangely presenting Himself. How many times have we thought we heard from the Lord, only to find out that it was maybe not so from the Lord? Either someone gave us a "word" or advice, or we thought we heard the Lord in our minds, etc., and it didn't pan out how we expected. Gideon needed to be sure that if He followed the words of this Messenger, he would not be misguided and that this was indeed the Lord calling him into this daunting task for himself, his family, his tribe, and his nation.

You can sense, though, that Gideon suspects this is a messenger (an Angel) of the Lord. So he is going to do something that will help to confirm this.

He is going to prepare a meal for this Messenger. This is a form of hospitality that Gideon is following based on similar instances of messengers of the Lord having visited the ancestors of the Israelites. For example, when Abraham was visited by three angels while sitting in the doorway of his tent when he perceived that they were Angels of the Lord, he ran out, bowed to them, and offered to wash their feet and provide bread for them to eat. Abraham even addressed the angels with similar rhetoric.

> *The Lord appeared to Abraham near the great trees of Mamre while he was sitting at the entrance to his tent in the heat of the day. 2 Abraham looked up and saw three men standing nearby. When he saw them, he hurried from the entrance of his tent to meet them and bowed low to the ground.3 He said, "If I have found favor in your eyes, my Lord, do not pass your servant by. 4 Let a little water be brought, and then you may all wash your feet and rest under this tree. 5 Let me get you something to eat, so you can be refreshed and then go on your way—now*

> *that you have come to your servant."" Very well," they answered, "do as you say."6 So Abraham hurried into the tent to Sarah. "Quick," he said, "get three seahs of the finest flour and knead it and bake some bread."7 Then he ran to the herd and selected a choice, tender calf and gave it to a servant, who hurried to prepare it. 8 He then brought some curds and milk and the calf that had been prepared, and set these before them. While they ate, he stood near them under a tree.*
>
> *Genesis 18: 1-8*

Gideon confirmed and honored this Messenger in the same way that his ancestor Abraham did. In both cases, we see that the Messengers agreed to allow the meals to be prepared for them. In each case, it took a reasonable amount of time to prepare the meals, but the messengers assured Abraham and, in turn, Gideon that they would wait.

We also see in the encounter with Gideon, though, when presenting his meal, the Angel responds differently to receiving the meal than the encounter with Abraham. The Angels sat down with Abraham and ate the meal together, but with Gideon, we see a completely different way the Angel received the meal. The Angel instructed Gideon to set the meat and unleavened bread on a rock near them and to pour the broth over it, and Gideon followed the instructions. Then the Angel extended his staff, touched the offering, and fire flared from the rock and consumed the meat and bread. Then, the Angel of the Lord immediately disappeared.

When the Angel of the Lord instructs Gideon to lay the meat and unleavened bread upon a rock close by and pour the broth upon it; the rock has now become an altar for an offering, not just a meal for a typical traveler or prophet. When the Angel touched the meat and the unleavened bread soaked with broth, the fire from the rock instantly consumed the offering.

This further established confirmation of the Angel's authenticity. Then the Angel of the Lord supernaturally disappeared out of Gideon's sight: not proceeding on his journey, as would have been logical for a traveler or prophet, but vanished immediately. Gideon now realized that this was not a typical visit from a man, or prophet, nor was he just an angelic spirit, but that this was the Angel of the Lord!

Gideon realized that he had looked in the face of the Lord and now had a holy fear that he may die. Gideon knew the scriptures and story of Moses, which we discussed in a previous chapter when the Lord God told Moses that He would put Moses in a cleft of a rock and put His hand over to cover Moses and then pull His hand away as He passes by so that Moses would only see the back of the Lord God's glory. The Lord told Moses that no man shall see his face and live!

In Judges 6:23, we see the Lord reassure Gideon,

> *But the Lord said to him, "Peace! Do not be afraid. You are not going to die."*

The Lord reassured Gideon that He was not Gideon's enemy and that the Lord God intended to partner with Gideon in this endeavor, allowing Gideon to be in His presence and sparing his life, which attests to this partnership! Gideon's mind is blown; he is completely overwhelmed and astounded. Gideon wanted to honor this moment, this experience, this encounter with the Angel of the Lord.

> *So Gideon built an altar to the Lord there and called it The Lord Is Peace. To this day it stands in Ophrah of the Abiezrites.*
>
> *Judges 6:24*

Gideon did this as a supplication and memorial. He was no longer in dread of God, as demonstrated by the title given to the altar: The LORD-Is-Peace. (Jehovah Shalom) It seems that Gideon has received a revelation that the sight of God does not lead to death but life and peace. Gideon now knows beyond a shadow of a doubt that the Lord God is NOT his enemy and can trust His word, His calling, and the partnership with and for the mission that the Lord God has assigned him.

The altar that Gideon built was to be a memorial and a witness to the revelation of God that Gideon received, as well as the physical evidence that Jehovah was Peace. It was to serve as a memorial that not only did the Lord bestow peace on Gideon, but also that the Lord God would not destroy Israel in wrath for their disobedience, but the Israelites would also be partakers in the Lord God's peace. The assurance of peace that He had given to Gideon also confirmed His announcement that Gideon would conquer the Midianites in the strength of God and deliver Israel from its oppressors.

How many of us have had this kind of experience with the Lord God? Can we get to a place with the knowing and personal interaction with him to build our altar and memorial and give it the name The LORD is Peace- Jehovah Shalom? Can we get to the point that we pass from hearing about the things of God into personal contact? Can we say, I have listened to YOU by the hearing of my ear, but now I have been in Your presence, and now I am at peace?

Now that Gideon and the Lord God are beginning to come into alignment and have established trust, it is time to get the people of Israel in alignment. Up to this point, the Lord has.

- Heard the cries of the people.
- Their oppression is not due to the might of the Midianites but through the disobedience of serving the gods of the inhabitants.

- That the Lord has chosen Gideon to free the people from their oppression.
- That the Lord God is going to partner with Gideon in this endeavor.
- That Gideon, the people, and God have the same enemy, and the Lord is not their enemy.
- That Gideon and God have the same harvest.

The Lord is now going to begin the process of destroying the things that have separated His people from right standing with Him. Now that Gideon has made his requests for confirmation to the Lord and the Lord has allowed Gideon's initial confirmations to establish trust for him and the Lord to begin working together, the Lord will start the first realignment of Gideon and the people.

> *25 That same night the Lord said to him, "Take the second bull from your father's herd, the one seven years old. Tear down your father's altar to Baal and cut down the Asherah pole] beside it. 26 Then build a proper kind of altar to the Lord your God on the top of this height. Using the wood of the Asherah pole that you cut down, offer the second] bull as a burnt offering."27 So Gideon took ten of his servants and did as the Lord told him. But because he was afraid of his family and the townspeople, he did it at night rather than in the daytime.28 In the morning when the people of the town got up, there was Baal's altar, demolished, with the Asherah pole beside it cut down and the second bull sacrificed on the newly built altar!29 They asked each other, "Who did this?" When they carefully investigated, they were told, "Gideon son of Joash did it." 30 The people of the town demanded of Joash, "Bring out your son. He must die, because he has broken down Baal's altar and cut down the Asherah*

pole beside it."31 But Joash replied to the hostile crowd around him, "Are you going to plead Baal's cause? Are you trying to save him? Whoever fights for him shall be put to death by morning! If Baal really is a god, he can defend himself when someone breaks down his altar." 32 So because Gideon broke down Baal's altar, they gave him the name Jerub-Baal that day, saying, "Let Baal contend with him."

Judges 6:25-32

When Gideon made himself responsive to and aligned with God, God began guiding him to the next level to Destroy. The Lord directed Gideon to tear down the altar of Baal that his father had: In Gideon's community, Baal and Asherah were worshipped alongside Yahweh. God was calling Gideon to get his own house in order first. It would appear that Gideon's father, Joash, was the keeper of the altars of Baal and the Asherah Pole.

Baal and Asherah were pagan gods represented by statues or poles carved by human hands and considered idols in the Bible. Baal was considered the God of life and fertility and was believed to bring rain to the lands. Asherah was considered the female mother goddess to Baal and was considered the fertility goddess. Worship to her usually included illicit sex acts and ritual prostitution.

At times, human sacrifices would be made to appease Baal and Asherah. What proverbial idols are we knowingly or even unknowingly clinging to? Money? Job or career? Alcohol, drugs, an affair? What evil or dysfunction have we allowed into our lives that have taken the place of the Lord or that we are exalting alongside the Lord that needs to be destroyed?

Gideon decided to perform this task of destroying the altar to Baal and the pole of Asherah at night, under cover of secrecy, probably because he feared that his father's household and the men of the city would try preventing him from doing what needed to be done- to carry out the work entrusted to him of setting Israel free, Gideon needed to first purify his father's house from idolatry, and sanctify his own life and calling to Jehovah by sacrificing a burnt offering. Until sin is pardoned through sacrifice, there is still the separation between Israel and God.

The Lord instructed Gideon to tear down the idols' places of worship and build a proper altar for sacrifice. The Lord directed Gideon to set things in order by building an altar for the Lord in the prescribed manner and using the wood of the Asherah to burn the sacrifices.

Two bulls were offered. The first bull was burnt as a sin, offering to redeem the household of Gideon's family and the Israelites for their idolatrous behavior. The second bull was burnt as a consecration offering. The second bull was a seven-year-old born when the Midianites began their oppression. It was now to be slain to indicate that their oppression of seven years was about to end and to re-establish Gideon, his clan, his tribe, and the Israelite people back to what the Lord intended-concentrated- set apart unto Him over all other nations.

The following morning when the town's people found the altar of Baal destroyed. The Asherah upon it cut down, and the bull sacrificed upon the newly erected altar, still smoldering; they asked who had committed this act and soon learned that Gideon was the one who had committed it. They called Joash to send his son Gideon out to be put to death for destroying Baal's altar.

Why were the people so zealous in pleading for Baal through whose worship they experienced such terrible afflictions? Even Gideon's father, Joash, had been a worshipper of Baal for the last seven years, seemingly going with the flow of the people, with the altar of Baal on his estate. But he was convinced of his sin, possibly through hearing Gideon's encounter with the

Angel. Gideon had received the divine commission, and his call to action, which disrupted the spell upon his family and the people, had been lulled under. Now, Joash resolutely declares himself on the side of the God of Israel. When the people demanded that his son should be put to death for casting down the altar of Baal, he boldly demanded, according to the law of Moses, that whatever man should plead for Baal should be put to death, idolatry being a capital offense!

Joash renewed in his revelation of the foolhardiness of his past actions for the last seven years, declares, "That if Baal is a god, let him plead for himself," — as the Lord God of Israel has often done when any indignity or injury has been imposed upon Him. But Baal has now demonstrated that he is not inclined to help the people nor himself and, therefore, is not worthy to be bowed down to. Joash's resolute answer was necessary to stop the people's wrath, and it was realized by the sense of his son's extreme danger and the confidence that God would plead his son's cause and use his son to rescue his people. It was the words and rebuke of Joash that the veil over the eyes of the people was lifted, and their eyes were opened, to see the impotence of the false god whom they had worshipped, lo' these seven years! In comparison with what they had heard and knew of the God of Israel had frequently done in vindication of His honor, they might reasonably conclude how inferior Baal was to Jehovah, that Baal was nothing, a mere nonentity.

From that day forward, Gideon has his name changed from Gideon, which in Hebrew means "to cut down," to Jerub- Baal, which in Hebrew means "let Baal contend with him." His name has now become a challenge, a taunt to Baal to come and contend with him!

All it takes to stand against the oppressors of our time, both in the spirit and the physical realm, is one person to stand up and say I choose the Lord God over anything and everything in this world! Through this, we can break the spell, the yoke, the hold that contends against the children of God, which will then turn the hearts of men and ultimately a nation from their spell, from their wicked ways, turn their faces back to the Lord God, and for revival to return to the land! Hallelujah!

Chapter 12

Is Your Fleece Wet or Dry?

Gideon (Jerub-Baal) and the Israelites have returned to right standing with the Lord God. They have torn down the altar of Baal and the Asherah pole and destroyed the place of idol worship. They have correctly built the altar of the Lord and sacrificed the first bull on it to atone for their sins, and then sacrificed the second bull seven years of age to consecrate, set apart, to reestablish themselves as His chosen people and to signify that the season of oppression will soon end. Through this series of realignments, the stronghold of idolatry and the influence of these pagan gods have been **destroyed.** The Israelites have had the veil over their eyes lifted, of even wanting to put Gideon to death for the destruction of the pagan places of worship, to restore their focus, faith, and trust in Jehovah, the One True God of Israel!

Now that the problem of what has caused their oppression has been solved- pagan worship, it is time to deal with the physical oppressors, the Midianites.

33 Now all the Midianites, Amalekites and other eastern peoples joined forces and crossed over the Jordan and camped in the Valley of Jezreel. 34 Then the Spirit of the Lord came on Gideon, and he blew a trumpet, summoning the Abiezrites to follow him. 35 He sent messengers throughout Manasseh, calling them to arms, and also into Asher, Zebulun and Naphtali, so that they too went up to meet them.

Judges 6:33-35

We see here that the Spirit of the Lord God came upon Gideon and laid itself around him like a mantle. Gideon then blew the trumpet to call Israel to battle against the enemy, and Abiezer responded to the call. Abiezer is the clan of his own family. He immediately acknowledges Gideon as the deliverer of Israel and the fighter of Baal. He is the first to recognize that they are safe from Baal's revenge and the first to gather around Gideon. The Abiezrites example was then followed by all Manasseh, the tribe of Gideon, and then with the tribes of Asher, Zebulun, and Naphtali. Through the power of the Spirit of the Lord coming upon Gideon, he could stir the people's hearts to rally around him to begin to resist the Midianites. Gideon gathered an impressive number of troops on short notice; around 32,000 men came to follow him into battle.

While the people gathered to rally around Gideon, and before Gideon went into the battle with the assembled army, Gideon paused to ask for confirmation from God for the success of this undertaking. His request was not from a place of doubt or lack of faith, but for his newly gathered army might be an encouragement for those who were with him as a public demonstration that the Lord would be with them as an army in this endeavor.

36 Gideon said to God, "If you save Israel by my hand as you have promised— 37 look, I will place a wool fleece on the threshing floor. If there is dew only on the fleece and all the ground is dry, then I will know that you will save Israel by my hand, as you said." 38 And that is what happened. Gideon rose early the next day; he squeezed the fleece and wrung out the dew—a bowlful of water. 39 Then Gideon said to God, "Do not be angry with me. Let me make just one more request. Allow me one more test with the fleece, but this time make the fleece dry and let the ground be covered with dew." 40 That night God did so. Only the fleece was dry; all the ground was covered with dew.

Judges 6:36-40

There are several things to consider in this passage.

- Firstly, the place into which Gideon is performing this request. He is not doing this in hiding, not doing this in a winepress; he is performing this request possibly in the most visible place in the entire area, the threshing floor, which is up on a high place that can be seen from the surrounding landscape. The days of cowering from the enemy are over!
- There is tremendous significance to this being performed on the threshing floor for more than just visibility; it is also symbolic of the process by which this entire story is being established- Threshing and Harvest! As with the harvest of the people of Israel for their crops, so too will the Harvest of the Lord be performed of his people from their oppressors.
- The Fleece. The fleece is from a sheep. Sheep, particularly lambs, are significant throughout the history of Israel for atonement and redemption. The fleece has also been a

symbolic reference to Israel. The fleece in this scenario represents Gideon and the ground, and the threshing floor represents the people of Israel.

- The dew. In the region of Gideon's dwelling place, dew falls in copious amounts overnight. The symbolism of dew is that it often goes unnoticed, and this subtle gift from God speaks of his steadfast love – his mercies that come new every morning. The Bible references dew as primarily of bounty and divine blessing. It is seen to descend similarly to the manna and the quail God provided for his children in the desert. Dew is a refreshing gift and a continued message from heaven – a source of life. Dew arrives every morning indeterminately. It brings gentle nourishment and sustenance to the earth. it appears daily, no questions asked... just like the unconditional love of God. In Gideon's request, the dew will be used to confirm to Gideon and the Israelites that the Lord God will save Israel through the hand of Gideon.

When Gideon lays out the fleece on the threshing floor, He asks the Lord to have the dew fall only on the fleece and keep the ground dry. This request, in the natural, would be an impossibility. This act has to be from the Lord. Dew naturally falls everywhere, and to only fall precisely on the fleece and not the surrounding area would be a sure sign from the Lord. The Lord honors Gideon's request that night, and the dew only falls on the fleece. The ground and the surrounding area are completely dry.

When Gideon and the people get up the following day to check, the fleece is the only surface the dew fell upon, and the ground is completely dry, just as requested. Gideon picks up the fleece, which is so soaked and saturated with dew that when he squeezes it, there is a bowlful of water. The significance of this is that the Lord so saturated, so blessed, so anointed the fleece that it contained a bowlful of overflow of blessing and anointing. The fleece represented Gideon, and the dew upon it was the confirmation of blessing and anointing that the Lord would defeat the Midianites by the hand of Gideon. The Lord is the Lord of abundance, and He demonstrated that He will surely defeat the Midianites by the hand of Gideon, and there will be an overflow of blessings and victory.

Gideon then goes a step further with his test.

Gideon petitions the Lord to allow him a second test or confirmation. Gideon requests that he lay the fleece out a second time onto the threshing floor, and this time, instead of the dew falling only onto the fleece, the Lord makes the dew fall on all of the surrounding ground and leaves the fleece dry. The Lord honored Gideon's second request and covered the ground with dew, and the fleece was completely dry. Again, this was a supernatural act, signifying to Gideon and the Israelites that the Lord's blessing, anointing, and victory would extend to the people, the ground representing the people- the Israelites.

So here we are, Gideon and Israel are now back in alignment and right standing with the Lord God.

- Gideon has been chosen and called and qualified to be the Mighty Man of Valor that will defeat the Midianites through the empowering of the Lord.
- The places of worship and the idolatry of the house of Gideon and the people of Israel have been eliminated.
- The proper altar has been built, and the sacrifices of atonement for their sins and the second sacrifice of the consecration of the people back to the One True God of Israel have been reestablished.
- Through the confirmation of the fleece, Gideon and the people of Israel have been assured of their partnership, that the Lord God will be with them, and in overthrowing their common enemy.

- Gideon and the 32,000 soldiers are gathered together and ready to take on the Midianites in battle, and even though the Midianites are so numerous that they nor the camels can be counted, they are encouraged that they now can perform this task of defeating them!

SO LET'S DO THIS!!!

But not so fast...

The Lord has allowed Gideon and the people to request and has complied with various affirmations to establish realignment and right standing and assure them that He is with them, but now the Lord has some requirements of His own for them to proceed. Now, the actual threshing will begin!

> *1 Early in the morning, Jerub-Baal (that is, Gideon) and all his men camped at the spring of Harod. The camp of Midian was north of them in the valley near the hill of Moreh. 2 The Lord said to Gideon, "You have too many men. I cannot deliver Midian into their hands, or Israel would boast against me, 'My own strength has saved me.' 3 Now announce to the army, 'Anyone who trembles with fear may turn back and leave Mount Gilead.'" So twenty-two thousand men left, while ten thousand remained.*
> *Judges 7:1-3*

Before we proceed on...

It would be beneficial to ensure we understand the threshing process to see its metaphorical application in this story and, ultimately, in our walk, journey, and mission.

> It is one thing to grow the grain in the field, but it takes a lot of work after the grain had grown to get it ready to grind into flour and be used for making food, primarily bread. For thousands of years, ancient farmers

used a basic three-part system of threshing, winnowing, and sieving to get the grain to the point where it could be ground into flour. After harvesting, the first stage in making grain suitable for grinding into flour was threshing.

Threshing

Threshing is the process of removing the kernels barley or wheat from the stalk and husk. The threshing was completed in various ways, depending on how much grain there was and the tools the farmer had available to him. A "threshing floor" was essential, a flat area of hard dirt or rock on which freshly harvested wheat could be piled. The threshing floor was usually set on higher elevations, such as a hill or high mound, making the process accessible to the wind.

When there is just a tiny amount of wheat to thresh, the kernels of grain could be knocked off the stalk with a stick, which is what Gideon was most likely doing when harvesting some wheat in the winepress. A much more common and efficient way of threshing was to pile it on the threshing floor, where cows or oxen were driven back and forth over it. Their feet threshed the grain from the stalk. Many ancient farmers also owned a "threshing sled," a piece of equipment that looked like a wide toboggan, with metal or stone set in the bottom so the wheat could be cut off the stalk faster. As the oxen or threshing sled went over and over the large pile of harvested wheat, the stalks would be cut up into pieces, and the heads of grain knocked off the stalk and often even separated from the husk. Now, the kernels are prepared for winnowing.

Winnowing

This was the process that separated the mixed kernels, twigs and husk so that the edible grain could be sifted and separated. For this process, the farmer gathers up the pieces of the wheat or barley he had just threshed and casts it all up into the air, allowing the wind to blow the light pieces of the stalk to the side while the kernels, which are both heavier and roundish, fell almost straight back down to the floor. Thus, over time, the threshing floor was covered with three quite distinct piles of material. The kernels of grain, which were dense of a more significant substance, fell almost straight down or were not blown far at all. The larger pieces of stalk, or "straw," would blow a little way off to the side, and the small pieces, called the "chaff," would blow even further away.

The farmer used a winnowing fork or a winnowing shovel to throw the threshed grain into the air. The winnowing fork and shovel were used like farmers today to move loose hay with a pitchfork or broad shovel. The winnowing fork was usually about the size of a pitchfork but with flat wooden tines to catch more of the grain. Since the grain crops ripened in April, May, and June, it was not unusual that there was too little wind to winnow during the daytime. That meant the farmer would usually wait until there was a slight wind, which often came in the evening.

After winnowing, the valuable grain was gathered and stored, while the straw and chaff were handled differently. Sometimes, the straw and chaff were ignored and left to blow away. Sometimes, straw and chaff were used to make mud bricks because they helped bind the mud together, as when Pharaoh forced the Israelites to make bricks with "straw" (Ex. 5:7-18). The straw and chaff were sometimes used as fuel for household ovens because they burned fast and hot and got the ovens hot quickly.

The Sieve

It was sieved or sifted just before the grain was ready to be ground into flour. This was necessary for many reasons. For one thing, it was expected when harvesting that weed seeds would get mixed in with the wheat, and the threshing and winnowing processes did not separate the different seeds, and the winnowing process usually did not get all the chaff from the grain. Dust and pebbles may be mixed in with the grain when gathering the grain off the threshing floor.

In the biblical culture, the grain sieve was round and relatively large, usually two to three feet in diameter. The sides were wood, often 3-5 inches high, with a bottom frequently made of woven reeds, grasses, or thin interwoven pieces of wood.

In ancient times it was the women who sifted—they would set themselves on the ground with their feet and legs spread apart, grabbing a large but slender sieve, some two and a half feet across. Having placed a small amount of wheat in the sieve, she begins by giving it some vigorous shakes, to sift the chaff and tiny pieces of crushed twigs to the surface, which she removes with her hands. After this, the main part of the work begins, which is done with much skill. Holding the sieve at an angle, she shakes it up and down, while forcefully blowing across the top of it. The results are.

- First, the dust, earth, small seeds, and small imperfect grains of wheat fall away through the meshes of the sieve.
- Secondly, using vigorous blowing, any crushed straw, chaff, and light refuse are either blown away to the ground or collected.

- Thirdly, the good kernels goes together in the middle of the sieve, while the tiny debris or pebbles are brought into a separate little pile on the part nearest to her chest. The pebbles, chaff, and crushed straw are cleverly removed from the grain, mainly by the angle at which the sieve is held and how it is jerked up and down, and are removed. she carefully removes any slight impurities that may remain with her fingers, and process of sifting is complete."

  This process ensured that all the other debris that was once necessary for growth, maturing, and ripening of the plants were no longer needed, and are stripped away- the stalks and chaff, dirt, debris, and the weed's seeds. The most valuable substance, the wheat, and the grain kernels were collected. The whole process of planting, tending, and harvesting the wheat was to glean the most important part of the grains to provide food for the people.

As we jump back into the story, we see where the Lord is about to begin this process with his people to destroy the Midianites.

The Harvest has taken place through the Spirit coming upon Gideon, and he has gathered (harvested) the 32,000 men to stand with him through his blowing of the shofar. So now that the harvest has been gathered, it is time to begin to sort out the stalks and chaff from the valuable grains. The Lord will perform this threshing process for His purpose and glory. The Lord tells Gideon that he has too many men and that with the number they have gathered, the Israelites could say that it was by their might and strength that they prevailed against Midian. Even though at 32,000 men, Gideon's army was vastly outnumbered, there may still be the mindset that they could succeed as underdogs, that through their extraordinary bravery or excellent strategy, they could win the day. This was not acceptable to the Lord. The Lord wanted this great deliverance to be so miraculous. That there would be no doubt, either to Gideon, the Israelites, the enemy, or all the other nations when they heard of it, that it could be nothing but the Lord that prevailed!

So the Lord instructed Gideon to thresh the gathered men. The Lord instructed Gideon to offer the men the that they may return to where they came from if they trembled in fear. Gideon may have thought that a few hundred or even a few thousand men may leave, but they still have enough to complete this mission. But when 22,000 men left, it had to be a shock! With 32,000 men, it would be difficult, and even then, it would take the Lord to be on their side to defeat the overwhelming, incalculable number of Midianites, but now there were only 10,000 men against an entire throng.

There was another reason for the removal of the 22,000.

The Lord said that they could go if anyone were trembling with fear. Fear is infectious, and overwhelming (trembling) fear can be debilitating. Once the fighting begins and the heat of the battle has ensued, the last thing you want is for those 22,000 men to retreat when you need them the most. Fear is not of the Kingdom of Heaven; faith is of the Kingdom of Heaven, and, as His people, we are called to live by faith and not by fear. So the most fearful, the trembling, overwhelmed and ruled by it, and possibly unable to allow faith to overcome their fear, have been threshed and winnowed from the rest.

So Gideon has to process this turn of events and resign himself to the fact that the most fearful men have been removed and are now left with 10,000 men who will activate their faith over their fear. Gideon now assumes he will defeat the Midianites with 10,000 men of faith! Though he would prefer more, he is ready to proceed with less.

As Gideon has just reconciled and resolved to proceed with significantly fewer 10,000 fighting men, the Lord will require more and sifts them again.

> *4 But the Lord said to Gideon, "There are still too many men. Take them down to the water, and I will thin them out for you there. If I say, 'This one shall go with you,' he shall go; but if I say, 'This one shall not go with you,' he shall not go." 5 So Gideon took the men down to the water. There the Lord told him, "Separate those who lap the water with their tongues as a dog laps from those who kneel down to drink." 6 Three hundred of them drank from cupped hands, lapping like dogs. All the rest got down on their knees to drink. 7 The Lord said to Gideon, "With the three hundred men that lapped I will save you and give the Midianites into your hands. Let all the others go home." 8 So Gideon sent the rest of the Israelites home but kept the three hundred, who took over the provisions and trumpets of the others.*
>
> *Judges 7:4-8*

God had already reduced Gideon's army from 32,000 to 10,000. Here, He reduced them even further to 300. For the Lord's purposes 10,000 were still too many men. The Lord instructed Gideon to bring the men down to the water, and He would thin them out for Gideon. This seems a strange test, and there are different ideas about why God used this method to sift the soldiers. Possibly it was because those who cupped the water in their hands would make better soldiers. After all, they kept their eyes on their surroundings even when drinking.

I call this THE AWARENESS TEST. The men who bent over to drink directly from the stream, similar to the way a horse would, would have the disadvantage of potential surprise attack through not being aware of their surroundings, less prone to being alert, have their focus on their own needs, and who may think first of convenience or the easy way. It was more accessible and more convenient to stoop down and suck the water directly from the stream rather than to scoop water with their hands, their heads up, surveying their surroundings while getting the water they needed. The men who lapped the water from their hands were using a less efficient method and would have had to do it significantly more often to get the amount of water needed to satisfy their thirst than those who bent over and drank. But they possessed the critical characteristic and a Kingdom Principle that the Lord God expects- AWARENESS! The Hebrews in the desert during the Exodus had to maintain this same awareness. When the fire or cloud moved, they were to follow; when the fire or cloud was stationary, they were to remain stationary.

The composition of the remainder of Gideon's army to fight against the Midianites is to be synonymous with the metaphorical army of the Lord, to fight Satan's hosts,

- To be faithful and overcome their fear with the faith that the Lord has instilled in them.
- To be aware of their situation, times, and surroundings, but also where God is and to move and align with Him and His purposes as He moves, and to be effective and impactful.
- To be responsive.
- To be obedient.

Through this threshing process, the Lord has gleaned the most valuable part of the harvest: the grains, the substance. The stalks, the chaff, the weed seeds, the pebbles, and the debris have all been removed, and the most substantial part of the army will be used to deliver the Israelites from their enemy. The Lord declares that He will deliver the Israelites with 300 men! Through this we can see the principle, "Many are called, but few are chosen!

The Lord's process of threshing has.

- Reduced 70% of the 32,000 men who were called and gathered but trembled with fear in the initial threshing to 10,000.
- He further reduced 97% of the remaining 10,000 men by determining their awareness to a mere 300!
- This equates to .09375% of the initially called 32,000, less than 1%!

Where do we see ourselves concerning the different levels of threshing described here in the story of Gideon?

- Have we been called and responded but are so fearful of the world or the enemy that we tremble and run in fear at the first point of resistance?
- Or are we those who have faith but are so prone to the comforts and conveniences in life that we are more self-focused and less God-focused? Then, when the attack comes or God moves, will we be either blindsided and not realize what has happened or how to respond?
- Has God moved, and we are still in our comfortable place, but we are not feeling His presence anymore, and wonder if God cares about or even notices us? Then, we become even more self-conscious until, eventually, we are alone and isolated and are now searching for anyone or anything to affirm us, which could include returning to Baal and Ashtoreth.
- Or can we, through desire for and seeking to become so plugged in and in relationship with the Lord God, that we know His voice, His presence, His love that when He says I have a mission, whom shall I send, can we say, "Here am

I, send me?"

The Lord assured Gideon that victory was inevitable, even with 300. Gideon's army was less than 1% of its original size, and the proportion was over several hundred Midianite to each Israelite. Gideon could only trust in God because there was nothing else to trust.

Chapter 13

When Your Enemies Dream About You!

The Lord has assured Gideon that victory was inevitable, even with only three hundred fighting men. The Israeli army was less than one percent of its original size, and the estimated proportion was hundreds of Midianite soldiers to each Israeli soldier. Gideon could only trust in God; there was nothing else to trust. I am sure Gideon is fearful, more than a little skeptical, and in the natural, physical circumstances, is thinking that there is no way that 300 men can logically defeat a whole nation of Midianites! In this case, Gideon is correct; there is no logical way to defeat the enemy, given the odds of over 400 enemy soldiers to one.

Let's be sure we see and notice the progression of the change and transformation that has transpired in Gideon. When the Angel first appeared and addressed Gideon, declaring him a mighty man of valor and saying that he would deliver the Israelites from the Midianites, their oppressors for the last seven years, Gideon was full of protest, of challenge, and borderline "snarkiness" in his dialogue with the Angel. With statements such as.

- "If the Lord is with us, where are all of His miracles?"
- "The Lord has now abandoned us into the hand of Midian."
- "How can I save Israel? My clan is the inadequate in Manasseh, and I am the most insignificant in my family."

To,

- "Give me a sign that You, Lord, are talking to me."
- "Please do not go away until I return and bring my offering and set it before you."
- "Sovereign Lord! I have seen the Angel of the Lord face to face!"

To,

- Tearing down the altars and places of worship for Baal and Asherah.
- Rebuilding the proper altar and sacrifice to the Lord God.
- Blowing the trumpet (Shofar) to call and gather the men to go against the enemy.
- Asking the Lord for public confirmation through the fleece on the threshing floor and the dew- in two separate and different requests.

We noticed that Gideon did most of the talking through the initial call to confirm the fleece. Now we see that Gideon is not saying much as the Lord begins threshing the 32,000 men.

Up to this point, the Lord has allowed Gideon, and in turn, the people, to become a level of what He has called them to, and allowed the doubt, fear, dysfunction, and disorder to be processed through first; from the people crying out, to challenging and skeptical speech, to the requesting of confirmation. Now, through hearing and responding to their cries, addressing their fear, and bringing in function and order, the Lord has reestablished Gideon and the people back to right standing in His sight.

With this critical foundational step completed, the Lord makes His requirements known by commanding the threshing of the 32,000 men. Through this sorting process, we see that the Lord is now doing all of the talking, and Gideon and the people are submitting to and obedient to the Lord through their silence.

Now that the threshing process is complete and the Lord is ready to proceed with Gideon and his 300 men, the Lord has one more secret errand for Gideon and intends that Gideon should hear something to inspire further, activate, and embolden his courage and that of his troops.

> *Now the camp of Midian lay below him in the valley.*
> *9 During that night the Lord said to Gideon, "Get up, go down against the camp, because I am going to give it into your hands. 10 If you are afraid to attack, go down to the camp with your servant Purah 11 and listen to what they are saying. Afterward, you will be encouraged to attack the camp." So he and Purah his servant, went down to the outposts of the camp. 12 The Midianites, the Amalekites and all the other eastern peoples had settled in the valley, thick as locusts. Their camels could no more be counted than the sand on the seashore. 13 Gideon arrived just as a man was telling a friend his dream. "I had a dream," he was saying. "A round loaf of barley bread came tumbling into the Midianite camp. It struck the tent with such force that the tent overturned and collapsed."*
> *14 His friend responded, "This can be nothing other than the sword of Gideon son of Joash, the Israelite. God has given the Midianites and the whole camp into his hands."*
> *15 When Gideon heard the dream and its interpretation,*

he bowed down and worshiped. He returned to the camp of Israel and called out, "Get up! The Lord has given the Midianite camp into your hands"
Judges 7:9-15 (NIV)

God allowed Gideon to witness an incredible conversation into the exploit He was about to perform. It was not a coincidence or an accident that the soldier dreamed of that dream on that specific night. It was no accident that he told his friend about it at just that precise moment and that Gideon and his assistant came to the exact place amongst the multitude camped there that night where he could overhear the telling and interpretation of this precise dream!

It must have both thrilled and humbled Gideon beyond measure to know that his enemies recognized who he was, and that God would use the sword of Gideon to defeat the entire Midianite army! Even the enemy knew that the Lord God and Gideon were partners! God used this divine appointment to bring into complete revelation to Gideon, once and for all, that He is with Gideon, that they are partners against a common enemy, and that the enemy's defeat is a foregone conclusion; the enemy is even having nightmares about it! This event so touched Gideon and affected him that all he could do was bow down and worship God. This is the point to where Gideon has finally BECOME what the Lord has called him to be- A MIGHTY MAN OF VALOR! Gideon has finally arrived for this time and this place, and he has now conditioned his mind, spirit and identity to what the Lord has called him to be!

As we revisit the dream of the Midianite, a fundamental principle we should consider is that the Hebrew word, **shorim**, occurs nowhere else in the Bible, translating, "Of barley bread." This seems to intentionally refer to the most typical of bread, the food of only the poorer classes, indicating the perceived insignificant station of Gideon and the Israelites that the Midianites held. Wheat was generally used for human consumption, and barley was typically used to feed their cattle. This interpretation of the dream was logical. Gideon is mentioned explicitly as the leader of the Israelites. The barley loaf was usually the food of the poorer classes. This reference to Israel, especially after the Israelite's seven years of oppression, had ground them down to the point that they would have to use the grains that they would usually feed their cattle to sustain themselves. The barley loaf can be interpreted as the symbol of Israel, which was disdained among the nations. But under Gideon, the ascending of Israel was not a mystery to the Midianites since all of the gathering and threshing of his army was performed on the threshing floor, a place of high visibility, and no doubt had filled them with fear. Therefore, in this dream, their fear might easily assume the form of their defeat or desolation and destruction of their camp by Gideon.

The tent mentioned in the dream can be interpreted to be synonymous with a general's tent to indicate the total and entire destruction and overthrow of the tent, symbolic of the route and destruction of the whole Midianite army. This instills not only the obviousness of the symbolism but also the dread in the Midianite ranks of Gideon's distinction as the one who will lead this destruction as an instrument of the Lord God. A subtle terror began building and creeping over the Midianites, manifesting and confirmed through both the dream and its interpretation. The tiny loaf's impact was disproportionate to its size; a giant boulder thundering down the hillside might have the mass and momentum enough to level a line of tents, but one simple poor man's loaf to cause such catastrophe? Something more majestic is at work than just a band of rebels rising, and the Midianite soldier, therefore, interprets that God will deliver the army into Gideon's hand.

Gideon came away so emboldened by what he had just witnessed that when he returned to his camp and commanded them to wake up, the Lord was about to do what He had promised and set the 300 men into motion!

> *15 And so it was, when Gideon heard the telling of the dream and its interpretation, that he worshiped. He returned to the camp of Israel, and said, "Arise, for the Lord has delivered the camp of Midian into your hand." 16 Then he divided the three hundred men into three companies, and he put a trumpet into every man's hand, with empty pitchers, and torches inside the pitchers. 17 And he said to them, "Look at me and do likewise; watch, and when I come to the edge of the camp you shall do as I do: 18 When I blow the trumpet, I and all who are with me, then you also blow the trumpets on every side of the whole camp, and say, 'The sword of the Lord and of Gideon!' "19 So Gideon and the hundred men who were with him came to the outpost of the camp at the beginning of the middle watch, just as they had posted the watch; and they blew the trumpets and broke the pitchers that were in their hands.*
>
> *Judges 7:16-20 NKJV*

So if I imagine that I am one of the 300 men and Gideon and Purah come running back to camp full of excitement, waking us all up in the middle of the night and telling us that now is the time, let's go to battle and that the Lord has delivered the enemy into our hands! Then, giving us the battle plan, we would be separated into three companies, spread out around the camp of the enemy to cover more territory, which makes sense; after all, we are taking on an army so numerous that we can't even count their camels, then instructing us to arm ourselves.

I would think, "OK, I need a helmet, a shield, and a sword, and I'm ready to go." So, as I am going through the line to get my weapons, I receive a trumpet, an empty pitcher, and a lighted torch inside the pitcher. Before I can challenge the decision-making process, I hear Gideon giving more instructions for us to look and watch him and do whatever he does, and when he comes to the edge of the enemy's camp, I am to do likewise. We are to watch, and we are supposed to do as he does... when he blows the trumpet, we blow the trumpet, and then we are to yell, "FOR THE SWORD OF THE LORD AND OF GIDEON!" Then we are to smash our pitchers?

WAIT... WHAT??? This sounds more like a celebration after the battle has been won, than a plan for the battle! But that's precisely what happened!

> *20 Then the three companies blew the trumpets and broke the pitchers—they held the torches in their left hands and the trumpets in their right hands for blowing—and they cried, "The sword of the Lord and of Gideon!" 21 And every man stood in his place all around the camp; and the whole army ran and cried out and fled. 22 When the three hundred blew the trumpets, the Lord set every man's sword against his companion throughout the whole camp; and the army fled to Beth Acacia, toward Zererah, as far as the border of Abel Meholah, by Tabbath.23 And the men of Israel gathered together from Naphtali, Asher, and all Manasseh, and pursued the Midianites.*
>
> *Judges 7:20-2*

This was a surprise attack! It was the middle of the night; it was time for the changing of the guard, so the Midianite soldiers' attention would have been distracted, and all of a sudden, the Midianite soldiers awoke to a roar of noise, light, and movement coming down on them from all directions. It must have seemed that they were being attacked by an army even more significant than they were. Gideon and his 300 men blew their shofars and shouted, "The sword of the LORD and Gideon!" continuously. This shout demonstrated the Midianites were primed to fear the sword of Gideon, that and along with the previous conversations through the camp that the Lord would deliver them into his hand, and through the sound of the trumpets, the shouting, and the sight of the torches... it perpetuated the Midianites to such fear that a panicked frenzy overtook them.

The LORD then set every Midianite's sword against his companion throughout the camp: The first phase of the battle didn't even commence between Israel and Midian, but rather, it was through the Midianites fighting themselves. As the Midianites fought each other, Gideon's army continued blowing their trumpets, shouting, and running towards them with their torches. This all led to the Midianites turning and fleeing the area in full retreat!

Before proceeding with the battle, let's take a breath and not breeze past some fundamental Kingdom principles embedded in the setup and commencement of this battle... Once Gideon was emboldened by the dream and the interpretation of it, we can assume that he received divine instructions from the Spirit of God concerning the strategy that he explained and then implemented with his men.

- The first instruction was for the men to watch Gideon and follow his lead.

  We can see here why the Lord sorted out these 300 men through drinking from their hands. These men had their heads up and were aware of their surroundings, and Gideon was calling on that trait for this battle.

- The handing out of the instruments they would use for the battle was different from the instruments that any logical plan would call for.

  A clay pitcher with a lit torch in it. This was used so they could sneak up to the enemy camp without the torch's light giving them away; it was hidden in the vessel. This can be symbolic of us as Christ's followers. We are the vessels made of clay that have the light and fire of the Holy Spirit inside us waiting to be activated. Once Gideon and the 300 men surrounded the enemy camp, they were to break the jars and the light of their torches would blaze bright, disorienting and confusing the Midianites into thinking that there were more soldiers than was the case.

- A trumpet (A shofar or rams' horn) was in their other hand.

  The shofar is mentioned and has many significant meanings throughout the scriptures. It could be used as an alarm to warn of enemy attacks, as an announcement for ceremonial events, and as in this case as an instrument of warfare, particularly of spiritual warfare.

> *9 "When you go to war in your land against the enemy who oppresses you, then you shall sound an alarm with the trumpets, and you will be remembered before the Lord your God, and you will be saved from your enemies.*
> *Numbers 10:9*

The shofar was also used when Joshua and the Israelites had marched around Jericho for six days, and on the seventh day, they marched around seven times. Then the priests blew the shofar, and the Hebrews shouted, and the walls of Jericho fell, and were defeated.

- The sword that the Lord gave Gideon was not physical.

  Gideon and the Lord needed to use the same sword, and in this case, it was the Sword of the Spirit, which, in Ephesians 6:17, tells us that this is the WORD of God. In both battles of Joshua at Jericho and with Gideon against the Midianites, the SHOUT was the instrument that tumbled the walls at Jericho and set the Midianites into a panicked frenzy. We have to ensure we have the same sword as the Lord God! When we try to use the sword of our strength, not the Sword of the Spirt, we can mess up the divine strategy and battle plan against our enemies. When Peter grabs his sword and chops off the Roman soldier's ear as they come to take Jesus away to be crucified from the Garden of Gethsemane, Jesus instructs Peter to put away his sword. Because as long as we rely on our swords, the Lord won't use His Sword.

The Midianites were startled from their slumber (their comfort, contentment, and their confidence in their oppressive dominion over the Israelites) by the sound of the trumpets in the middle of their imposed "darkness" (the oppression and fear) along with the shouts of the faithful, chosen, and empowered Mighty Men of Valor and the piercing lights of the glory of the Lord that has burning inside of them. It was like walking into a dark room and switching on the lights- all of the cockroaches scattered! Chaos ensued throughout the Midianite camp, and the enemy was rendered into a state of confusion.

The Lord caused the Midianites to turn on each other with their swords! Isn't it easy for the oppressor to be so smug and regal when they have the dominant numbers, and they can keep you in check through seven years of fear and oppression and assume and expect that you will continue to submit to their tyranny over you? But once you have:

- Cried out to and have been heard by the Lord.
- Have received clarification from His prophet, reminding us why we are in this state of oppression.
- Receive an audience from the Angel of the Lord declaring to us that we are Mighty Men (and women) of Valor and that He will give the Midianites into our hands.
- Has us tear down our idols.
- Reestablishes proper alignment and right standing with Him.
- Then confirms to us with a fleece.
- Threshes us so that we stand in faith and not fear, ensuring that we are aware and in tune with Him.
- Gives the enemy dreams about how the Lord will deliver them through us... so much so that the enemy knows your name and recognizes that you and the Lord are partners.
- And now the fear that they have lorded over you for the last seven years is about to be overturned.

And you can sense the Lord God encouraging you, "Now! Let ME show YOU how WE will deliver YOU and turn your night into day, your mourning into dancing, from slaves to children of the King!" Then, when the enemy has camped just over the horizon, getting a good night's sleep, expecting to wake up the following day and raid your harvest, and expect that you will just step aside and allow them into your fields and slaughter your cattle. At the same time, you go running and hide in your little caves and dens like scared little rabbits, just as you have done for the last seven years...

Your Father walks into the room and turns on the lights by smashing us -as earthen vessels so that His light shines through and out of us so brightly that even though the number is only 300 seeds of barley grain, our lights shine so bright... His glory illuminates so blazingly... that 300 torches of His glory send hundreds of thousands of cockroaches scurrying and exposes what they are: vermin and scavengers!

When the Lord God... our Father in Heaven... decides to step in and deliver us... He so disrupts, so startles, so resist, and assails the enemy.... that He causes them to turn against each other and to flee from the "Sword of the Lord and of Gideon!" or "The sword of the Lord and (Your Name!)"

The enemy turns on each other and the swords of oppression they once used on you.... are now being used on each other! Oh what a mighty and awesome God we serve!

> *22 When the three hundred trumpets sounded, the Lord caused the men throughout the camp to turn on each other with their swords. The army fled to Beth Shittah toward Zererah as far as the border of Abel Meholah near Tabbath. 23 Israelites from Naphtali, Asher and all Manasseh were called out, and they pursued the Midianites. 24 Gideon sent messengers throughout the hill country of Ephraim, saying, "Come down against the Midianites and seize the waters of the Jordan ahead of them as far as Beth Barah." So all the men of Ephraim were called out and they seized the waters of the Jordan as far as Beth Barah. 25 They also captured two of the Midianite leaders, Oreb and Zeeb. They killed Oreb at the rock of Oreb, and Zeeb at the winepress of Zeeb. They pursued the Midianites and brought the heads of Oreb and Zeeb to Gideon, who was by the Jordan.*
>
> *Judges 7:22-25 NIV*

The Lord used the 300 men for the deliverance of the Israelites by breaking their clay jars, holding their torches high, and shouting, "For the sword of the Lord and of Gideon!" startling the Midianite's camp to a state of confusion and chaos, the Midianites turn their swords on each other and eventually began to flee, attempting to escape back across the Jordan river.

As the Lord initially called and conditioned Gideon and then the 300, now he is using the 300 to encourage and embolden the remaining Israelite tribes to join in the chase and to participate in the deliverance from their oppressors. Gideon sends messengers to the tribes of Manasseh, Nepthal, and Asher in the nearby region to get involved. He also sent messengers to Ephraim throughout the hill country near the Jordan River to seal it off so that the Midianites could not escape across it. Ephraim sealed the escape route and even captured and killed two of the Midianite leaders and brought their heads to Gideon.

Often, when there is a new move of God, there is an initial fear of the unfamiliar and the uncomfortable that can freeze many into inaction. But when a few faith-filled people are brave enough to trust, partner, and come alongside the move of God, there is a momentum that activates and emboldens those standing by the sidelines watching and waiting. They will be motivated to join forces when they see the movement is working and know it is real. But sometimes, while we are operating in the move of God, things aren't always as they seem, and we see here that Gideon is coming against resistance, but not necessarily from where you would expect. The tribe of Ephraim had just ambushed the fleeing Midianites as they were attempting to cross the Jordan, and they fought and prevailed against them and captured and killed two of their leaders. Still, some of the Midianites made it past Ephraim and made it across the Jordan River. When Gideon caught up to them, Ephraim handed off the heads of the leaders to him, and

Gideon was about to cross Jordan in pursuit of the Midianites. Ephraim wanted to take this opportunity in the middle of the battle and the pursuit to bring up some concerns with Gideon.

> *Now the Ephraimites asked Gideon, "Why have you treated us like this? Why didn't you call us when you went to fight Midian?" And they challenged him vigorously. 2 But he answered them, "What have I accomplished compared to you? Aren't the gleanings of Ephraim's grapes better than the full grape harvest of Abiezer? 3 God gave Oreb and Zeeb, the Midianite leaders, into your hands. What was I able to do compared to you?" At this, their resentment against him subsided.*
>
> *Judges 8:1-3 (NIV)*

Now, you would think that after such a mighty turn of events where an apparent miracle of God is taking place, freeing the nation of Israel from an "Intense" seven years of oppression. You now have the oppressor in full retreat; the remaining tribes of Israel have locked arms with Gideon and the 300 men and are now participating in their deliverance; you would expect a high level of camaraderie and unity in purpose for this extraordinary move of God. However, although Ephraim is engaged and has cut off most of the Midianites, Ephraim has an issue with Gideon and wants to address how and when he involved them.

Ephraim wants to know why Gideon treated them like this and didn't reach out to them at the very beginning when he went to fight with the Midianites. And Ephraim challenged him vigorously!

What is this all about? Why is the leaders of Ephraim addressing Gideon this way?

Have you ever had a sibling or family member who always seems to lord their status over you or remind you that because of their past successes or their position in the family, or their career, or their networks, you should consider them before going off on your own, particularly if it is going to be something incredible or successful?

This was the case with the tribe of Ephraim. Gideon was from the tribe of Manasseh. These two tribes are descended from the sons of Joseph. Manasseh was Ephraim's older brother. At a young age, Joseph brought his two sons to his father and the boy's grandfather, Jacob, who was on his deathbed to bestow the patriarchal blessing on them. The patriarchal blessing is customarily granted to the oldest child first, and they are to receive the double portion, and then any succeeding heirs are to split the remaining. In this case, Jacob who preferred the younger Ephraim over the older Manasseh, gave the double portion blessing to the younger Ephraim, to the protest of Joseph. So, over centuries, the tribe of Ephraim has grown haughty and arrogant against the lesser tribe of Manasseh.

This arrogance was reinforced by Joshua, who was part of the tribe of Ephraim. Joshua led the Israelites for 40 years in the desert, crossing the Jordan River into the Promised Land, and through many campaigns to possess the promised land. In the eyes and perspectives of Ephraim, Gideon had seemed to advance his tribe, Manasseh, and to depress theirs.

Isn't it funny how those who will not attempt to venture anything for the move of God are the most ready to quarrel with those who are willing to? They are willing to argue and ridicule the ones who are obedient, humble, and responsive to His call; they are also the ones who are the most reserved, fearful, and standoffish to His call, and they are the most offended when they don't receive the credit. The tribe of Ephraim was venting toward their ambitions.

Gideon's response to Ephraim not only diffused their haughty anger and entitled expectations but also gives us an example of how the self-denial and humility of Gideon to be

less "self-focused" and more "God-focused" amid a remarkable victory to which the Lord used Gideon as the chief instrument. Gideon could have easily succumbed to his natural instinct and desire to defend his right to the accolades for his part. Still, for the sake of the common good, he receives the reproach without anger, humbles himself before them, and then magnifies their part as the superior achievement. This act disarms their anger through humility and haughtiness through meekness and allows Ephraim the right to accolades.
In Proverbs 15:1, we see that,

> *"A soft answer turns away wrath, but a harsh word stirs up anger."*

When we operate as a product of the world, of the flesh, or carnal nature, we will usually respond in a worldly manner, which will bring about worldly consequences. But Gideon, through his transformation, is now operating from a "Kingdom of heaven" perspective and respond through Kingdom principles, obedience, humility, meekness, and love. Gideon realizes he is called to a higher mission, purpose, and destiny.

Jesus calls us today to deny ourselves, pick up our cross, and follow Him (His example). He is calling us to become what He has paid for through His sacrifice for us. To become children and heirs to the King and no longer slaves to this world, to be IN the world but not OF the world.

On a practical level, Gideon also understood that this was no time for silly bickering over status, position, or accolades. There was still an enemy to pursue, who was getting further and further away the longer they bickered!

> *4 Gideon and his three hundred men, exhausted yet keeping up the pursuit, came to the Jordan and crossed it. 5 He said to the men of Sukkoth, "Give my troops some*

bread; they are worn out, and I am still pursuing Zebah and Zalmunna, the kings of Midian." 6 But the officials of Sukkoth said, "Do you already have the hands of Zebah and Zalmunna in your possession? Why should we give bread to your troops?" 7 Then Gideon replied, "Just for that when the Lord has given Zebah and Zalmunna into my hand, I will tear your flesh with desert thorns and briers." 8 From there, he went up to Peniel and made the same request of them, but they answered the same way the men of Sukkoth had. 9 So he said to the men of Peniel, "When I return in triumph, I will tear down this tower." 10 Now Zebah and Zalmunna were in Karkor with a force of about fifteen thousand men, all that were left of the armies of the eastern peoples; a hundred and twenty thousand swordsmen had fallen. 11 Gideon went up by the route of the nomads east of Nobah and Jogbehah and attacked the unsuspecting army. 12 Zebah and Zalmunna, the two kings of Midian, fled, but he pursued them and captured them, routing their entire army.

Judges 8: 4-12 (NIV)

The men of Gideon were exhausted from pursuing the Midianites across the Jordan, and as they came upon the towns of Sukkoth and Peniel, Gideon and his men were asking the leaders of these towns for assistance. These towns were towns of the Israelites, and they were not enemy towns. Gideon requested these towns not to join the fight but to give the men food, shelter, and rest. But as we read in these scriptures, the men of these towns- Israeli towns not the towns of the enemy, declared that they would not provide support until Gideon had the kings of Midian captured and as prisoners. They refused support, food, shelter, and rest until the battle was won.

It would seem that if Gideon and his troops were in the process of delivering his fellow citizens from seven years of oppression of the Midianites, there would be a sense of camaraderie, patriotism, or at least gratitude, but what Gideon and his men received from Sukkoth and Peniel was not only refusal of essential support, food and rest in their state of weariness and hunger, which was not out of faith or even fear, but callous indifference and were indirectly aiding their enemy through their nonsupport.

Due to the lack of support of these towns, Gideon declared to them that when he did return in triumph, he would deal with Sukkoth with thorns, and for Peniel, he would tear down their tower. Gideon, then pursued and routed the entire Midianite army and captured and killed their two kings. He then returned to Sukkoth and Peniel to make good on his promise.

> *13 Gideon son of Joash then returned from the battle by the Pass of Heres. 14 He caught a young man of Sukkoth and questioned him, and the young man wrote down for him the names of the seventy-seven officials of Sukkoth, the town's elders. 15 Then Gideon came and said to the men of Sukkoth, "Here are Zebah and Zalmunna, about whom you taunted me by saying, 'Do you already have the hands of Zebah and Zalmunna in your possession? Why should we give bread to your exhausted men?'" 16 He took the elders of the town and taught the men of Sukkoth a lesson by punishing them with desert thorns and briers. 17 He also pulled down the tower of Peniel and killed the men of the town.*
>
> *Judges 8:13-17 (NIV)*

Gideon, who was called to perform in the role of a Judge, was not only called to deliver the Israelites from their oppressors but was also responsible for rendering judgment on those who were resisting or fighting against the will of God, which included the Israelites who were a people set apart for God.

The leaders of Sukkoth and Peniel were not just being rude to Gideon and his men, but through their lack of hospitality, they were resisting the move of God. They were actively refusing the threshing of the Lord for their deliverance and restoration.

The Hebrew word for threshing is *deshe*, which translates to tear; threshing can be described as tearing. Since the men of Sukkoth and Peniel were resisting the threshing of the Lord's **deliverance and restoration** to return them to right standing with Him, they would suffer the flip side of the coin for threshing, which is the judgment, the curse, the punishment. For Sukkoth, they would have their flesh torn (threshed). They were whipped and had their flesh torn by the briers, thorns of the wilderness, as a public rebuke. For the men of Peniel, their threshing was that they had their tower torn down and killed all of the men of the city. Gideon's execution of the Lord's judgment onto the leaders of Sukkoth and Peniel was to **Expose, Destroy, Heal, and Replace** the perceived alliances with the Midianites so that they would stand as an example to those who would resist the will of God, and so that their behavior wouldn't affect the rest of the Israelites for the potential to follow their poor behavior. The Lord God is judicious in His expectations of His chosen people.

> *6 For you are a people holy to the Lord your God. The Lord your God has chosen you out of all the peoples on the face of the earth to be his people, his treasured possession. 7 The Lord did not set his affection on you and choose you because you were more numerous than other peoples, for you were the fewest of all peoples. 8 But it was because the Lord loved you and kept the oath, he swore to your ancestors that he brought you out with a mighty hand and redeemed you from the land of slavery, from the power of Pharaoh king of Egypt. 9 Know therefore that the Lord your God is God; he is the faithful God, keeping*

his covenant of love to a thousand generations of those who love him and keep his commandments. **10** *But those who hate him he will repay to their face by destruction; he will not be slow to repay to their face those who hate him.* **11** *Therefore, take care to follow the commands, decrees and laws I give you today.*

Deuteronomy 7: 6-11

When God moves to advance His Kingdom, He will thresh His people to establish alignment, proper worship, deliverance, and restoration, or He will thresh for judgment and punishment. The men of Sukkoth and Peniel had the opportunity to get on the right side of God's move but instead chose to take their chances with the Midianites, the enemy of the people of God and, therefore, an enemy of God. They put themselves in a position to be an enemy of God!

Gideon fulfilled the call the Lord God had assigned to him to be a Mighty Man of Valor and to deliver Israel from their oppressors. Gideon was very successful in completing this call.

28 Thus Midian was subdued before the Israelites and did not raise its head again. During Gideon's lifetime, the land had peace forty years. 29 Jerub-Baal son of Joash went back home to live. 30 He had seventy sons of his own, for he had many wives. 31 His concubine, who lived in Shechem, also bore him a son, whom he named Abimelek. 32 Gideon son of Joash died at a good old age and was buried in the tomb of his father Joash in Ophrah of the Abiezrites,

Judges 8:28-32 (NIV)

This is a fantastic story of how God called a person who was threshing wheat in a wine press, who was the least in his tribe and the least in his family, but through the process of threshing, the Lord conditioned Gideon into the vessel, he needed for what he called him to. When the Angel visited Gideon and declared Gideon a Might Man of Valor, Gideon was not yet what he was being called. But the Lord made Gideon, He threshed Gideon, He fashioned Gideon into what the Lord was to use Gideon for. In turn, the Lord God also fashioned the Israelite people into what they needed to be, for the Lord to be able to deliver them. During Gideon's lifetime, Israel was peaceful for forty years. Hallelujah!

The Lord God is seeking those among us whom He can call, thresh, and use for the purposes He has for us now! What in our lives, families, and culture must be delivered from our oppressors? What strongholds have we been living with for years, even decades, that we need to have the Lord deliver us from- to **Expose, Destroy, Heal, and Replace**? What idol worship and altars need to be torn down in our lives? How do we re-establish the proper altar and approach to worship the One True God? How do we become so aligned with God that our name has been changed to Jerub Baal-he, who contends with Baal? What in our lives needs to be threshed, beaten, and thrown into the air to blow away all of the wasted chaff that has built up in our lives and then to sift us for the few fine, valuable kernels of grains- the essential substance that the Lord God can use in us? How do we get to where the Lord God gives the enemy dreams about us, that they know our name, that we are partners with the Lord, and we can shout, "For the Sword of the Lord and of (Your Name!)"? Is it time that we align with the move of God in our life for His purposes and His will to further His Kingdom?

"But" you may say, "I am the least in my family, the least in my circle of influence, I don't have the pedigree, I am too young or too old, or my guilt and shame is too much!" Gideon said those things too. And the Angel waited for him to bring his offering of submission to Him. Is it time to lay your burdens at His feet and put away those thoughts? What He is calling you to may seem overwhelming and so great that you cannot see yourself able to fulfill it. But the Lord God is saying to you...

> *"My grace is sufficient for you, for my power is made perfect in weakness."*
> *2 Corinthians 12:9*

As with Gideon, He is calling us into the mission, purpose, and destiny that He has for us, and like Gideon, we may fall short of what He is calling us for. But He doesn't call the qualified; He qualifies the called. He will realign us as partners.

A word of caution... A final note in the story of Gideon.

> *22 The Israelites said to Gideon, "Rule over us—you, your son and your grandson—because you have saved us from the hand of Midian." 23 But Gideon told them, "I will not rule over you, nor will my son rule over you. The Lord will rule over you." 24 And he said, "I do have one request, that each of you give me an earring from your share of the plunder." (It was the custom of the Ishmaelites to wear gold earrings.) 25 They answered, "We'll be glad to give them." So they spread out a garment, and each of them threw a ring from his plunder onto it. 26 The weight of the gold rings he asked for came to seventeen hundred shekels,[b] not counting the ornaments, the pendants and the purple garments worn by the kings of Midian or the chains that were on their camels' necks. 27 Gideon made the gold into an ephod, which he placed in Ophrah, his town. All Israel prostituted themselves by worshiping it there, and it became a snare to Gideon and his family. 28 Thus Midian was subdued before the Israelites and did not raise its head again. During Gideon's lifetime, the land had peace forty years 29Jerub-Baal son of Joash went*

back home to live. 30 He had seventy sons of his own, for he had many wives. 31 His concubine, who lived in Shechem, also bore him a son, whom he named Abimelek. 32 Gideon son of Joash died at a good old age and was buried in the tomb of his father Joash in Ophrah of the Abiezrites. 33 No sooner had Gideon died than the Israelites again prostituted themselves to the Baals. They set up Baal-Berith as their god 34 and did not remember the Lord their God, who had rescued them from the hands of all their enemies on every side. 35 They also failed to show any loyalty to the family of Jerub-Baal (that is, Gideon) in spite of all the good things he had done for them.

Judges 8:22-35 (NIV)

Despite all the exploits in the deliverance of the Israelites that the Lord God provided through the hand of Gideon from the Midianites, there are still some considerations that we need to address. Even after their deliverance and restoration, there were still issues that the Israelites needed to have **Exposed, Destroyed, Healed, and Replaced**, which we should take as a warning in our journeys.

1. **The Israelites wanted to make Gideon their king.** This seems harmless at first glance and would be a great honor to bestow on Gideon as a reward for such great exploits, but Gideon refused to be exalted as king over Israel or for his sons to be exalted king over Israel and proclaimed that the Lord would rule over them. Gideon was putting this line of thinking from the Israelite people back into perspective. The Israelites had a special privilege in that the Lord God ruled them. No other nation had this arrangement- For the Lord God, the King of the universe, to rule over His chosen and select

people. The people's thought process came from the Israelites' desire to be like the other nations, who had kings ruling over them, and possibly thinking that if they had a strong king to rule over them, they could hedge themselves against recurring troubles with oppression in the future. In both cases, the Israelites were mistaken; who better to rule over them than the King of the universe? Their captivity was never really about being overrun by a stronger nation; it was about whether they were following the Lord God with their whole heart and not turning away from Him and worshipping false gods.

2. **Gideon asked for a portion of the jewelry from the plunder to make a gold ephod.** The jewelry gathering in and of itself was not so much of an issue or even a sin. What Gideon did with it became a snare for the Israelites though. The priests of Israel wear a garment over their torso called an ephod, and it seems that Gideon created it as a reminder or memorial for the Israelite people to ensure they remember the miracle of the Lord God delivering them. It had the opposite effect though, and the people began to worship it, making it a form of an idol.

   The people of Israel reveled in making the ephod the center of idolatrous worship. The magnificent and extravagant ephod became a snare to Gideon, his family, and Israel.

   The craftsmanship of incredible beauty impresses us and gives us a sense of awe; often, it can distract our focus from the LORD due to its beauty. In Exodus 20:25, God commands that His altars be made of unfinished stone so that no one's attention is focused on the beauty of the stone carver's work but on the Lord God Himself.

3. **When Gideon died the Israelites immediately re-established the altar to Baal, worshipped him as their god, and did not remember their Lord God.** The Israelites enjoyed freedom from their oppressors throughout Gideon's lifetime and had peace for forty years. Through his life, calling, and journey, we see Gideon as a man who descended from extraordinary faith and obedience to a point of negligence against God. It seems that Gideon handled the challenge of the act of deliverance better than the complacency of success. Gideon's attraction and appetite for success, riches, and prominence became a snare for him and his family. Gideon's excess living included having seventy children, one of whom was even born from his concubine. Gideon's family became a product of Gideon's excess and dysfunction. This led to a complacency concerning the things of God, which progressed to a point over the forty years of peace that led to the Israelites immediately returning to idol worship upon the death of Gideon.
4. **The Israelites failed to show loyalty to Gideon's family.** Not only the Israelites returning to idol worship was a falling away of allegiance from the Lord God, but a falling away of loyalty to Gideon and his freeing of the Israelites from their oppressors, the Midianites, and a disregard towards the family of Gideon. Gideon's family, though, was itself very dysfunctional, and Abimelech, the son of Gideon and his concubine concocted a scheme to become ruler over them, scheming undercut of the people considering the remaining seventy sons of Gideon.

> *Abimelek son of Jerub-Baal went to his mother's brothers in Shechem and said to them and to all his mother's clan, 2 "Ask all the citizens of Shechem, 'Which is better for you: to have all seventy of Jerub-Baal's sons rule over you, or just one man?' Remember, I am your flesh and blood." 3 When the brothers repeated all this to the citizens of Shechem, they were inclined to follow Abimelek, for they said, "He is related to us." 4 They gave him seventy shekels[a] of silver from the temple of Baal-Berith, and Abimelek used it to hire reckless scoundrels, who became his followers. 5 He went to his father's home in Ophrah and on one stone murdered his seventy brothers, the sons of Jerub-Baal. But Jotham, the youngest son of Jerub-Baal, escaped by hiding. 6 Then all the citizens of Shechem and Beth Millo gathered beside the great tree at the pillar in Shechem to crown Abimelek king.*
>
> *Judges 9:1-6 (NIV)*

Not only did Abimelek undercut and disrespect the family of Gideon, but he also conspired with the citizens of Shechem, who funded Abimelek from the treasury of the temple of Baal, which Abimelek used to hire scoundrels to participate in the rounding up of the rest of his seventy brothers and execute them on one stone in Gideon's hometown of Oprah!

One brother escaped, though, and that was the youngest son of Gideon, Jotham. Jotham then climbed up on the top of Mount Gerizim and shouted to them,

> *16 "Have you acted honorably and in good faith by making Abimelek king? Have you been fair to Jerub-Baal and his family? Have you treated him as he deserves? 17 Remember that my father fought for you and risked his life to rescue you from the hand of Midian. 18 But today you have revolted against my father's family. You have*

murdered his seventy sons on a single stone and have made Abimelek, the son of his female slave, king over the citizens of Shechem because he is related to you. 19 So have you acted honorably and in good faith toward Jerub-Baal and his family today? If you have, may Abimelek be your joy, and may you be his, too! 20 But if you have not, let fire come out from Abimelek and consume you, the citizens of Shechem and Beth Millo, and let fire come out from you, the citizens of Shechem and Beth Millo, and consume Abimelek!" 21 Then Jotham fled, escaping to Beer, and he lived there because he was afraid of his brother Abimelek.

Judges 9:16-21 (NIV)

Jotham was calling out and reminding the citizens of Shechem that his father, Gideon, had fought for them and risked his life to rescue them. And through this act of revolt and executing his sons had dishonored the family of Gideon.

Abimelek reigned over the region of Shechem for three years, which ended through a revolt against Abimelek's cruelty. In the battle, Abimelek was killed by a woman dropping a mill stone and crushing his skull. What a tragic end to the house of Gideon.

The warning.

How can we be sure we don't fall into the same snare that Gideon did? The key is not becoming complacent and comfortable and thinking we have arrived. Our mission is on-going. Gideon was still responsible for grooming, training, and building up the next generation of followers, especially in his family. How much different would his legacy had been if he had stayed as diligent, obedient, and impactful to passing the mission on to his children? This isn't as exciting, glamorous, or adventurous as fighting with and expelling the enemy, but

I submit it is as important and impactful. It is playing the long game and takes constant reliance upon and anointing from the Lord God to achieve. We, like Gideon, must guard against living a comfortable, luxurious, uneventful life; the Lord God has so much for us to do in our short lives here on this earth.

Chapter 14

Three Kings and a Prophet

We are called to be a nation of kings and priests. To become what we are called to, we must learn what it means to be a "King" and a "Priest" and how to operate in these roles. These two distinct roles are almost opposed to each other. When He granted Israel a king over them, the Lord declared that the two offices of King and Priest were to be separate and not under one person. But when He sent His Son Jesus (Yeshua) to the earth to restore and redeem mankind through His dying on the cross and His shed blood. We are now being called to be a nation of Kings and Priests.

> *Your Kingdom come, Your will be done, on earth as it is in heaven.*
> *Matthew 6:10 (NIV)*

> *But you are a chosen people, a royal priesthood, a holy nation, God's special possession, that you may declare the praises of him who called you out of darkness into his wonderful light.* **10** *Once you were not a people, but*

now you are the people of God; once you had not received mercy, but now you have received mercy.
1 Peter 29-10

The original intention for this calling can be found in the Garden of Eden, where The Lord created mankind in his image to reflect His glory. Man was crowned with honor and glory (Ps. 8:5), given authority to have dominion (Gen. 1:28), and was given priestly authority for serving in his Garden (temple) (Gen. 2:15; cf. Num. 3:8). This has become the template of royal priesthood from which all other priestly roles is to be conformed to. Over time, as the priesthood is established in Israel, it refers back to the template from Eden through the times of the Patriarchs. However, the Law of Moses separated priestly and kingly roles. Only Jesus, the second Adam, can join the Kingdom and priesthood again.

King

The King is a ruler who has a kingdom, a domain that he rules over.

- He is to ensure the safety, welfare, economy, and continued stability and to have the ultimate authority and dominion over his Kingdom.
- The King is a possessor; he possesses what he has authority over and takes possession of what he has been bestowed, granted, or entrusted to or has acquired through conquest.
- The King defends his Kingdom. He defends his Kingdom against enemies who try to oppress, steal, kill, or destroy the sanctity of the Kingdom.

- The King ensures that his followers understand his Kingdom's rules, laws, and expectations and that they represent him and his will for his Kingdom.

In the sense of a righteous king, the Lord God is the ultimate King, and His Kingdom is the entire universe. He has assigned to us dominion over certain aspects of His Kingdom. The word kingdom is based on combining the words "Kings- Domain," The Lord God has chosen to allot to us a particular realm (domain) to oversee and to rule over and to represent Him as the King of kings, to ensure that His laws, rules, commands, expectation of His Kingdom are followed.

Priest

When man through Adam fell and became separated from God's glory, he was expelled from the Garden- destroying any chance of him serving alongside God as King and priest. Because of the fall, Adam's sin made sacrifice necessary, as death was the punishment for sin, and blood was the price to pay for sin and death. Therefore, from this time forward, we needed someone to stand before God and serve as a mediator.

From Eden to Sinai is known as the time of the Patriarchs, and the firstborn sons were expected to be advocates for their families. Abraham, Isaac, and Jacob weren't officially priests but integral to the earthly priest functions, without a legal title.

The official return of priestly glory that was lost in the Garden began at Mount Sinai when the Lord chose the sons of Aaron to stand before Him in the Tabernacle and serve at His altar. As Exodus describes, these priests were adorned in beautiful apparel intended to match the glory of the Tabernacle. They were officially Stationed to function between

God and man. In the series books of Exodus, Leviticus, and Numbers, we ascertain how the priesthood of Israel is established, beginning with the sons of Aaron. Then, God assigned the Levites to the sons of Aaron to assist them in serving the Lord's Tabernacle and God's people. Often, we merge priests and Levites today, assuming that all Levites are priests. Still, the Levites only assisted but were not allowed to draw near to God's altar—not without severe consequences. Any time a priest, Levite, or King drew near to God without authorization, wrath resulted.

In Deuteronomy 33:8–11, Moses outlines the protocols of the Levites and the priests; these instructions focused on their hierarchy of nearness to the altar, service in the Tabernacle, and mediation for the people performing the duties necessary for the Holy Lord to be among the Israelites and to mediate the people's access to God. Principally, the Levitical doctrine emphasizes the part that priests played in the application of the blood sacrifice to each altar type (Lev. 1–7), to instruct the laws to the people (Lev. 10:10–11), to sanctify the Tabernacle of God (Lev. 16:1–34), and to notify them of the Lord's blessings (Lev. 26:1–46; cf. Num. 6:22–26).

The priest's role was to be an overseer in God's house, make sacrifices for the sins of God's people, and instruct the people in order to bask in the Lord's blessings. When priests did their job, God blessed his people, but God's curses fell on them when they failed. Time and again, the priests showed themselves unfaithful. One pivotal example is the fall of Levi's house, which is observed in the early times of Israel's era of the kings, when Eli's sons provoke the judgment of God, and their judgment comes through a prophet (1 Sam. 2:31–35). After that, the fate of Israel is tied to the vacillating efficacy of the priesthood. Throughout Israel's history, this pattern recurred and, due to their inability to faithfully serve, has shown that a new and better priest(hood) was ultimately needed.

In response to the inconsistency of faithful priests, God promised to raise a new priesthood. Zechariah 3:1–10 is the most extravagant presentation of this promise.

> *Then he showed me Joshua, the high priest standing before the angel of the Lord, and Satan standing at his right side to accuse him. 2 The Lord said to Satan, "The Lord rebuke you, Satan! The Lord, who has chosen Jerusalem, rebuke you! Is not this man a burning stick snatched from the fire?" 3 Now Joshua was dressed in filthy clothes as he stood before the angel. 4 The angel said to those who were standing before him, "Take off his filthy clothes." Then he said to Joshua, "See, I have taken away your sin, and I will put fine garments on you." 5 Then I said, "Put a clean turban on his head." So they put a clean turban on his head and clothed him, while the angel of the Lord stood by. 6 The angel of the Lord gave this charge to Joshua: 7 "This is what the Lord Almighty says: 'If you will walk in obedience to me and keep my requirements, then you will govern my house and have charge of my courts, and I will give you a place among these standing here. 8 "'Listen, High Priest Joshua, you and your associates seated before you, who are men symbolic of things to come: I am going to bring my servant, the Branch. 9 See, the stone I have set in front of Joshua! There are seven eyes on that one stone, and I will engrave an inscription on it,' says the Lord Almighty, 'and I will remove the sin of this land in a single day. 10 "'In that day each of you will invite your neighbor to sit under your vine and fig tree,' declares the Lord Almighty."*
>
> *Zechariah 3:1-10 (NIV)*

The prophet Zechariah received a vision from the Lord in which he saw Joshua, the high priest, unclean and accused by

Satan. (This is not the Joshua that led the Hebrews out of the wilderness into the promised land) Yet, instead of destroying him as He could have, The Lord sanctifies and reestablishes him to service. In this passage and Zechariah 6:9–15, the future expectation of a priest-king is confirmed. Thus, the Old Testament finishes with a glorious expectation of a king who will serve as a priest and a high priest on the throne (Zech. 3:5; Zech. 6:13). To be sure, this combination of priest and King was not allowed under the Law of Moses, but God is declaring in Zechariah that He is going to bring a new covenant, using a new royal priest.

This vision of Joshua, the high priest, being redeemed by the Angel of the Lord is also a depiction of all of us. We, too, have Satan standing next to us, accusing us, pointing out our sins, our uncleanness, and our unworthiness to even be considered for the high calling of King and priest. And the Angel's response to Satan is what Jesus does for us and declares,

> *2 The Lord said to Satan, "The Lord rebuke you, Satan! The Lord, who has chosen Jerusalem, rebuke you! Is not this man a burning stick snatched from the fire?"*
> *Zechariah 3:2 (NIV)*

The example of the Angel of the LORD demonstrates a template for spiritual warfare – that we should constantly battle from the authority of the Lord. In God's authority, we battle from a **position** of victory rather than **for** victory; the battle has already been won. The Lord fights for us when Satan calls us to account.

We are also like Joshua in that we were a burning stick SNATCHED from the fire, a burnt, burning, smoking ember, a scorched, sooty piece of wood still smoking in the ashes. It isn't worth much and will be entirely consumed if not **plucked** from the fire. But the Lord snatched us out of the fires of this fallen world, our past, and Satan's desire to destroy us.

The Lord justifies why Joshua could stand before Him because He chose Joshua and saved Joshua from the fires that were about to consume him. The Lord has also snatched us from the fires we have and are about to be consumed with! Now that that has been settled, the Lord will redeem Joshua.

> *" 3 Now Joshua was dressed in filthy clothes as he stood before the angel. 4 The angel said to those who were standing before him, "Take off his filthy clothes." Then he said to Joshua, "See, I have taken away your sin, and I will put fine garments on you." 5 Then I said, "Put a clean turban on his head." So they put a clean turban on his head and clothed him while the angel of the Lord stood by.*
>
> *Zechariah 3:3-5 (NIV)*

As Joshua stood in the presence of the LORD, Satan accused him on legitimate terms – Joshua was guilty of standing before God in filthy garments. Nevertheless, the LORD addressed the problem by cleansing Joshua, taking away the filthy clothes and the defilement, the iniquity of Joshua that they represented. The Lord has Joshua's filthy garments removed and replaced with the RIGHTEOUS robes of the Lord! Joshua received FINE clothes, and then Joshua was given a clean turban for his head. The Lord has now made Joshua into the opposite of everything that Satan was there to accuse and condemn him of. Joshua is no longer the burning brand snatched from the fire, standing in front of the Lord, filthy and unclean. He has now been made clean and righteous, in right standing, before the Lord! Hallelujah!!! We need to see ourselves through the lens of the blood of Jesus, who has saved, cleansed, redeemed us, and put us in the right standing with the Lord.

And now the Lord gives Joshua the reason, mission, purpose, and destiny He has to carry out. In Joshua's case, this is before Jesus comes to the earth to redeem mankind, so the Lord is not only doing this for Joshua's mission. Still, he also uses this as a prophecy of the coming of Christ and what He will do for all mankind who accept and believe in Him what the Lord did for Joshua.

> *6 The angel of the Lord gave this charge to Joshua: 7 "This is what the Lord Almighty says: 'If you will walk in obedience to me and keep my requirements, then you will govern my house and have charge of my courts, and I will give you a place among these standing here. 8 "'Listen, High Priest Joshua, you and your associates seated before you, who are men symbolic of things to come: I am going to bring my servant, the Branch. 9 See, the stone I have set in front of Joshua! There are seven eyes on that one stone, and I will engrave an inscription on it,' says the Lord Almighty, 'and I will remove the sin of this land in a single day. 10 "'In that day each of you will invite your neighbor to sit under your vine and fig tree,' declares the Lord Almighty."*
>
> *Zechariah 3:6-10 (NIV)*

The fulfillment of all this prophecy comes into focus in the life, death, and exaltation of the Messiah Jesus Christ. Christ's priestly glory is veiled as Jesus enters the world in humiliation and obscurity. Now, as a commandment-keeping son of the tribe of Judah, under the old covenant, He is not allowed to be a priest. But through the New Testament, His access to the priesthood restores his perfect sonship, justifying the supremacy of His priesthood, inaugurating a superior priestly covenant that now includes us!

Hebrews chapter 5 records Yeshua's position as a high priest through His sonship. Hebrews chapter 7 records that His priesthood is in the order of Melchizedek, who is given the right to sit at God's right hand because of his blamelessness here. His priesthood justifies a superior covenant (Heb. 7:12) through His dying on the cross, shedding His blood as the price, sanctifying all to have access to this royal priesthood.

Not only has Jesus recovered the royal priesthood, but now we have access to the same role. As He is the Royal Priest in heaven through His ascension, His Holy Spirit can empower us for royal priestly service. t.

While priesthood is a theme that runs through the Bible, Hebrews is the most essential book for understanding the priesthood.

King and Priest

Putting the two roles together, we can see this in the Garden as God's original intention for man was to be a Royal Priesthood tending His Garden Sanctuary. After the fall of man, we see this role one more time in the Old Testament in the person of Melchizedek.

> *17 After Abram returned from defeating Kedorlaomer and the kings allied with him, the King of Sodom met him in the Valley of Shaveh (that is, the King's Valley). 18 Then Melchizedek, king of Salem, brought out bread and wine. He was priest of God Most High, 19 and he blessed Abram, saying, "Blessed be Abram by God Most High, Creator of heaven and earth. 20 And praise be to God Most High, who delivered your enemies into your hand." Then Abram gave him a tenth of everything.*
>
> *Genesis 14:17-20 (NIV)*

Melchizedek: whose lineage and origins are unknown, or how he came to be a worshipper and priest of the true God, and how Abram came to know about him was the King of Salem. His name means *King of Righteousness*. He was Salem's King, the city of Salem's original name of Jeru*salem*, and Melchizedek was the priest of the Lord Most High. He was a priest and worshipper of the true God, ruling over Jerusalem.

A defining point that makes Melchizedek unique is that he was both a king and a priest. Melchizedek was the priest of God Most High. Melchizedek worshipped the Lord God, a priest of the Lord God, yet his heritage was not of God's chosen people.

Melchizedek served Abram bread and wine. As the priest of God Most High, Melchizedek mediated between Abram and worshipping God. Melchizedek demonstrated that as a priest, he was the conduit with the Lord God and Abram and minister to the Lord God.

> *This Melchizedek was King of Salem and priest of God Most High. He met Abraham returning from the defeat of the kings and blessed him, 2 and Abraham gave him a tenth of everything. First, the name Melchizedek means "king of righteousness"; then also, "king of Salem" means "king of peace." 3 Without father or mother, without genealogy, without beginning of days or end of life, resembling the Son of God, he remains a priest forever.*
>
> *4 Just think how great he was: Even the patriarch Abraham gave him a tenth of the plunder! 5 Now the law requires the descendants of Levi who become priests to collect a tenth from the people—that is, from their fellow Israelites—even though they also are descended from Abraham. 6 This man, however, did not trace his descent from Levi, yet he collected a tenth from Abraham and*

blessed him who had the promises. 7 And without doubt the lesser is blessed by the greater

Jesus Like Melchizedek

11 If perfection could have been attained through the Levitical priesthood—and indeed the law given to the people established that priesthood—why was there still need for another priest to come, one in the order of Melchizedek, not in the order of Aaron? 12 For when the priesthood is changed, the law must be changed also. 13 He of whom these things are said belonged to a different tribe, and no one from that tribe has ever served at the altar. 14 For it is clear that our Lord descended from Judah, and in regard to that tribe Moses said nothing about priests. 15 And what we have said is even more clear if another priest like Melchizedek appears, 16 one who has become a priest not on the basis of a regulation as to his ancestry but on the basis of the power of an indestructible life. 17 For it is declared:

"You are a priest forever, in the order of Melchizedek."

18 The former regulation is set aside because it was weak and useless 19 (for the law made nothing perfect), and a better hope is introduced, by which we draw near to God.

20 And it was not without an oath! Others became priests without any oath, 21 but he became a priest with an oath when God said to him:

"The Lord has sworn and will not change his mind: 'You are a priest forever.'"

22 Because of this oath, Jesus has become the guarantor of a better covenant.

23 Now there have been many of those priests, since death prevented them from continuing in office; 24 but because Jesus lives forever, he has a permanent priesthood. 25 Therefore he is able to save completely those who come to God through him, because he always lives to intercede for them.

26 Such a high priest truly meets our need—one who is holy, blameless, pure, set apart from sinners, exalted above the heavens. 27 Unlike the other high priests, he does not need to offer sacrifices day after day, first for his own sins, and then for the sins of the people. He sacrificed for their sins once and for all when he offered himself. 28 For the law appoints as high priests men in all their weakness; but the oath, which came after the law, appointed the Son, who has been made perfect forever.

Hebrews 7:1-28 (NIV)

Ok, that is a lot to take in. But this is so critical and foundational to renewing our minds and transforming our lives through getting knowledge and understanding so that we can live what Jesus paid for...

18 Then Jesus came to them and said, "All authority in heaven and on earth has been given to me. 19 Therefore go and make disciples of all nations, baptizing them in the name of the Father and of the Son and of the Holy Spirit, 20 and teaching them to obey everything I have commanded you. And surely I am with you always, to the very end of the age."

Matthew 28: 18-20 (NIV)

So here we are, we have been called to be a Royal Priesthood, kings and priests to represent the Lord God to the world, and to represent the world to the Lord God. Not much pressure, huh? This is what we are to become.

God doesn't call the qualified; He qualifies who He calls!

The Becoming...

We have to learn to operate and be conditioned in this role. For most of us, though, we have been conditioned to operate as survivors. We will need to have our minds renewed and our lives transformed to operate in what we have been called from and into. We live as survivors partly because our parents and grandparents were born during or just after the Great Depression. Therefore, our parents and grandparents taught us and brought us up in the thought process of lack, making do, not wasting, and preparing for the worst.

So, our parents' generation taught our generation the ways and thinking needed for their time, but not necessarily for our time. They were preparing us for things and situations we may never see. Their mentality and paradigm assumed that our generation would be based on survival, lack, and getting by, not success, plenty, and abundance. Our parents trained us for worst-case scenarios and survival preparation; therefore, we have been brainwashed into not expecting success.

The challenges our generation faces are not the challenges our parents face. We have been taught to prepare for decrease and not increase. We have been raised, trained, and conditioned by minimalists, and through this conditioning and thinking, this is what we have become. We are a generation that believes and declares increase but lives and operates on the principles of decrease and survival.

Most of us have also been conditioned to have a "follower" mentality, not a "leader" mentality. We submit ourselves to the environment, circumstances, and situations holding us down-when we have been called to correct and fix. We have been conditioned to give in and give up on problems or challenging situations because we never had the example or instruction to be correctors of the issues.

We have been called, blessed, anointed, equipped, and released for our mission, purpose, and destiny that the Lord God has given us, but we are trying to step into and fulfill our mission as a survivor rather than a king. We often have a new mission that the Lord has called us to that requires a particular mindset, structure, process, or network, and we need to be a specific type of vessel designed explicitly for the calling. Still, we bring out old, previous structures to carry out our new mission. The problem is that we can't put new wine in old wineskins.

> *17 Neither do people pour new wine into old wineskins. If they do, the skins will burst; the wine will run out and the wineskins will be ruined. No, they pour new wine into new wineskins, and both are preserved."*
> *Matthew 9:17 (NIV)*

Compared to how our parents and grandparents have conditioned us for their generation and circumstances, are we training, conditioning, and indoctrinating our children and grandchildren for the things of our generation that they may never see? Or are we teaching them what they will face for their generation and calling?

Another concern is that we humans will surround ourselves with friends and colleagues who have the same limitations and shortfalls. We do this to cope and soothe our plight because we those around us "Understand" what we are going through. The problem with this is that it enables us, gives us permission to stay where we are, and keeps us in a faulty condition. Our network may not have the capacity, anointing, or bandwidth to fulfill the mission we have been called to effectively. So even though we have been called, motivated, confirmed, and released, our default operating system is limited to being a survivor and not a succeeder.

When a survivor takes on a mission that requires a succeeder, usually the survivor will attempt to accomplish the mission as a "One-man band." Overextending and stressing themselves due to trust issues, a fear or phobia of delegating, allowing others in, or locking arms with a network that can succeed. Instead, they take it all on themselves and either never accomplish anything or become so isolated that there is no impact on the mission in the first place.

To become what we need for the Lord to use us for the next mission and dimension, we need to renew our minds and transform our lives from that of a survivor to kings!

Three Kings and a Prophet

Looking at this story in 2 Kings, we see how these characters have been put together to complete a call and mission even though they had very little in common. But their unlikely alliance would catapult them into victory and a dimensional shift for God.

> *Joram son of Ahab became King of Israel in Samaria in the eighteenth year of Jehoshaphat king of Judah, and he reigned twelve years. 2 He did evil in the eyes of the Lord, but not as his father and mother had done. He got rid of the sacred stone of Baal that his father had made. 3 Nevertheless, he clung to the sins of Jeroboam son of Nebat, which he had caused Israel to commit; he did not turn away from them. 4 Now Mesha, king of Moab, raised sheep, and he had to pay the King of Israel a tribute of a hundred thousand lambs and the wool of a hundred thousand rams. 5 But after Ahab died, the King of Moab rebelled against the King of Israel. 6 So at that time, King Joram set out from Samaria and mobilized all Israel. 7 He also sent this message to Jehoshaphat, king of Judah: "The King of Moab has rebelled against me. Will you go with me to fight against Moab?" "I will go with you," he replied. "I am as you are, my people as your*

people, my horses as your horses." 8 "By what route shall we attack?" he asked. "Through the Desert of Edom," he answered. 9 So the King of Israel set out with the King of Judah and the King of Edom. After a roundabout march of seven days, the army had no more water for themselves or for the animals with them. 10 "What!" exclaimed the King of Israel. "Has the Lord called us three kings together only to deliver us into the hands of Moab?" 11 But Jehoshaphat asked, "Is there no prophet of the Lord here, through whom we may inquire of the Lord?"

2 Kings 3: 1-11 (NIV)

The three kings that were in alliance are Joram, the King of northern Israel, Jehoshaphat, and the King of Edom, whom the Bible doesn't name.

- Joram could be described as highly dysfunctional. His father, Ahab, was the most terrible king the Northern Kingdom of Israel had ever known, and his mother, Jezebel, was undoubtedly the worst queen Israel had ever known. Joram was better than his father and mother, but he was still wicked. He was the ninth consecutive evil Ruler over Israel's Northern Kingdom, which only had evil kings for its rule.
- Jehoshaphat was the King of Judah, a godly king who followed in the godly footsteps of his father, Asa. Jehoshaphat made peace with the Northern Kingdom, unlike his father, Asa, who fought against Israel.
- The King of Edom is not named, but I believe he was asked to join not only for the additional forces to add to their numbers but also to access the territory they chose to travel through to approach Moab.

It was time for Mesha, the King of Moab, to pay the Kingdom of Israel, as the Moabites were under tribute to Israel, initiated by Joram's father, King Ahab. King Ahab died, which presented an opening to end the tribute the King of Israel was enforcing and now refused to pay the tribute. King Joram was mobilizing his army and asked King Jehoshaphat to join forces with him in this endeavor, and the King of Edom was also enlisted to enforce the tribute payment.

Joram appealed to Jehoshaphat, who was more experienced in military matters, as to which route they should choose towards Moab. Jehoshaphat recommended they approach Moab through the Desert of Edom, probably because the Moabites wouldn't expect them to come by that route as it was inhospitable.

As they were making their way through the Desert of Edom, after seven days, they realized that they were in trouble. They had found themselves in the middle of nowhere and no water for their men or the animals with them. They were in a dire situation, and at the edge of Moab's boundary, they may die of thirst. Whenever the Lord is about to move in our lives and usher us into the next dimension of what He has for us, He will often put us in a dry place. Before Israel was to take possession of the Promised Land, they were taken to a dry place. David had to go to a dry place for seven years when he was anointed King. When Jesus was about to launch His ministry, immediately after He was baptized, the Spirit led Him for 40 days in a dry place. A dry place is a place of disruption from our everyday routines, devoid of comfort, devoid of the things of this world, a place of shifting focus and conditioning. The three kings found themselves at a dry place, a place of disruption, of shifting focus on their strength, and about to be conditioned.

Isn't it funny that when we get into a desperate or serious situation, whatever behavior or characteristic in us manifests itself in wholesale? We see this in Joram and Jehoshaphat's responses. Joram was operating from a place of fear, self-focus, pitifulness, and survival; you can see it in his speech.

> *"What!" exclaimed the King of Israel. "Has the Lord called us three kings together only to deliver us into the hands of Moab?"*
> *2 Kings 3:10 (NIV)*

When faced with a challenging situation, Joram whined and talked about defeat, desperation, and fear. On the other hand, Jehoshaphat was operating from a different place entirely; he was operating from faith, and his speech demonstrated it.

> *But Jehoshaphat asked, "Is there no prophet of the Lord here, through whom we may inquire of the Lord?"*
> *2 Kings 3:11 (NIV)*

While facing the same challenging situation, Joram and Jehoshaphat believed their current crisis had a spiritual, divine element. Joram believed God was to be avoided because of the crisis, while Jehoshaphat believed God should be sought. One operated as a spiritual pauper, while the other operated as a spiritual king.

> *An officer of the King of Israel answered, "Elisha son of Shaphat is here. He used to pour water on the hands of Elijah]." 12 Jehoshaphat said, "The word of the Lord is with him." So the King of Israel and Jehoshaphat and the King of Edom went down to him.*
> *2 Kings 3:11-12 (NIV)*

Elisha was Elijah's humble and practical servant. This service to Elijah prepared Elisha for further spiritual service and the legacy of Elijah, the great prophet. Jehoshaphat recognized the name of Elisha and was familiar with his exploits for the Lord, stating, "The word of the Lord is with him." This was also an act of humility by these three kings. Typically, kings demanded that others come to see them. These three were willing to go to the prophet.

When the three kings arrived at the camp of Elisha, the greeting they received was not exactly what they were expecting.

> *13 Elisha said to the King of Israel, "Why do you want to involve me? Go to the prophets of your father and the prophets of your mother." "No," the King of Israel answered, "because it was the Lord who called us three kings together to deliver us into the hands of Moab."*
> *2 Kings 3:13 (NIV)*

Elisha made it clear that he didn't want anything to do with Joram and was openly disgusted with him. Elisha sarcastically told Joram to go to the prophets of your mother! Elisha was referring to the 450 prophets of Baal that Joram's mother Jezebel brought with her from her country and how they were killing off the prophets of the Lord wherever they found them. Finally, there was a showdown at Mount Carmel with Elisha's mentor Elijah, who singlehandedly took on the 450 prophets to once and for all see which God was supreme. Elijah, with the power of the Lord, prevailed over the 450 prophets and their impotent gods when fire from heaven came down and licked up the entire sacrifice that had a trench dug, filled with water and everything, the trench, the altar, and the sacrifice saturated the fire consumed the sacrifice, all of the water, the wood, the stones, and the soil! Then Elijah had the 450 prophets executed, and for that, Jezebel put a bounty on the head of Elijah, which drove Elijah to hide out in a cave for forty days. Elisha was not going to accept the presence and request

of Joram, whose mother and father so relentlessly pursued and killed the prophets of the Lord and badgered his mentor so relentlessly. King Joram continued his pleading with Elisha with the same pitiful speech, which still wasn't convincing Elisha.

Elisha finally concedes to helping the three kings and explains why he would even consider helping.

> *14 Elisha said, "As surely as the Lord Almighty lives, whom I serve, if I did not have respect for the presence of Jehoshaphat king of Judah, I would not pay any attention to you.*
>
> *2 Kings 3:14*

Whoa! That is pretty straightforward. Elisha, in one statement, showcased the dichotomy of these two kings. Elisha had no respect, no sympathy, or no mercy for Joram. But on the other hand, he was honoring the presence of Jehoshaphat and his character as the reason he is not going to leave the whole army of Israel to be Moabite fodder!

Let's look at these two kings to see why Elisha is responding the way he is.

King Joram

- He came from a lineage beyond dysfunctional, his father being Ahab, arguably the worst King Israel has ever had. His mother was Jezebel, who could be considered even worse than Ahab.
- The book of 2 Kings describes Joram as one who did evil in the sight of the Lord, but not quite as bad as his father and mother.
- Joram was the ninth evil King of the Kingdom of Israel. He had done away with Baal worship but instituted a false worship of Yahweh as an idol of an Ox.

- In spiritual matters, he appears to have been undecided, neutral, in between, never seeming to take a stand or genuinely able to declare where he is concerning his faith. He removed the Baal idol of his father and mother but fell short in real belief or trust in the Lord God.
- Joram possibly put away Baal worship out of wrong motives due to fear of remembering the judgment against his father, Ahab, and his brother, Ahaziah. He wanted to impress Jehoshaphat, the Judean king, and enlist him in the coalition.

King Jehoshaphat

- Jehoshaphat was from the lineage of King David.
- He was pronounced King over Judah at 35, the fourth king of Judah.
- He was considered one of the most successful rulers of Judah because He followed God.
- He followed the steps of his father Asa, and Jehoshaphat and his father were two honorable kings who did not do evil in the sight of the Lord.
- He abolished idolatry and renewed the worship of the One True God.
- He strengthened the military of Judah by increasing the installations and forts and expanding the army's infrastructure.
- He solidified peace between Judah and Israel and built an alliance.
- The people and nation of Judah experienced a great measure of prosperity and blessings of God under the rule of Jehoshaphat.
- Jehoshaphat was known as a faithful follower of Yahweh.
- He was known for consulting God's prophets before making decisions.

- He was known for crediting and honoring God for every victory.
- He was a consistently victorious military leader.
- He was honored by other nations and was made wealthy from their tributes.
- He obeyed and followed the commands and will of God.
- He would not put anything ahead of God.
- He was unashamedly consistent in his reliance and dependence on God as the only way to rule over his Kingdom.

This is why Elisha responded the way he did towards Joram with contempt and disgust, why he had respect for the presence of Jehoshaphat, and why he was even convinced to help them get a word from the Lord.

> *15 "But now bring me a musician." Then it happened, when the musician played, that the hand of the Lord came upon him. 16 And he said, "Thus says the Lord: 'Make this valley full of ditches.' 17 For thus says the Lord: 'You shall not see wind, nor shall you see rain; yet that valley shall be filled with water, so that you, your cattle, and your animals may drink.' 18 And this is a simple matter in the sight of the Lord; He will also deliver the Moabites into your hand. 19 Also you shall attack every fortified city and every choice city, and shall cut down every good tree, and stop up every spring of water, and ruin every good piece of land with stones."*
> *2 Kings 3:15-19 (NKJV)*

For Elisha to quiet himself and be more attuned to the leading and voice of the Holy Spirit, he requested a harpist. This demonstrates the tremendous spiritual power of music. Elisha had to clear his mind, angered with holy anger at the sight of wicked Joram. Having the harpist play pulled his focus away from his circumstances. It refocused on the presence of God, and as the music soothed and refocused Elisha so that he could hear the still small voice of the Lord God, the Holy Spirit came upon him and gave him the prophetic message to speak to the three kings. Elisha then spoke to the kings and told them,

> *"You shall not see wind, nor shall you see rain; yet that valley shall be filled with water."*

This seemed a strange promise from God. The water would be provided without any apparent rain or storm, so the blessing of water would not come in the usual natural way. But it was intended to go through a miraculous event.

Then Elisha told them to,

"Make this valley full of ditches."

The Lord would miraculously fill the valley with water, but He required them to dig the ditches to accommodate His provision. By faith and the word of the Lord through the prophet, they were to dig the troughs before the water was available to demonstrate their faith and alignment with the Lord God when the provision came. A couple of points to consider: the three kings and their armies had made camp at the edge of a dry riverbed. So it begs the question, why didn't the Lord restore the dry riverbed to what it used to be? The riverbed was insufficient for the blessing the Lord wanted to bestow on the three kings. For them to contain the level of blessing the Lord would bring, they would have to create the space and infrastructure to hold it. The Lord won't perform an old miracle for a new mission.

I am sure when the three kings returned from visiting Elisha and then told their commanders to have the men dig ditches, that it was not well received by the severely thirsty, near-dead men in the middle of the desert being asked to begin the hard work of digging ditches in dry ground. But if they were to receive the blessing that the Lord spoke, they were expected to be active participants in receiving the blessing. The Lord will fill us to the level of our capacity.

> *"Let him who thirsts come unto Me and drink."*
> *John 7:37 (NIV)*

The more we thirst for the things of the Lord, and the more capacity we create, the more He will fill. In this case, with the three kings, the blessing the Lord was planning for them was not only to bless and save them from their circumstances but to bless them so that they could carry on with the mission that He had called them to. Many times, we ask for the Lord to bless us, to anoint us, to save us from the dire circumstances that we find ourselves in, and He may do that, but the Lord also will bless us so that we can progress on with the purpose that He has tasked us for.

If we have been brought up with and conditioned to be survivors, when we seek the Lord and the Lord responds to bless or anoint us, and He blesses us out of our difficult circumstances, then we are contented, no longer seek the Lord, and progress no further. But suppose we have had our minds renewed and our lives transformed to be and have a "Kings" mentality. In that case, we will prepare and expand our capacity for the blessing and use the overflow of that blessing to do greater and mightier exploits for the Lord to expand His Kingdom.

Elisha told the three kings to dig ditches to increase their capacity to contain the blessing, the anointing He was about to give them. The Lord commanded the three kings and their men to dig so that they would be partners in receiving the blessing. He needed them to expand their capacity in obedience, trust, and belief to operate in a new dimension of calling and mission.

The Lord used the desert, the dry place the three kings thought would kill them, as a platform to establish the conditioning necessary to increase their capacity to hear, understand, receive, and operate on a new level, a new dimension with Him.

> *18 And this is a simple matter in the sight of the Lord; He will also deliver the Moabites into your hand. 19 Also you shall attack every fortified city and every choice city, and shall cut down every good tree, and stop up every spring of water, and ruin every good piece of land with stones."*
>
> *2 Kings 3:18-19 (NIV)*

This is a simple matter in the sight of the LORD: The three kings approached Elisha for water. God wanted to fulfill more than their immediate need, more than immediate provision; He also wanted to give them complete victory over their enemies. When God blesses, He blesses to the full and to overflowing. He intended not only to guide the forces of nature so that the physical, practical needs of the armies would be supplied but also to crown their expedition with victory over their detractors, for they were so weakened and discouraged by the great drought that they had no hopes of proceeding in the offensive war and thought it sufficient, if it were possible, to defend themselves from the Moabites. They were in SURVIVAL mode! They needed to be in SUCCEDER mode. But the words that Elisha spoke are to be considered as a prediction of their success, encouraging and confirming to them that their victory should be so complete, that they should be so refreshed, anointed, and empowered to have the strength to lay the country of the Moabites to waste with fire and sword, as an easy thing. What an extravagant move of the Lord; they were expecting water and rescue from dying of thirst, but the Lord was providing a refreshing victory over their enemies!

> *20 Now it happened in the morning, when the grain offering was offered, that suddenly water came by way of Edom, and the land was filled with water. 21 And when all the Moabites heard that the kings had come up to fight against them, all who were able to bear arms and older were gathered, and they stood at the border. 22 Then they rose up early in the morning, and the sun was shining on the water, and the Moabites saw the water on the other side as red as blood. 23 And they said, "This is blood; the kings have surely struck swords and have killed one another; now therefore, Moab, to the spoil!" 24 So when they came to the camp of Israel, Israel rose up and attacked the Moabites, so that they fled before them; and they entered their land, killing the Moabites. 25 Then they destroyed the cities, and each man threw a stone on every good piece of land and filled it; and they stopped up all the springs of water and cut down all the good trees.*
>
> *2 Kings 3: 20-25 (NIV)*

The water, the blessing, and the anointing were available only because the three kings and their armies were obedient to digging the ditches. The ditches collected the water from the move of God. They would have never realized their blessing if they had disobeyed and didn't follow God's instructions to dig the trenches. They were instructed to prepare to receive His provision. God often moves us to do things that may or may not make much sense, but they will prepare us for what He will do in the future.

The availability of water directly correlated with their faith and obedience. The more of quantity and size of the trenches, the more water was provided. Though it was hard and unpleasant work, when they were at their thirstiest and most desperate state, the more they did, the more blessings they received.

The ditches themselves were not the blessing, and they were not the victory, but they were critical for both the blessing and the victory. When the Lord wants us to prepare for a provision and victory, the kings should understand that digging was not the provision. Without the miraculous grace of God, the trenches were worthless, and without the ditches, the expansion and blessing would have been circumvented.

Not only did their efforts capture the water, but they also kept their respective armies from dying of thirst. But it also confused and defeated their foe, the Moabites misunderstood the reflection on the water and thought it was blood from the three armies fighting each other. The Lord defeated the Moabites by providing the provision.

In this story, we see the examples of each significant character, the dichotomy of Joram and Jehoshaphat, and each person's behavior, character, mentality, and spiritual capacity. Joram is a survivor, a spiritual pauper, who does not trust the Lord and does not have the spiritual capacity to function as a KING. This has been passed down to him from his even more dysfunctional and evil parents.

Jehoshaphat, on the other hand, is well respected as a good and honorable KING, who is recognized by other nations, and all those who have interacted with Jehoshaphat, including Elisha, as a king who followed the commands of the Lord with his whole heart. He followed the example of his father, Asa, who was also a good king and not too far removed from King David, whom God called a man after his own heart. So, we see the things that hinder and make wrong, inadequate, and poor representatives of kingship in Joram. We also see an example of what makes an honorable, mature, spiritually sound, godly representative of kingship in Jehoshaphat.

The third character that we are introduced to is the prophet Elisha. He is the prophetic successor of the mighty prophet Elijah. Elisha benefited from the richness of his mentor's anointing, instruction, and, ultimately, a double portion of Elijah's Spirit. He knew then that he was to carry on the great work of Elijah, spread the knowledge of God, bring relief and blessing to his people, and teach them to be in the warning of the things of God.

Elisha picked up the mantle Elijah had cast off when he was ushered into heaven. He felt the Spirit of Elijah within him. God called this mighty prophet to perform extraordinary feats and bring stern and unwanted messages to God's rebellious people. Elisha served as the mediator between God and man and, in turn, between man and God. He was the spiritual connector and mediator. So, although Elisha was often in the presence of kings and royalty, he wasn't accountable to them but to God directly.

Elisha's anointing was so powerful that he did double the number of miracles as his mentor, Elijah. The legacy of the prophet Elijah was carried on through the prophet Elisha. What a great testament to the succession of the anointing and power they possessed to fulfill the calling of the Lord. What is sad, though, is that Elisha did not mentor his next successor. There was no one to pass the mantle- the anointing of Elijah onto to carry on the fantastic calling of these two prophets. The anointing was finished when Elisha died. The anointing on Elisha was so powerful and so impactful that it was still upon Elisha, even in his death.

> *20 Elisha died and was buried. Now Moabite raiders used to enter the country every spring. 21 Once while some Israelites were burying a man, suddenly they saw a band of raiders; so they threw the man's body into Elisha's tomb. When the body touched Elisha's bones, the man came to life and stood up on his feet.*
> *2 Kings 13:21 (NIV)*

This points to the fact that Elisha's anointing on his life was not finished. Even the bones of Elisha contained such an anointing that when a dead man was inadvertently thrown into the same tomb and his dead body touched the dead bones of Elisha; it brought the man back to life. The anointing wasn't finished, but there was no one to pick up the mantle of Elisha to carry on the calling. Elijah's and Elisha's calling and ministry died with Elisha. There was no one that Elisha groomed to become his successor.

Through this story, we see the call of each office, the "King" and the "Priest," and we have been shown examples of honor and dishonor. We must take the lessons from this story and ensure we account for it in our calling of...

> *But you are a chosen people, a royal priesthood, a holy nation, God's special possession, that you may declare the praises of him who called you out of darkness into his wonderful light. 10 Once you were not a people, but now you are the people of God; once you had not received mercy, but now you have received.*
> *1 Peter 29-10*

Chapter 15

Get Your Provisions Ready!

In this chapter, we are finally getting ready to explore the **doing** of our mission He has for us after the process of **becoming** the vessel He needs. As human beings, our nature is TO DO. DOING equals PROGRESS; if necessary, we will usually figure it out as we go. As we have learned through exploring the previous chapters of this book, though, inadvertent **doing** is a principle of the world- of this fallen skewed kingdom. When we just set off on our own, we are, in effect, telling the Lord- "I am going to do this; I need You to either to- stop me if You don't want me to DO it- or make it all work out." We are asking the Lord to align with our agendas, goals, and purposes, we are asking the **Lord of the Universe** to follow us. But since our journey through this book, we have had our minds renewed to understand that God's ways are not our ways, and we are to follow Him! He will lead the way.

Up to this point in the previous chapters, the premise of the **Expose-Destroy-Heal-Replace** journey has been about becoming. It has been renewing our minds and transforming our lives to become the vessel the Lord needs to be able to use us for the mission He has for us. It has been about understanding who God is, who we are, and what is our purpose. It is recognizing what the world and the devil have conditioned us into and what the Lord is endeavoring to **Expose- Destroying- Healing- Replacing** what we were created to be, His children, and for ruling and reigning with Him. Now that we have trekked through the principles of this ongoing process of renewing our minds and transforming our lives to align with Him, it is time to.

TO GET OUR PROVISIONS READY!

We begin this process at the base of Mount Nebo, in the plains of Moab on the east side of the banks of the Jordan River. We are going to listen in on a man's journey into a handover of leadership.

All of Israel has been weeping and mourning these last thirty days. Moses, the Great servant of the Lord God, climbed up the mountain to die as the Lord God commanded him. The nation has been mourning the loss of someone who has become so paramount and a part of our lives that it's inconceivable that he is no longer with us, and we will no longer hear his voice! The Lord had decreed that Moses would not be the one to lead us across the Jordan River, that he would die on Mount Nebo, and that I would be given the daunting task of succeeding Moses and being the one who would lead the nation across the Jordan and to receive the land that was promised to our forefathers.

Before Moses ascended the mountain, the Lord had Moses speak to all the people to remind and prepare us for when we cross over the Jordan. Moses instructed us not to forget how God brought us out of Egypt and parted the Red Sea. How we walked across dry ground to escape the enemy, and then the Lord closed the waters upon Pharaoh and his army and

destroyed our enemies so that we no longer had to fear them. The Lord sustained and led us through the wilderness with our clothes never wearing out, manna every morning, and water from the rock to quench our thirst. How the Lord was with us when we defeated the Kings Sihon and Og, who came out against us and once defeated, the Lord gave their lands to us; to the tribes of the Gadites, the Reubenites, and the half-tribe of Manasseh. We were also warned that the consequences if we departed and turned away from the Lord God and bowed to other gods, He would turn His face from us and allow us to be destroyed by our enemies.

Then Moses brought me up before Eleazar, the High Priest, and the assembled nation of Israel and announced to the people that the Lord had forbidden Moses to go into the promised land. I could hear the collective groanings of sorrow and disappointment throughout the assembly. Still, Moses pressed on and explained that it was because he had broken faith with the Lord in the presence of the people at the waters of Meribah Kadesh in the Desert of Zin and did not uphold the Holiness of the Lord to the people. Therefore, the Lord God Himself will lead us across the Jordan, and I, Joshua, have been appointed to succeed Moses as the Lord's servant to lead them. More confused murmurs and groanings from the assembly ensued, me included. But Moses, ever being the leader, the shepherd, the comforter over us, raised his hands to quiet the people and then told us to be strong and courageous, not to be afraid of our enemies or fear being abandoned. That the Lord God goes before us and is with us; He will never leave us or forsake us!

Then Moses had me stand beside him and spoke to me in the presence of Eleazar the High Priest and all Israel and told me that I am to be strong and courageous and that I must lead the people into the land that was promised to our ancestors Abraham, Isaac, and Jacob that the Lord promised to them. I must divide the land to the tribes as their inheritance according to this promise. Then Moses laid his hands upon me, looked into my eyes, with tears in his eyes but also with strength and the Spirit of the Lord in them, and told me, "The Lord will never leave ME and will never forsake ME," and he shook me for emphasis and told me, "Do not be afraid! Do not be discouraged!" I then felt a power flow out of Moses and into me with such intense energy that it filled me from the top of my head to the soles of my feet until I was tingling all over and trembling with an overwhelming presence so strong that I fell to my knees. Then Moses explained that some of his authority and the Spirit of wisdom he possessed had been passed down to me so that the Israelites would obey me. I have received some of the "Glory" the Lord showed Moses.

Now that Moses is gone, I cannot conceive that I am worthy or ready to lead these people. Moses has always led us. These last thirty days of mourning with the rest of the people, I remembered the great servant of God, Moses, and the journey of the previous forty years. No one has been like Moses; his story and destiny amaze me beyond words to this day. During the thirty days of mourning, we would sit around the fires throughout the camp. I would tell the stories of Moses, how he was born a Hebrew during the time of Pharaoh's decree to kill all of the Hebrew males who were children by throwing them into the Nile to drown, how Moses was hidden in a reed basket that floated up to where Pharaoh's daughter was bathing. She found him and had favor for the child, took him as her own, and raised him as an Egyptian prince.

I would tell of the time when Moses, who now was an Egyptian Prince at forty years old, wanted to see his people, the Hebrews, and found the harshness of their circumstances and witnessed an Egyptian beating one of the Hebrew slaves. How, when no one was looking, Moses murdered the Egyptian. Then, fearing he would be found out, he fled from Egypt to the back side of the desert to Midian to hide and was there for forty years, living with the Shepherd and Priest Jethro, who became his father-in-law, tending Jethro's flocks and raising a family.

I would tell how Moses when shepherding his father-in-law's flocks near Mount Horeb, the mountain of God, encountered the Lord God in the burning bush that would never burn up. The Lord God spoke from the burning bush and told Moses to remove his sandals, for he was standing on holy ground. There, the Lord God called Moses to go to Egypt and Pharaoh, that Moses was to bring the Israelites out of Egypt. Then, the Lord performed extraordinary signs through Moses using his shepherd's staff or rod and brought the ten plagues onto Pharaoh and the Egyptians.

The first plague turned the Nile River into blood, which lasted seven days and became a dreadful stench in the land. The second plague was the plague of frogs. The frogs invaded everything:

- The palace.
- The Egyptian officials' homes.
- The Egyptian people's homes.
- The Hebrews' homes.
- All the food stores.

They were everywhere. The frogs soon died and were gathered into heaps, and the land had a dreadful stench.

The third plague was the plague of gnats. The Lord turned the dust of the land to gnats, and they swarmed everywhere and over every person and animal; everything was covered with gnats. I explained how I remembered how the gnats would cover my whole body and get into my eyes, nose, and mouth. My family was so irritated by them that they begged the elders to request Moses to appeal to the Lord God to end the plague. Finally and thankfully, through the cries of the Hebrews,

Pharaoh, and Egyptians, the Lord sent the gnats away upon Moses' request. Both nations experienced these first three plagues: the Egyptians and the Israelites.

Then the Lord brought the fourth plague, swarms of flies even more numerous than the gnats. But the Lord instructed Moses to tell Pharaoh and the Hebrews that this time, the Lord would treat the Land of Goshen differently where the Israelites lived. In Goshen, there will be no swarms of flies, and the Lord will distinguish between the Lord's people and the Egyptians, and it was so; the flies swarmed the Egyptians and did not affect Goshen. I explained at the fireside that at a much later time, while we were in the wilderness, I asked Moses why the Israelites had to experience the first three plagues. Moses explained that the trials of these first three plagues forced both nations to turn their eyes to the Lord God to appeal for relief. The purpose of this for the Israelites was to teach us after 430 years of slavery and the conditioning of the Egyptian ways, behaviors, beliefs, mannerisms, and culture, the plagues were a disruptive shift for the Hebrews. It forced the Israelites to begin turning away from Egypt, Pharoah, and the Egyptian gods who could not stop the plagues, and to seek and believe in the Lord God for their relief and deliverance.

The fifth plague was the killing of all of the livestock in Egypt. All of the animals in Egypt, their cattle, horses, donkeys, and camels died, but no animals died in Goshen. I explained that I remember seeing Pharaoh coming into the land of Goshen and seeing for himself how all the animals of Goshen were alive and well and how frustrated he became. However, Pharaoh still refused to free the Israelites so they could go and worship the Lord God. The sixth plague was of boils. The Lord instructed Moses to gather ashes from the furnace and throw them into the air, and fine dust would cover the land of Egypt, and festering boils broke out on all the Egyptians.

For the next set of plagues, the Lord had Moses tell Pharaoh that the coming plagues would be more severe than the previous plagues and would come with such force that had never been seen before over all the earth. But Pharaoh continued to resist and would not release us, so the Lord brought the worst hailstorm ever since the beginning of the Egyptian empire. The storm was very intense, with large, insistent hail, fire, and lightning. The hail destroyed anything left out in the open; all of the crops and trees were stripped bare, and all of the ripened barley and flax were damaged. The wheat and spelt were spared because they had not grown to fullness yet. But the land of Goshen did not receive any hail or lightning.

The eighth plague was locusts. The Lord brought in swarms of locusts so thick that the ground was black. They ate every plant left over after the hail, the wheat and spelt, and every tree of its greenery or fruit until no crops were left in Egypt. The Egyptian land was ruined, and so was their economy due to the severity of the plagues. There would be no harvest of any kind in Egypt.

The ninth plague was of darkness. The Lord brought darkness to the land of Egypt. It was a darkness that was so intense it could be felt and lasted for three days. No light could be seen in Egypt; the Egyptians stayed put for fear of getting lost or hurt. But in Goshen, there was light. When all of these plagues had been completed, Pharaoh still would not release the Israelites to go to and worship the Lord.

The Lord had one more plague for Egypt. The Lord told Moses that the Pharaoh would drive the Israelites out entirely after this final plague. When he did, the Lord told Moses to instruct the Hebrews to ask the Egyptians for silver and gold articles, which they would freely give to us. This tenth plague was to kill all the firstborns of the Egyptian people. The Lord had Moses instruct all of us Israelites on what we must do to protect the Hebrew's firstborn; and became the first Passover.

For all of the other plagues, the Lord didn't require anything from the Israelites other than to look to Him, believe and trust in Him, and He would protect us. But for this last plague, the Lord required our participation.

I remember that I went out to pick the lamb as Moses had instructed. We picked one that had no bad spots and was healthy and took it back to our home. I carried it the entire way home; I would not let the lamb get dirty or hurt, as the lamb needed to stay perfect. The night of the plague, I killed our new lamb, which broke all of our hearts. It was late, but I made us all get dressed and ready to travel; I mixed the lamb's blood with hyssop, took a small broom, and smeared the blood on the two sides and over the mantle of our doorway as Moses had instructed. We then roasted the lamb along with the other ingredients Moses commanded, bitter herbs and bread with no yeast, and made us eat everything until it was all consumed as Moses had instructed.

It was midnight, and we were all dressed and prepared to travel. We were all getting sleepy and wanted to lie down, but I ensured everyone stayed awake. Then, a hush fell over our home; we all felt a heavy, ominous presence surrounding our dwelling that was pressing down upon us. I reached out and pulled the family towards me closely and tightly. The presence caused the air to chill and made us all hold our breaths, and my blood ran cold inside me. My family began whimpering; I could feel their tears falling onto my cheek. I started to tear up, and my grip tightened; I was pleading under my breath for YHWH to have this presence pass us over. The presence pressed more intensely, and I felt my breath catch. But then it subsided and left us. Death had passed over us. We all let out a collective sigh; we were all so relieved, but I felt myself trembling from the aftereffects.

We were saved, but we began to hear the screams and wails piercing the night throughout Egypt! Their firstborn sons were

not so fortunate. "The Lord is true to His Word," I said, "For the Israelites, he spared our sons, like He said He would..." I paused for a few seconds and then finished, "For the Egyptians, he took their sons... Like He said, He would."

The sun was peeking over the horizon, and all Hebrews were gathering. Earlier that night, Pharaoh had summoned Moses and was told to have the Israelites leave Egypt. So, we began the procession of over a million people walking out of Goshen and Egypt. As we were leaving, the Egyptians were urging us to go quickly so that no one else would die! I watched in amazement as the Egyptians gave us their jewelry, silver and gold. Each of our family members had so much to carry that we kept dropping items; those following behind us would pick them up.

Moses explained that the Lord would lead us out of Egypt with a cloud by day and a pillar of fire by night. We followed the cloud and pillar through the desert until we reached the Red Sea. As the Sea surrounded us, we heard a great commotion behind us on the backside of the camp. We saw in the distance a vast dust cloud trailing towards us and realized that it was Pharaoh's entire army on horses and with a multitude of chariots pursuing hard after us. The people began to panic; you could hear throughout the camp yelling and complaining to Moses that we should have stayed in Egypt and that it would have been better for us to serve the Egyptians than to die out in the desert. Moses comforted the people, "Do not be afraid... and to stand firm.... and they shall see the deliverance of the Lord."

Moses then stood on the edge of the Sea and stretched out his hand and rod over the Sea, and the Lord brought a strong east wind which drove the Sea back, divided the waters, and we were able to walk on dry ground through the Sea with walls of water on our right and left sides. During this time, we could see the Angel of the Lord holding back Pharaoh's army with the cloud of darkness. The cloud finally lifted, and the Egyptian army pursued us, chasing after us through the Red Sea. They were well into the channel while all of us Israelites made it through on the opposite shore. Moses stretched out his rod again, and the sea waters went back to their place, covering and drowning the entire Egyptian army!

I couldn't take my eyes off the Sea; I was awestruck! As I stared out over the waters, I could see hundreds and even thousands of soldiers floating on the surface, eventually washing up on the shore. I had never seen so many dead bodies before. My friend Caleb came and stood beside me. He put his hand on my shoulder, and I looked at him.

"We have seen the Mighty hand of the Lord this day," he said. "The God of Abraham, Isaac, and Jacob has caused the plagues to come to pass just as He declared they would. He caused death to pass over us like He said it would. The Lord lead us out of Egypt and through the desert to the Red Sea with a cloud by day and a pillar of fire by night. Then, with our backs against the Sea and Pharaoh's army in full pursuit, the Lord made a highway for us to pass through. Then, the Lord annihilates our enemy in one moment by closing the Sea over Pharaoh's entire army so we will never see them again. Oh, what a mighty God we serve! Praise Adonai and his servant Moses!"

Over the years, as Moses was mentoring me, I would ask him so I would understand the deep reasons why the Lord delivered the Israelites the way that He did. I wasn't challenging or questioning God; I just wanted to understand the Ways of God better. Moses would explain to me that the Hebrews had been slaves for 430 years. We had become so disenchanted with our state of affairs that we had lost hope, and to this point, we doubted the Lord could break the stronghold of the bondage of Pharaoh, his army, or the many gods of Egypt. We had become so indoctrinated in their culture, in their ways, that we had come to believe in the superiority and strength of their many gods who seemed more able to hold us captive than in our belief that the One True God of Israel could deliver us.

So when God sent Moses to deliver the message to Pharaoh to let the Israelites go, he also brought the message to the Israelites that now is the appointed time, which had been prophesied to Abraham, that his descendants who would be slaves to Egypt for 430 years, but would be brought out with great possessions. I thought, how precise is the Lord in all He prophesies? He foretold this exact moment 430 years earlier.

Moses explained that the Lord had him bring the message to the Hebrews to confirm that the God of Abraham, Isaac, and Jacob, the One True God of Israel, is here and keeps His promises. He is worthy to be worshipped, trusted, and able to deliver us and show us that Pharaoh, Egypt, and all the other nations- that their armies and gods are no match to resist Him! The event of the plagues, for the Hebrew people, demonstrated to us that we can have faith and trust in the Lord God to deliver us over our fear of oppression of Pharoah, his armies, and their gods.

I then asked Moses why the Lord led us to the Red Sea and caused Pharaoh to pursue us when He could have easily led us on another route that wouldn't have trapped us. Moses explained that the Lord decided not to take the quicker and more manageable path through the country of the Philistines. Even though it had accessible roads and was a trade route where food and water could be bought, the all-knowing Jehovah perceived that if we came up to resistance by the Philistines and had to face war against them, in our fragile emotional state, we might have changed our minds and returned to Egypt.

Moses said the Lord spoke to him, saying, "The Israelites are to camp by the sea so that we appear to be wandering around the land in confusion, hemmed in by the desert.' And I will harden Pharaoh's heart, and he will pursue them. But I will gain glory through Pharaoh and all his army, and the Egyptians will know I am the Lord."

Not one Egyptian survived because the Lord closed the Sea over the them and their chariots, the horsemen, and the entire army. That day, the Lord saved the Hebrews from the hands of the Egyptians, and when we saw with our own eyes the Egyptians lying dead on the shore, we saw the mighty hand of the Lord displayed against the Egyptians. That day, we then feared the Lord and put our trust in the Lord God and Moses, his servant.

As I reminisced around the fires during the grieving time, I could see that the Passover and the miracle of the Red Sea were linked together. If not for the victory at the Red Sea, the redemption at Passover would have been for nothing. But we would have never made it to the Red Sea without the miracle of God's redemption at Passover. The two works of deliverance went hand in hand.

Through the Passover, we experienced the deliverance from the judgment of God against us as by the lamb's blood. But as we experience this event of Passover, God was still on the outside and separated from us in Egypt. But the Passover brought us peace as we were sheltered under the covering of the blood, feeding on the Lamb, as we prepared to leave Egypt. The foundation of all God's deliverance on our behalf was based on the lamb's blood.

On the journey to the crossing through the Red Sea, we experienced a symbolic cleansing of a nation. By these events, God was now with us in the pillar and cloud. The pillar and cloud gave us direction and protection by initially dividing the Israelites from the Egyptians. On our side, it was a light even at night, but to the Egyptians, it was a cloud and darkness, even during the day. Now, God, instead of being against us, is for us. Our access to Him was made good in judgment against us through the Passover and has redeemed us, His people, back to Himself. He has been glorified through the Red Sea through Pharaoh and all his hosts! So, just as everything that would typically be against us, the rod, the cloud, the fire, the waters, and death have all become the means of our deliverance because Jehovah is now for us!

The events of Passover and the crossing through the Red Sea confirmed that our deliverance from Egypt was absolute and complete. As an oppressed people, it would be difficult to believe that we were genuinely free while our tyrants still lived. The Lord God wanted us to know that our oppressors were dead. The Lord also exalted Moses through the Red Sea event. By the Lord using Moses as His instrument and Moses raising his rod, it showed us that Moses was indeed the servant of God and not the enemy of Israel. This was God's vindication of Moses. We had previously accused him while in Egypt of the lowest of intentions and a deceiving heart by accusing him of bringing us out of Egypt so that we could die in the desert! By performing these works through Moses, God showed the nation of Israel that Moses was our chosen leader. This we must never forget.

Now, after thirty days of mourning the great servant of God, Moses, I find myself standing on the edge of the Jordan River just as the sun was coming up in the cool of the spring morning. I was looking down and watching the water occasionally lap up over my sandaled feet. There was a chill in the air, and it smelled clean and cool with the mist hovering over the rushing water as it flowed down from the mountains. The spring rains had caused the river to overflow its banks, and the current was strong as it coursed through its channel. Looking across the river, I could make out the edge on the other side of the river in the predawn light. Further up the embankment on the top of the cliffs, I could barely make out the top of the gate of the walls of the city of Jericho overlooking the river as there was just enough light.

I turned my gaze away from the river to my old companion Caleb, who now stood next to me. "I don't remember this much water and the banks overflowing like this," he observed. The river was flooding, with three times more water flowing than when we were here 40 years ago. We both looked out over the water to the distant shore and were quiet for a few minutes, deep in our thoughts. We have been through so much together. We are two men standing on the banks of a river, but that is not all we are standing next to. We are also two men standing on the edge of two environments, two dimensions, two eras, two generations, two worlds, and so much more; we are standing at the edge of a proverbial portal that has been a journey of forty years in the making.

On one side of the river, the East side, the side we are standing on, is the desert. It is a wilderness, barren with extreme temperatures during the day and frigid temperatures at night, with water so scarce that few plants or creatures, let alone human beings, can live there. On the other side of the river, the West side is a lush, abundant land full of crops and fruit trees, cattle, grassland, mild temperatures, cities, and towns throughout the land, with wells of water in each town available for any who desire to quench their thirst, all the way to the Sea.

We are two men who have seen and experienced both worlds. An experience no other man from our nation has ever experienced, at least during our lifetime. We had been here 40 years before as spies along with ten other men. Based on our findings from exploring the west side of the river for 40 days, we found it so abundant, lush, and fruitful that we even brought back huge samples to show off the abundance of the land. But even though my friend Caleb and I gave a good report describing that the land is everything we had been led to believe and more and that we could possess it through our faith in the Lord God to bring it about! The other ten men sabotaged the whole outcome of the expedition with their fear! They reported that the inhabitants in the region were too strong, too mighty, and too numerous to overcome! They spread their report and fear throughout the camps, and eventually, the entire nation was convinced that even with all the victories and breakthroughs that we had seen and experienced through the hand of our Lord God, there was no way to prevail. So, sadly, the opportunity was missed, and we were incarcerated for 40 years of wandering, for the Lord could not trust and would not allow this unbelieving generation to cross over.

I can remember this event as if it were yesterday. The people were in total rebellion, grumbling and crying out their sad mantra, "If only we had died in Egypt or this wilderness!" They conspired to choose another leader to take them back to Egypt. Moses and Aaron fell on the ground on their faces to intercede to the Lord on behalf of the nation's rebellion so that He might not wipe us off the face of the earth in judgment!

The Lord told Moses that the Lord had forgiven them, but that not one of them who saw His glory and the signs He performed in Egypt and the wilderness, who disobeyed Him and tested Him these **ten times**... will ever see the land that He promised as an oath to their ancestors. But then the Lord said that because Caleb has a distinct spirit and follows the Lord wholeheartedly, He will be allowed to enter the land, and Joshua will be allowed to enter the land. Then the Lord declared that anyone of this generation, other than Caleb or myself, that was twenty years old or older would die in the wilderness, per the very words that they repeatedly had said. Their children were destined to wander in the wilderness for forty years until all of the first generation died- one year for each of the forty days the land was explored.

After this event, I later asked Moses what the Lord meant when He said that this nation had tested Him these ten times. When were the ten times, and what were the offenses? Moses explained to me that the ten tests the Lord referred to were.

1. When we, the Israelites, were trapped between Pharaoh's army behind us and the Red Sea in front of us, the people cried out to the Lord and even complained to me, saying, Have you led us into the wilderness to die because there are no graves in Egypt? The Lord heard their complaints, but He parted the Red Sea, and we crossed over on dry ground.
2. After the Israelites had been in the Wilderness of Shur for three days without finding water, we came to Marah. Marah had water but was so bitter that no one could drink it. So, the people complained against Me again. The Lord heard their complaints again, but still, the Lord showed me a tree that, and when I cut a branch and cast into Marah's bitter waters, it was made sweet.
3. On day 15 of the second month, after we departed from Egypt, the Israelites grew hungry and complained against me and my brother Aaron, complaining that we would be like the Lord. We stayed in Egypt; we sat by kettles of meat and ate bread to the full. Now, we are in this wilderness to kill us all with starvation. The Lord heard their complaints, but still, the Lord began sending manna every morning except the weekly Sabbath morning.
4. When God sends the Israelites manna to eat every morning, I warn them against saving some of their daily portions and eating them the next day. Even with the warning, however, some try it and learn that the manna draws insects and spoils if left overnight. The Lord saw this disobedience, but still, despite their blatant attempts

to break the rules the Lord commanded concerning the manna, He continued sending it.

5. Also, concerning the gathering of the manna, I tell them to gather double for the morning before each Sabbath because God won't send the manna on the Sabbath. Still, even though the Sabbath is to be a day of rest, some Israelites gather manna. Of course, they find none. The Lord saw this disobedience, but still, despite their blatant attempts to break the rules the Lord commanded concerning the manna, He continued sending it.
6. When the Israelites came to Rephidim, they complained because there was no water. They complained to me, Why have you led us out of Egypt? Was it to kill our children, livestock, and ourselves with thirst?" Their complaints were severe enough that I thought they would stone me! The Lord heard their complaints and saw their disobedience. Still, the Lord had me strike a particular rock with my staff, after which water rushed.
7. When we were all encamped at the base of Mount Sinai, I went up into the mountain to be alone with God and receive revelation. I am gone for 40 days, and the people assume I will never return. So they, with the help of my brother Aaron, created a golden calf to serve as their new God. They worship it and offer sacrifices to it. The Lord saw their disobedience and told me what was happening in the Israelite camp. Again, He agrees to show the nation mercy. There was punishment, though; the Lord destroyed them when 3000 men stood up to revolt. The rest of the nation, He had me grind the golden calf to dust and had us mix it with water and drink it as a punishment.
8. In the second year, three days after we departed from Mount Sinai, the Israelites complained again. The people are grumbling and complaining concerning the hardships

of living in the desert in the hearing of the Lord, and their complaints were infuriating enough to the Lord to cause Him to burn some of the people to death with fire. With His patience growing short, He kills a small portion of the people as a warning rather than the entirety.

9. Shortly after the killing by fire, the Israelites complained again about not having enough food. This time, they are sick of eating the manna and long for Egypt's fish, cucumbers, melons, leeks, onions, and garlic. The Lord hears their complaints, but still, He brings an enormous coveys of quail into Hebrew's camp to be eaten for food so that they would have their meat, but He punishes a number of them to death by way of plague.
10. When Hebrew's twelve spies return from studying the land of Canaan, ten of the spies tell the people that Canaan is a land of giants that devour those who try to inhabit it. This caused the people to complain against me and my brother Aaron, saying, "If only we had died in the desert or Egypt. Why were we brought to this land to die by the sword and watch our wives and children become orphans? Wouldn't it be better if we all just returned to Egypt?" Then, the people started planning to select a new leader who would lead them back to Egypt. The Lord hears their complaints and sees their disobedience. The Lord tells me that the Israelites will wander in the wilderness for 40 years. During this time, every Israelite 20 years old or older (except for you, Joshua, and Caleb) will die over time so that the Hebrew's second generation can eventually conquer and settle Canaan.

Moses goes on to explain to me that the first generation had been delivered out of Egypt and out of slavery, and while in the desert, the Lord God was conditioning the Israelites so that they could go forth and possess the promised land. We had been set free, reordered, re-established from slaves of Egypt and of Pharaoh to be the chosen people of God called to inherit the land promised to our ancestors. We had been cleansed, purified, set apart, blessed, and taught in the ways of God in the wilderness. We had been given the Ten Commandments and the Law to ensure our obedience and diligence as His chosen people, with a new government, a new priesthood, and an orderly way to sacrifice and worship Him. We were taught to remember judgment spared and deliverance achieved, and we have now been prepared for possession. We had experienced the Lord God's presence and provision, and He guided us to follow into prosperity, success, and promise.

Yet our unbelief prevented an otherwise prepared people from receiving God's promise. We could not become the vessel He needed for the next dimension He had for us- **Promise possessors**. During our time in the wilderness, the Lord would test our faith to see if it would overcome our fear. We need to see if, when the pressure was on, we, the Israelites, operated in faith, believing and trusting the Lord to deliver before we received the deliverance. To be able to live by faith and not by sight. In each instance, instead of honoring God for each miraculous miracle performed and progressively believing and building faith from each experience, we were dishonoring God by gradually responding with increasing grumbling, complaining, disobedience, unbelief, and dishonor. This culminated in ten times that we failed and tested the patience of the Lord and refused to honor and magnify him. In Hebrew, the significance of the number ten is the number of fulfillments, so the first generation's level of unbelief and dishonor was deemed complete and absolute, as tested ten times. Therefore, the Lord judged the first generation that we demonstrated were not able or worthy to become the possessors of the promise, and this privilege would be passed down to the second generation for them to prove that they can become the possessor generation. How sad.

I broke from my reverie and asked my old friend, Caleb, "Are the people ready to break camp?"

Caleb also returned from his thoughts and responded, "Yes, they should be ready and lined up to move the camp from the base of Mount Nebo to the edge of the Jordan. We await your instructions. I will go and do a last-minute walk-through and instruct the leaders."

As my old companion set off to ensure the logistics of the camp, I couldn't shake the feeling that even though this moment, which had been prophesied, promised, and the destiny for our people was just on the other side of this river, the immensity of the moment and my role in it was overwhelming me!

Then, all of a sudden, I heard a voice I had never heard before. It seemed inside my head, but I could hear it audibly. I began to look around to see who was speaking to me, but I saw no one. Then I heard the voice again, "Moses, my servant, is dead." A chill went down my spine! This could only be the voice of one person, but not a person. This was the voice of Jehovah! I listened more intently; the voice was still and quiet, barely above a whisper. I heard it again, "Moses, my servant is dead." I took off my sandals, got down on my knees, and responded, quivering, "Yes, Lord."

Then the Lord spoke again, "Now then, you and all these people, get ready to cross the Jordan River into the land I am about to give them- to the Israelites. As I promised Moses, I will give you every place where you set your foot. Your territory will extend from the desert to Lebanon and from the great river, the Euphrates- all the Hittite country- to the Mediterranean Sea in the west. No one can stand against you all the days of your life. As I was with Moses so that I will be with you; I will never leave you nor forsake you."

My breathing was rapid; tears began rolling down my face. The Lord God, who spoke to Moses, is now talking to me. I could hear the echo of the voice of Moses when Moses spoke to me and told me that the Lord would never leave me nor forsake me with his hands on my shoulders, shaking them for emphasis, and now I am hearing these exact words from the Lord God Himself. No longer will I listen to the voice of Moses to instruct, mentor, or lead me... for as the Lord said- Moses is dead. From this point forward, it will be the voice of Jehovah that will instruct me, mentor me, and lead me. I could feel the weight of the responsibility to lead this nation across the Jordan and into the promised land and the weight of the tasks ahead of possessing and taking the land.

Forty years before, I had spied out this land of abundance with my own eyes, me and eleven other men. The land was full of inhabitants who were numerous, strong, well-organized, and well-equipped to defend against any campaigns against them. At the young age of 40, I was confident in my strength and ability for combat, but now, forty years later, I am an 80-year-old man chosen to lead this nation to conquer and take back what the Lord had given to our ancestors. My confidence is not quite as ambitious as it had once been.

The Lord told me again, "Be strong and courageous because you will lead these people to inherit the land I swore to their ancestors to give them. Be strong and very courageous. Be careful to obey all the law my servant Moses gave you; do not turn from it to the right or the left, that you may be successful wherever you go. Keep this Book of the Law always on your lips; meditate on it day and night so that you may be careful to do everything written in it. Then, you will be prosperous. Have I not commanded you? Be strong and courageous. Do not be afraid; do not be discouraged, for the Lord your God will be with you wherever you go." I almost felt the Lord shaking my shoulders for emphasis as Moses had; He is now *MY* God and will be with *ME* wherever *I* go! Then, the Lord gave me detailed instructions on how to prepare to cross the Jordan.

Later that evening, I could hear the arrival of the people and the setting up of their camps near the river. Everyone was gathering along the banks to see the water. It was quite an impressive amount of water in its flood state, and for a nation that has only known the desert for the last 40 years, it was a stunning curiosity. The children ran up and down the river's edge, splashing and frolicking. The animals could smell the water from quite a ways off and were gathered on the banks, their nuzzles in the water, taking long drinks. Many of the adults were staring out at the water, watching their children and livestock enjoying the river, and sneaking glances of the city of Jericho high up on the opposite cliff with its high walls staring back.

My old friend Caleb found me and approached me, "Shalom Joshua, the people are setting up camp according to the tribes. They should be settled in for the night in a couple of hours, in time for the sun to go down," he reported.

"Shalom, my old friend, thank you," I replied. "When the camps are set, I want to gather the officers of each tribe in my tent. I have instructions I want to pass on."

"You heard from the Lord?" he asked.

"Yes, Caleb," I acknowledged with an air of restlessness.

"How was it? How did you hear Him? You look wonder-struck," he questioned.

"Yes, Caleb, it was a little overwhelming. I am still trying to recover but ready to serve Him and lead our people." I assured him.

"Of course," he said, touching my shoulder. "I will bring the men to your tent when the camps are set."

"Thank you, my friend," I said. Caleb went to attend to the settling of the people.

A couple of hours later, as the sun set, I had a big fire outside my tent. I could hear the officers meandering towards me. "Shalom!" they called out one by one.

"Shalom," I would respond to each as they gathered near the fire. Caleb must have spread the word because all of the officers were questioning,

"Joshua, have you heard from the Lord?" "What did He sound like?" "Were you afraid?"

I raised my hands to quiet the group and addressed them, "Shalom men, I trust that you have all gotten your families and tribes settled in for the night?" They all responded that all was good. "Good," I said, "For I have instructions from the Lord." I paused a minute and then continued. "Go through the camp and tell the people, 'Get your provisions ready.... Three days from now, you will cross the Jordan here to go in and take possession of the land the Lord your God is giving you for your own.'" The men excitedly began shaking their fists in the air and grunting satisfaction.

As they quieted, I had Caleb bring forward the officers for the tribes of Reubenites, the Gadites, and the half-tribe of Manasseh and spoke to them, "Remember the command that Moses the servant of the Lord gave you after he said, 'The Lord your God will give you rest by giving you this land. Your wives, children, and livestock may stay in the land Moses gave you east of the Jordan, but all your fighting men, ready for battle, must cross over ahead of your fellow Israelites. You are to help them until the Lord gives them rest, as he has done for you, and until they, too, have taken possession of the land the Lord you are giving them. After that, you may go back and occupy your own land, which Moses, the servant of the Lord, gave you east of the Jordan toward the sunrise."

There was a quiet hush over the gathering, and the officers over the tribes of the Reubenites, the Gadites, and the half-tribe of Manasseh conferred among themselves for several minutes. After a while, Caleb and I looked at each other with concern. Were they going to be obedient to Moses' and the Lords' commands, or would they rebel? If there was rebellion, we may never enter the land, and the Lord may send a plague upon us. Caleb and I looked at each other again; then, we saw the three tribes finishing their conversation and turning to answer me.

One of the officers spoke for the three tribes, "Whatever you have commanded us, we will do, and wherever you send us, we will go. Just as we fully obeyed Moses, so we will obey you." Caleb and I looked at each other with relief, and I said a silent prayer of gratitude. The gathering lifted their hands in the air and shouted their acknowledgment. When the shouting calmed, the officer went on to say, "Whoever rebels against your word and does not obey it, whatever you may command them, will be put to death....," and the Officer looked directly at me and stated, "Only be strong and courageous!" Everyone in the group raised their hands, including Caleb and myself, and were chanting, "Yahweh! Yahweh! Yahweh!"

After all the men returned to their camps, I had Caleb bring two men to me. I had them cross the river to look over the land, especially Jericho, and to report back to me in three days. So they set out and swam across the river in the darkness. Caleb came and stood beside me as we watched the two men navigate the strong current and reach the other side, quite a ways further down the river, but they made it out safely. We both let out a sigh of relief.

Caleb was fidgety, and I could tell he wanted to talk more, so I asked him, "What is it, my friend? What troubles you?"

He looked at me and gave a sheepish grin, "That obvious, huh?" he asked. I shook my head and smiled back; Caleb was not known for his ability to hide his feelings. It was quite the opposite. "The words you told the officers, 'to get our provisions ready, in three days we are to cross the Jordan.' This is something that we are not accustomed to," he divulged.

"How do you mean," I asked, "these are the words of the Lord."

"I know," he replied, "and I believe and will obey every word, but, for forty years, we have never prepared more than a day's worth of provisions of the gathering of the manna, except for the day before the Sabbath. The people of this second generation have known nothing else. It will be quite an adjustment to go against that conditioning."

I understood what he meant and had questioned that within myself. This would be a significant unsettling shift in how the Israelites have been conditioned to live. Every day for 40 years, the second generation has only known the desert and followed the leading of the Lord God every day. We have had our food, our water, the same clothing that has never worn out, a cloud by day to protect us from the scorching sun, and a fire by night to keep us from the freezing temperatures. In this one statement, a whole generation of people of forty years of adaptation are now being directed to do the exact opposite of what they have been instructed to do their entire lives.

"We had been trained and disciplined to follow the instructions and lead of the Lord God," I started, "we fully believe and trust in him with our whole hearts. But now the Lord God is taking us into another dimension of who He is, who we are, and the purpose He brought us here. So I am sure the people will adjust and do as instructed. We are about to become **possessors**; it is what we have been waiting for through 430 years in slavery and forty more years of deliverance, wandering in the wilderness, to become that which the Lord God can use to possess the promise. We have been chosen for such a time as this, Caleb. We will be successful and victorious in all we set our hands to. The Lord God has assured me."

Caleb turned to me with a huge smile and slapped me on the side of the arm with such force that it knocked me off balance and stated. "That's all I needed to hear!" He chuckled and returned to his camp.

Three days had passed, and it was early morning. The sun was coming up, and the people of the camp had been preparing their provisions as instructed, and were anticipating the trek across Jordan. The spies returned the evening before and reported to me. They told me that the king of Jericho was told that the spies had been seen crossing the river and sent men out to find them. They told me that they had taken shelter in the home of a prostitute named Rehab. As the men were searching for them, Rehab hid them, tricked the men of Jericho by stating that they had left through the city gate, and then instructed the spies to hide in the woods for three days before crossing back over the Jordan. The spies explained that since Rehab had helped them, they had made an oath to protect her and her family, that we would be able to identify their home by the scarlet rope tied to the window in which she let the spies down to be able to escape. I agreed to uphold the oath that they committed to the prostitute, Rehab, and her family. The spies said, "The Lord has surely given the whole land into our hands; all the people are melting in fear because of us."

The Lord had given me more instructions, so I gathered the officers and explained it to them. For the last three days, the officers had been going throughout the camp, giving orders to the people: "When you see the ark of the covenant of the Lord your God, and the Levitical priests carrying it, you are to move out from your positions and follow it. Then you will know which way to go since you have never been this way. But keep

a distance of about two thousand cubits between you and the ark; do not go near it."

I had been walking throughout the camp the entire day, monitoring the progress, and I would tell the people, "Consecrate yourselves, for tomorrow the Lord will do amazing things among you!"

Early the following day, the time that we had been waiting for the last 430 years of slavery and 40 years in the wilderness; this day-today was the first day of a new era, a new dimension, the first day beginning the promise of the possession. Everyone was up early; all the tribes had broken camp before daybreak, and you could hear and feel the buzz of excitement. It's finally happening! I instructed the priests, "Take the ark of the covenant and begin ahead of the nation." The priests moved ahead of the people.

I was making my way to the front of the procession to the banks of the river. I could feel my heart in my throat. The river had not receded or slowed down and was still overflowing its banks. It had a powerful current and was extremely wide and treacherous. For the multitude of the Israelite nation to cross this river was not going to be easy and could potentially lose many lives, cattle, and possessions. If that happened, then what kind of leader would the people think me to be? One who puts their lives at stake at any cost? But I had been here before forty-plus years ago, and the Lord had Moses lift his rod to part the Red Sea, and the nation went over on dry ground; how much more could the Lord part a river?

There was one problem in my mind, though. I don't have a rod-like Moses. I won't be able to lift my arms for the river to part. I have been groomed and mentored by Moses, but I have been a warrior, a man of action all my life. Moses was the servant of God, the leader out of Egypt, the leader through the wilderness, the mediator between God and man, and between man and God. Moses was officially exalted in the eyes of the people when he parted the Red Sea. That is when the people saw the glory of the Lord in Moses for the first time, and that glory was for them and not against them.

But now we are standing in front of a rushing river, and all eyes are on me, Joshua. I am the one who now must lead the nation. I remember the Lord's words, "As I was with Moses, so that I will be with you!" Those words comfort me while anxiety still perturbs me. The Lord will be with me *AS* he was with Moses; the Lord didn't say *LIKE* He was with Moses. I must understand and learn to wear the "glory" that was on Moses, but I will need to wear and operate from the perspective of what I have been called to. Moses was called to *deliver*; I have been called to *possess*. So, I cannot imitate the methods and miracles of Moses, which were for deliverance from Egypt and sustaining in the wilderness; I will have to be conditioned to be authentic and understand that my glory is for leading the nation to possess the promise. But right now, I am not sure how that will come about. I guess that is what belief and faith are for: to believe and have faith in the outcome before I see and experience the outcome. Moses had a rod, but I have the *ARK OF GOD!*

My thoughts were interrupted by the voice of the Lord. He spoke to me and said, "Today I will begin to exalt *YOU* in the eyes of all Israel, so they may know that I am with you *AS* I was with Moses. Tell the priests who carry the ark of the covenant: 'When you reach the edge of the Jordan's waters, go and stand in the river.'"

I told the priests the Lord's instructions, and the priests did as instructed.

Then the Lord had me tell the Israelites, "This is how you will know that the living God is among you and that He will certainly drive out before you the Canaanites, Hittites, Hivites, Perizzites, Girgashites, Amorites, and Jebusites. See, the ark of the covenant of the Lord of all the earth will go into the Jordan ahead of you. Now, then, choose twelve men from the tribes of Israel, one from each tribe. And as soon as the priests who carry the ark of the Lord- the Lord of all the earth-set foot in the Jordan, its waters flowing downstream will be cut off and stand up in a heap. They will choose a stone from the riverbed where the priests stand with the ark and carry to the other side of the Jordan" I was quivering with the power of the Spirit of the Lord upon me

I motioned for the priests to take the ark and to step into the Jordan. They picked up the ark and walked towards the river; they stopped for just a second before stepping in to ensure their footing. The first priests in front, carrying the ark of the Lord, stepped into the water, with the current flowing strongly around their feet. They stopped again to ensure their footing and proceeded further until all of the priests stood in the rushing water up to their knees. They stood there for what seemed an eternity. Nothing was happening; the water was still pounding against their legs, and you could see the concentration on the faces of the priests as they were standing firm and resisting the rush of the water, determined not to be swept away or let the ark fall in the water. I looked over at Caleb, who had a concerned look on his face. I turned back to the priests and the ark, closed my eyes, and began saying a silent prayer to the Lord God, thanking Him that He will make a way when there seems to be no way.

When I opened my eyes, what I saw began to fill them with tears. The priests were struggling, but suddenly, the sound of the rushing water began to quiet. Then, the flow slowed significantly and began to lower; I could actually see the tops of the priests' feet. A few seconds later, I saw the riverbed and the water drying up, past the city of Jericho and back to the town of Adam at the edge of the mountains, I could see a wall of water piled up at a great height as if an invisible hand was holding it back. When I looked back at the priests, I saw that the riverbed was dry to the Dead Sea in the opposite direction. Oh, what an amazing God we serve!

I yelled to the priests, "Let's GO!!!"

Chapter 16

Don't Leave Your Anointing in Your Bones!

We have embarked on this journey to see how the Lord uses this template to **Expose, Destroy, Heal, and Replace** throughout the Bible to realign His children from our fallen state and our self-centered focus, which has corrupted and turned our eyes from Him, and how it restores us back to our intended created identity and mission purpose and destinies. We take this journey to understand who He is, who we are, and our purpose. We are to follow the example of our Lord and Savior, Jesus (Yeshua), who was in the order of Melchizedek to be a king and priest, a royal priesthood. This is one of the reasons that He died on the cross, to reconcile us to what was lost. We now have access to this calling and right standing with the Kingdom of Heaven. He paid for this and has adopted us to be children and heirs.

As believers and followers of our Lord through Jesus Christ (Yeshua Hamashiach), we are called to become kings and priests. This call is for everyone who believes. No one who believes is disqualified, no matter your history, your status in society, your age, whether you have a pedigree or not, whether you are rich or poor, man or woman, or whether you feel worthy or not worthy, we are all called to follow Jesus as he commanded us in all ways.

To step into this calling, we must surrender our past and defining moments, be obedient, and allow the Holy Spirit to renew us and transform us into this role. We cannot do this alone; we must have the Holy Spirit come into our hearts and minds and **Expose, Destroy, Heal, and Replace** our past defaults, patterns, thought processes, generational curses, guilt, shame, and worldly conditioning. We need to have our minds renewed and our lives transformed from spiritual paupers to spiritual kings and priests, from slaves to sin and the world to children and heirs to the King, from debtors to freedom. We need to have our spiritual and mental capacity increased, our prayer life, our anointing, our understanding, and our infrastructure, and to be in alignment with His will so that we can have the ability to receive this dominion as kings and to stand in the gap between God and man as priests.

We must step into this calling for ourselves, our children, and our grandchildren and leave a legacy and a future aligned with the Lord God and His Kingdom. We must raise, train, and support our children to grow into their calling as kings and priests for their generation and the succeeding generations for the issues they will face. Let's not commit the errors of the various examples throughout the scriptures highlighted in this book of those who dropped the baton.

- Like Gideon, who was mighty for the Lord in delivering Israel from its oppressors, but he lived and died so that his calling and anointing didn't pass down to his children.

- Or like Elisha, who died with his anointing and had no one to take up his mantle as he did with Elijah. He died with the anointing still in his bones. How many of us will have our anointing die with us still in our bones?
- Or like the first generation of Hebrews in the Exodus, who were delivered out of Egypt, but Egypt couldn't be delivered out of them. The first generation wasn't allowed to cross into the promised land because, despite all the miracles they had seen and all that the Lord God provided for them, they couldn't become what the Lord was trying to condition them into. They couldn't respond to the conditioning to become more than just slaves. The Lord could not allow them to possess the promised land because He needed people who could be leaders instead of followers, succeeders instead of survivors, and who could be delivered but not possessors. This generation had to wander the desert for 40 years and die, and it was their children who were allowed to possess the promised land.

The Lord is calling for those who would step out of their familiar structures and get in alignment with Him to pierce this darkness, to be the light in this darkness, to turn the hearts of men back to Him, and reestablish His Kingdom of love, grace, mercy, and redemption. The Lord calls for those who dare to walk alongside Him as coheirs and have dominion through Him! All for His glory and His Great Name as a Royal Priesthood!

We learned how.

- Like the Prodigal son, to recognize the defining moments, the trauma, the fears, the shame, the lies, the hurts, distractions, and deceptions that have affected us our whole life, so we don't ask amiss.

- Like the story of the Leper, to recognize the things that have kept us from hiding who we truly are and not allow our skewed belief that we grew up with or that has been thrust upon us to cause us to miss what Jesus has for us and not allow Him to walk by or out of our life!
- Like King David, we must recognize the things that have defined and hindered us from our purpose and mission here on this earth, be in His image, reflect His glory, and understand why the Lord considers us.
- As with Adam and Eve in the Garden, to recognize the masks, camouflage, and coverings we have created to hide who we have become, to cover our shame, guilt, and feelings of unworthiness, and not to run and hide from the Lord, but to immediately turn to Him to restore us and cover us with His grace!
- Like the story of Gideon, we will learn to recognize all of the self-centered agendas that skew our focus, beliefs, and perspectives where we can never see our true self, higher calling, or why we are here.
- Like Joshua, we need to be strong and courageous, and as the Lord was with Moses, He will be with us. The Lord is the same yesterday, today, and forever more! We must learn to believe and trust in the Lord before we see His blessings or miracles.

Our time on this earth is short; our mission that He has given us is critical! We live in a time of wars, rumors of wars, oppressive chaos, and misapplied anger. We also have a generation that is so inundated with technology and social media that it is causing us to become dysfunctionally more connected yet even more isolated. We live in a generation that is fearful, without hope, distracted, and has allowed a veil to cloud the ability to see and recognize who we are in these times! Our familiar structures, systems of politics, our culture, churches, ministries, and families are falling to pieces all around us. In this new dimension, this new era that we have been thrust into, we can't just wait it out and hope it will just pass or even rely on past experiences and the things that used to work in the old dimension to get us through. We have entered into an unusual moment of unveiling a new era of the Kingdom of God that will require us to align with God's latest move to navigate these times.

The world, our churches, our families, the Kingdom, and our God are looking for more than just leaders that spout history and tradition as answers; it's looking for the "Boat Rockers," the provocateurs IN you!

The Kingdom requires those who are spiritually aware of the times and events we are experiencing and the ability to understand where God is in it. It's looking for those who are willing to get in alignment with the flow of the Spirit of the Lord. WHO is now disrupting all of the familiar systems, structures, paradigms, and traditions. It is searching for those to be the conduits for the Lord to PIERCE the darkness, chaos, evil, and oppression on the earth during these tumultuous times. He is looking for those who perceive the shift that is happening and the direction the Lord is using to usher a revival to combat the spiritual forces of darkness who endeavor to destroy the kingdom of God!

When Jesus walked on the water to the disciples who were in a boat during a raging storm, the disciples thought He was a ghost, but Peter became aware of a new move, a new dimension, a new characteristic of Jesus, and was the only disciple willing to "rock the boat" to step out of what was familiar which was the safety of the boat-the structure, the system and what used to work that would generally allow them to traverse the elements to move forward. Peter stepped into a new dynamic and move of God with Jesus by walking on the water alongside Jesus in the chaos of the storm around them!

The Lord is calling for the BOAT ROCKERS to step out of their familiar structures and get in alignment with Him, to be strong and courageous, to pierce and be the light in this darkness, to turn the hearts of men of these tumultuous times back to Him and reestablish His Kingdom of love, grace, mercy, and redemption. The Lord calls those who dare to walk alongside Him as coheirs and have dominion through Him! All for His glory and His Great Name!

Let's go... BOAT ROCKERS!

> *"Then I heard the voice of the Lord saying, "Whom shall I send? And who will go for us?" And I said, "Here am I. Send me!"*
>
> *Isaiah 6:8 (NIV)*

About the Author

Kenny Brown

When not writing, Kenny is a husband, father, and grandfather, and enjoys spending time with his family, reading, traveling, going to the beach, and reflecting Christ to all he comes in contact with. Kenny enjoys spending one-on-one time with God. actively participates in men's group ministries, leading bible studies, and praying for and coming alongside people in their walk with the Lord.

Milton Keynes UK
Ingram Content Group UK Ltd.
UKHW020122070624
443692UK00013B/238/J